ARTES
VERITAS
SCIENTIA
LIBRARY OF THE
UNIVERSITY OF MICHIGAN
SI QUAERIS PENINSULAM AMOENAM
CIRCUMSPICE

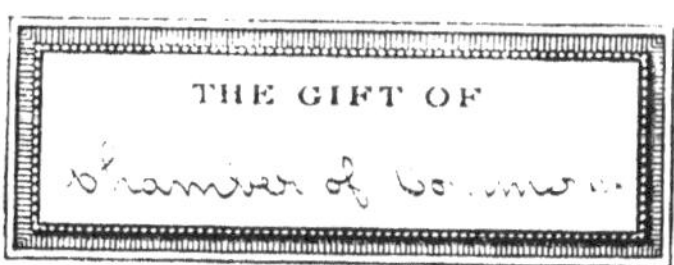

Alex. E. Orr

MEDAL PRESENTED BY THE CHAMBER OF COMMERCE TO THE RAPID TRANSIT COMMISSIONERS.

MEDAL PRESENTED BY THE CHAMBER OF COMMERCE TO ABRAM S. HEWITT.

RAPID TRANSIT

IN

NEW YORK CITY

AND IN

OTHER GREAT CITIES

Prepared for the

New York, CHAMBER OF COMMERCE OF THE STATE OF NEW YORK

By Its Special Committee on

RECOGNITION OF SERVICES OF MEMBERS OF THE CHAMBER
ON THE RAPID TRANSIT COMMISSION

1905

BLUMENBERG PRESS
NEW YORK

NOTE

The proceedings of the Chamber of Commerce authorizing the preparation and publication of this book will be found in the last chapter.

The book has been prepared by Mr. S. D. V. Burr, C. E., A. M., under the direction of the Chairman of the Special Committee.

CONTENTS.

CHAPTER I.

THE BEGINNINGS AND THE GROWTH OF NEW YORK CITY.

HENRY HUDSON

In the early part of the seventeenth century the Dutch were wonderfully prosperous, dealing on a large scale with the entire world. Motley mentions, in *United Netherlands,* that they had 100,000 sailors and 3,000 ships. Bryant, in his *History of the United States,* remarks that "The Dutch East India Company, the first of great trading monopolies, was formed by the consolidation of several small corporations, its charter granting it sole permission to trade for twenty-one years to the east of the Cape of Good Hope, and to sail through the Straits of Magellan." The Magellan route was long, and it became important to search for a passage across the northern hemisphere. Many expeditions were sent forth. So firmly rooted had become the belief that a passage existed north of the continent that one explorer, Henry Hudson, sent out by the Muscovy Company of England, had been instructed "to proceed directly across the pole." This was the second voyage of Hudson for the company.

In 1609 the Dutch East India Company engaged Hudson to make a third attempt. The ship *Half-Moon,* a vessel of 80 tons, was fitted out. The contract stipulated that Hudson was to receive a sum equal to $300 of our money for expenses and for the support of his family during his absence. If he did not return, his widow was to be paid $80 to indemnify her for his loss. If he found the passage, he was to receive a suitable reward, the exact terms of which were not stated in the agreement. He was instructed to proceed "around the north side of Nova Zembla"; also he was "to think of no other routes or passages, except the route around by the north and northeast above Nova Zembla."

HUDSON'S VOYAGE

The expedition sailed April 4, 1609, and early in May had reached the neighborhood of the island. Ice barred further progress in that direction, and, as the crew were insubordinate, most of them being unused to the extreme cold of that region, Hudson decided to disobey orders and sail west for the American shore. He skirted the coast of Newfoundland and New England and reached a point as far south as Chesapeake Bay; and returning sighted the Navesink Highland in

September. Before he sailed for home the Kills were explored, and also the Hudson to a point above Troy. The adventurers were delighted with the beauty of the country, and with its possibilities for agriculture and for trade with the natives.

The Dutch Government did not take advantage of the discovery to claim the territory; neither did it make an attempt, until long after, to develop and colonize it.

MANHATTAN

But the merchants of Amsterdam were not so indifferent. Two or three years after Hudson's visit they occupied the southern end of Manhattan Island, building there a crude fort and huts for the first settlers.

It did not call for the exercise of much insight on the part of the pioneers to appreciate the wonderful advantages of the location. While doubtless they never dreamed of the vast and thriving population that would in time occupy the Island of Manhattan, they knew that the harbor was not surpassed by any in Europe. They knew that the river would provide communication with a vast interior region. They knew, in some part, that the natural resources of the land were very great.

The Island of Manhattan was a rocky ridge extending north and south. The southern part was easily defensible. The country to the north was fit to be cultivated. The adjacent land in Jersey, Staten Island, and Brooklyn was of like character. The settlers sent their boats up the Hudson as far as the stream was navigable, south along the coast and north through the Sound, and rapidly established an extensive trade with the Indians. They entered also, in a modest way, upon the tillage of the soil.

The growth of the place was rapid. In 1700 the population was about 21,700. In 1800 it had grown to 60,489; in 1820, to 123,706. At this time the population of the State of New York was 1,372,812.

THE ERIE CANAL

At the date last mentioned a movement was set on foot to connect the waters of the Hudson with the Great Lakes by the Erie Canal. Mention of this enterprise is to be found in the minutes of the Chamber of Commerce of New York of January 3, 1786. In a memorial addressed to the Chamber by Christopher Collis he asks aid for the enterprise in the following prophetic language:

"Your memorialist has formed a design of opening an intercourse with the interior parts of the United States, by an artificial inland navigation, along the Mohawk River and Wood Creek to the Great Lakes, a design which must evidently extend the commerce of this city with exceeding rapidity beyond what it can possibly arrive at by any other means; a design which Providence has manifestly pointed out, and which, in the hands of a commercial people, must evidently tend to make them great and powerful; and which, though indefinite in its advantages, may be effected for a sum perfectly trifling when compared with the advantages."

CHAMBER OF COMMERCE

The memorialist declared that he had examined the ground "at the Cohoes, the Little Falls, and Fort Schuyler, and found that no considerable difficulty existed," and that he had secured "a number of respectable gentlemen as subscribers." He asked for the countenance and aid of the Chamber of Commerce. That body responded that, while it entertained a high idea of the feasibility of the scheme and wished it all success, it had no funds that could be applied to the purpose.

The physical features of New York and the value of this canal were summarized by the late Abram S. Hewitt when Mayor of the city. In a message to the Board of Aldermen in January, 1888, he said:

"The State of New York owes its pre-eminence among the States of the Union chiefly to the physical fact that within its territory the great Appalachian chain of mountains falls off, so that communication between the Great Lakes and the ocean may be secured on grades so low as to offer but little resistance to the tide of commerce in both directions. The City of New York owes its precedence among the cities of the Union to the fact that it has a great ocean harbor of unequaled proportions and of inexhaustible possibilities. These great natural advantages were turned to account by the foresight, genius and energy of one man, whose monument is to be found in the Erie Canal, and in the vast increase in the wealth of the city and State of his birth.

DE WITT CLINTON

"The name of DeWitt Clinton, the first graduate of Columbia College after the Revolution, Mayor of this city and Governor of this State, will always be held in grateful remembrance by the generations who enjoy the fruits of the incalculable benefits which he conferred upon the commonwealth. He laid the foundations of its prosperity upon an enduring basis. Since his day the introduction of railways has lessened, but has not destroyed, the natural advantages which New York possesses in low-grade lines to the interior, over other cities of the Atlantic seaboard."

Clinton started to dig his "ditch," 363 miles in length, on the 4th of July, 1817, amid much ridicule. But the undertaking, stupendous as it was, was pushed to completion in October, 1825.

RAILROADS

Thirty-five years later the construction of railroads that were to constitute great trunk lines was begun. The successive lines completed added to the importance of New York City as a commercial center. Its precedence, indeed, became such that railroads built between other seaboard cities and the West were obliged to ask for differential rates favorable to themselves. These rates were secured, and have lasted until our day. They have tended to build up other lines of transportation, but have not so far prevented the development of our city and commerce as to be the occasion of serious complaint here. The system of differential rates is, however, abnormal, and cannot be allowed to stand indefinitely.

LOCAL PROBLEMS

The people of New York City, while giving attention to problems of transportation between their city and other sections of the country north, west and south, have been obliged to meet local problems due to the physical conditions of their vicinage. The first settlement was at the extreme southern end of the island of Manhattan. This section remains until our day the center of the activities of our people. Population has increased year by year, and it has covered successively the district south of Wall street, south of Canal street, south of Twenty-third street, south of the Harlem, and it now extends north of the Harlem along the Hudson toward Yonkers, and along the East River toward the Sound. A great city has grown up on the Bronx. Neighboring great cities have grown up across the North and East Rivers. Our municipal government rules to-day the affairs of four millions of people. The metropolitan center, including the nearby cities of New Jersey, embraces a total population of four and three-quarter millions. It is the largest center in the world, save only London.

The growth from south to north to a distance of more than ten miles, always within bounds made by arms of the sea, and the growth across the waters contiguous to the island—the centre of commercial activity on the island itself remaining constant to its more southern parts—has created the local problems mentioned, and caused developments of a progressive nature that will be treated of in the following chapters.

DEVELOPMENTS

In a way the successive developments made have served to fix the commercial activities at the southern end of the island. It has been a case of "all roads lead to Rome." And this again has caused developments there that could not have been dreamed of in earlier days. One of these is a form of construction that permits of building to the height of twenty stories and more. This form of construction has gone forward so rapidly and to such an extent that it may be true to-day that the section of the city south of the City Hall gives accommodation to twice as many people as it contained twenty years ago.

A factor which should not be overlooked in the study of a problem of this nature is "the flat," which has done for certain residential districts what the skeleton-framed skyscraper later did for the commercial and financial district—increased the capacity of the ground area. One of these "Parisian novelties" had been built in 1865, and in 1870-71 two large apartment houses were erected on Eighteenth and Thirteenth streets. From this initiative the style spread, and has had much to do with increasing the density of population.

TABLET—CITY HALL STATION

CHAPTER II

PLANS FOR RELIEF

RAPID TRANSIT NECESSARY

The conditions existing in New York illustrate the proposition that city growth demands rapid and certain means of travel between different sections and the general center. In the absence of the progressive developments that have taken place during the last one hundred years, the growth of population would have been checked and business interests impeded in large measure. For purposes of commerce the people of a great business center are far more effective when they have the means to go to and fro as the occasion demands, with the least possible loss of time and the least inconvenience and fatigue.

At the beginning of the last century the people of New York had, for the time, reasonable facilities of transit. The city was so small that stages could reach readily all parts of the island then occupied. The two rivers were not barriers to movement. At a very early date people found it not inconvenient to do business in New York and to live on Long Island or in New Jersey.

STEAM VESSELS

With the introduction of vessels propelled by steam, about 1820, a noted development took place. Transit across the rivers was facilitated, and residential places of importance grew up on the opposite shores and along the rivers well to the north and east. The ferries and the steamboat lines established were very notable, surpassing any development of the sort elsewhere. They left little to be desired in that direction.

In 1850 the island population was served, so far as interior transportation was concerned, by stages and omnibus lines, and still later tram cars were introduced.

GRAND CENTRAL STATION

The first practical gain in rapid transit was made in 1875, when trains were brought into the Grand Central Station at Forty-second street over a four track system, two of which were intended for local trains.

The elevated railroads appeared in the seventies. A short section in Greenwich street was erected in 1870; but it was not until ten years later that the several structures were completed to the Harlem River.

ELEVATED ROADS

The elevated system was a very notable accomplishment. Criticism of it from an engineering standpoint were numerous and severe. When M. De Lesseps was whirled around the track at One-Hundred-and-tenth street he said, "American engineers are audacious." The precipitation of trains to the street was predicted freely. The record indicates that the elevated roads are safer than surface steam-roads. It was said that the constant jar and strain would impair the metal to such an extent that the structure would become unsafe. The original columns and girders are still doing duty. Fifteen years ago a thorough examination was made of the principal members, including tests of the steel. It was found that the physical properties of the metal had undergone no change.

The population north of Fourteenth street has increased threefold since 1870. Doubtless a large part of this gain is directly attributable to the elevated system.

BROOKLYN BRIDGE

The next advance was made in 1883, when the Brooklyn Bridge was opened. The territory adjacent to the Brooklyn end of the bridge, although so near to the business part of Manhattan Island, had remained largely undeveloped. The bridge and the system of elevated roads that followed closely upon its completion brought the outlying sections within reasonable traveling time to New York. The growth of Brooklyn has been rapid ever since. It was said, many years ago, that Brooklyn could afford to build a new bridge every ten years.

CABLE CARS

The system of propelling surface cars by cable was introduced in 1884. It answered its purpose admirably for some years, and was then displaced by the electric system. By these systems the cars were enlarged and movement accelerated.

THE FUTURE

It may be that ten years ago, or even five years ago, many people in New York believed that existing systems were the best that could be devised; that the electric cars on the surface and the elevated trains were entirely satisfactory; and that nothing remained but to extend accommodations as population increased. They had become used to the trouble of climbing to stations well lifted above the streets. They had forgotten about the dangers of "roads upon stilts." They ignored the discomfort to dwellers along the lines. They recognized how unsightly the structures were, but sank regrets in view of their utility. They equally minimized the objections that may be raised against the use of streets by a surface system that is noisy to a degree, that greatly inconveniences ordinary traffic, and that in each and every year maims and kills many victims. It is possible to-day to predict with safety that the elevated structures will all be taken down. It is at least possible to hope that the enormous cars now propelled rapidly over our streets by electricity will be disused in the more or less distant future, and a system of transportation introduced that will be more convenient and less objectionable. For it would be unreasonable to suppose that the evolution of the past in the matter of transit for cities is to end with the methods now in use. The ultimate goal is a system, or systems, that will be not unsightly, that will be noiseless to a reasonable degree, that will not cause undue inconvenience to any persons or interests, that will be safe for passengers and not dangerous to others, and that will be rapid. This is the goal; and in view of progress heretofore made, and in view of progress at large, one may say with confidence that it will be reached.

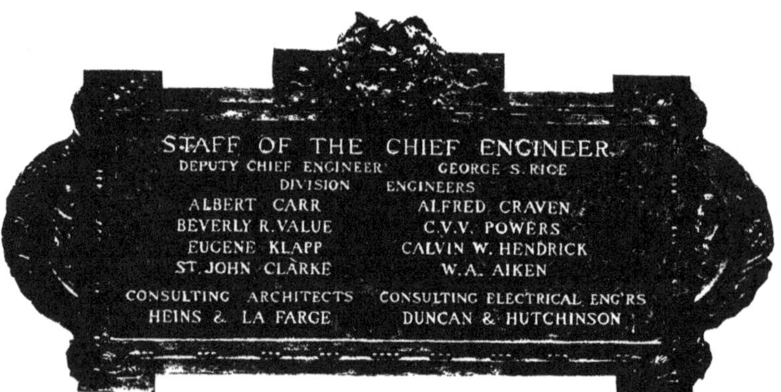

TABLET—CITY HALL STATION

CHAPTER III.

EARLY SUBWAY SCHEMES

During the period from 1868 to 1900 many subway schemes were brought forward in the effort to provide transportation that would be rapid and reliable, and would meet at least the demands of the times. Most of these are now historical incidents only.

NEW YORK CITY CENTRAL UNDERGROUND

In 1868, by an act of the Legislature, the New York City Central Underground Railway Company was incorporated. The line was to run from the City Hall to the Harlem River. The charter granted ample powers as to route, capital, and facilities for construction. Although the standing of the incorporators indicates that their purpose was serious, no practical result was reached.

NEW YORK CITY RAPID TRANSIT

Following this, in 1872, an act was passed by which Cornelius Vanderbilt and others were incorporated, as the New York City Rapid Transit Company, to build an underground road from the City Hall to connect with the New York & Harlem Railroad and with the New York Central. This company was duly organized and the necessary surveys and plans were made for the construction of the road. Adverse criticisms made at the time led Commodore Vanderbilt to decide that he would not construct the road. Many years later Mr. Hewitt said: "To this decision the members of his family, who succeeded in the management of the New York Central Railway, uniformly adhered; although they, as well as he, always insisted that the road ought to have been constructed and would have proven profitable, probably, to the New York Central Railroad." Of all the early endeavors to provide rapid transit this was the only one supported by sufficient capital.

OTHER SCHEMES

Other companies were incorporated as follows:

The Beach Pneumatic Transit Company in 1868.

The Central Tunnel Railway Company in 1881.

The New York & New Jersey Tunnel Railway Company in 1883.

The Terminal Underground Railway Company in 1886.

The Underground Railroad Company of the City of New York (a consolidation of two companies) in 1896.

The Rapid Transit Underground Railroad Company in 1897.

BEACH PNEUMATIC

Of all the plans brought forward the most interesting and perhaps the most important was the Beach Pneumatic, otherwise known as the Broadway Underground Railway. It was the only one upon which constructive work was done. A full-sized section of a tunnel was built on the line adopted, and is to-day in good condition. The route selected by the company had been advocated by every rapid transit board since that time, namely, from "the Battery, or Bowling Green, under Broadway to Madison Square; thence under Broadway to its junction with Central Park and Eighth avenue; with a branch under Madison Square and Madison avenue to and under the Harlem River."

The first company, the Beach Pneumatic Transit Company, incorporated in 1868, was empowered to "provide for the transmission of letters, packages, and merchandise in the cities of New York and Brooklyn, and the North and East Rivers, by means of pneumatic tubes to be constructed beneath the surface of the streets and public places."

THE CHARTER

The charter provided that the company must, as a preliminary step and to demonstrate the practicability of its plans, "first lay down and construct one line of said pneumatic tubes from the Post-Office in Nassau street, between Liberty and Cedar streets, in the City of New York, not extending above Fourteenth street, which shall be put in successful operation, and continue so for the period of three months, * * * before proceeding to lay down and construct any other lines of such pneumatic tubes."

As amended in 1873 the company was permitted to "construct, maintain, and operate an underground railway for the transportation of passengers and property." The capital stock of the corporation was fixed at $10,000,000. A two-track section, from Bowling Green to Fourteenth street, was to be finished in three years, and the remainder within five years thereafter. The act stated that the water and gas pipes and sewers must be maintained, and that street travel must not be interrupted during construction. The work was to be done under the supervision of a board of three engineer-commissioners, one of whom was named in the act, and two of whom were to be appointed by the Governor.

It was proposed to operate the tunnel by means of compressed air, the car being circular in cross section and approximately fitting the tube. This, as was pointed out at the time, would do away with the dust and obnoxious gases arising from the combustion of coal in a locomotive.

Work was begun on the tunnel at the corner of Broadway and Warren street, and a section was built under Broadway to the southerly side of Murray street. The curved portion at the corner of Warren street was constructed of cast iron plates, the straight portion being lined with brick to a diameter of 8 feet in the clear. The tunnel was built by means of a shield which was forced forward, 2 feet at a time, by hydraulic jacks.

EXPERIMENTAL SECTION

Early in 1870 the tunnel was thrown open for inspection, and a car was run from one end to the other, the object being to convince the public that the plans were safe and practicable. But all of the work done failed of successful issue. Engineers of prominence were divided in their opinion as to the possibility of building an underground road through narrow streets lined with heavy buildings. Even in the seventies the Beach plans were condemned because it was thought that the tube could not be constructed under the street in front of such a massive structure as the Astor House. Since the methods were not endorsed by engineers, financial interests were chary about investing money in it. Many believed that if built the returns would be insufficient to pay operating expenses and interest on the invested capital.

ELECTRIC TRACTION

The capitalists and engineers of those days should not be too hastily condemned as shortsighted. The needs of the people of our city for rapid transit increased greatly in the next thirty years; the population increased greatly; the city's wealth increased, and notable advances were made in the science of tunnel construction and of the movement of trains. A revolution was effected in the matter last named by the introduction of electric traction. We would have had no subway to this time if private enterprise had been relied upon.

TABLET — CITY HALL STATION

BROOKLYN BRIDGE—WILLIAMSBURGH BRIDGE IN DISTANCE.

CHAPTER IV.

BRIDGES TO BROOKLYN

THE BROOKLYN BRIDGE.

The concentration of business at the lower end of Manhattan, and the development of the district across the East River for residential and later for business purposes, caused attention to be given at an early date to the matter of better transit facilities in that direction.

BROOKLYN BRIDGE

A proposition to build a chain suspension bridge over the East River, with a clear span of 1,500 feet and a length of 2,100 feet between the "toll gates," was proposed as early as 1829. The structure was to have been 28 feet wide, the height of the granite piers from the water line to the roadway 160 feet, and from the roadway to the extreme point of the pier 65 feet. This and similar schemes came to naught, until, in 1867, the Legislature passed an act incorporating the New York Bridge Company. In May of that year John A. Roebling, who had, by designing and erecting the great Niagara Suspension Bridge, earned a high reputation in this branch of engineering, was appointed chief engineer. A survey of the line was made in the summer of 1869, and the Brooklyn tower located. It was while engaged in this work that Mr. Roebling met with an accident that resulted in his death. In the same year his son, Washington A. Roebling, was appointed to the position formerly occupied by his father, and under his supervision the work was carried to completion in May, 1883.

GOVERNMENT COMMISSION

In May, 1869, the War Department, in compliance with an act of Congress, appointed Generals Wright and Newton and Major King a commission of government engineers to examine into the feasibility of the project, and to report whether the bridge would be an obstruction to navigation. This resulted in changing the clear height to 135 feet above mean high tide, and in widening the bridge from 80 to 85 feet, in order to provide a double roadway on each side. In those days it was not contemplated to use the bridge for the passage of ordinary street cars, but to furnish it with a cable system of its own. The importance of the slight increase in width mentioned can hardly be overestimated, since it made provision for the vehicle and trolley traffic of the present time. In June, 1874, an act was passed changing the name to that of the New York and Brooklyn Bridge, and making it a public work to be constructed by the two cities, Brooklyn paying two-thirds of the cost and New York one-third.

FOUNDATIONS

The foundation of the Brooklyn tower was begun in 1870. The caisson, a rectangular chamber 102 feet wide by 168 feet long and having a solid roof 15 feet thick, was sunk to a depth of 44½ feet. Brick piers were then built in the air-chamber, which was finally completely filled with concrete. As the caisson was sunk the granite masonry forming the tower proper was built above it. The New York foundation was also carried to solid rock, the caisson in this case being slightly larger than the other, 102 feet wide by 172 feet long. The cutting edges were extended to a depth of 78 feet below mean high water, this being necessary because of the presence of extensive beds of quicksand resting on the rock. The roof was 22 feet thick and was surmounted by a cofferdam reaching to high water, thereby increasing the buoyancy and lessening the pressure on the frames during sinking.

THE TOWERS

The towers are not solid masses of masonry, but each is composed of three buttressed shafts joined together up to the roadway by four connecting walls. In the Brooklyn tower the course of the walls next the caisson is 17 feet thick; the thickness diminishes by offsets until at high water it is but 10½ feet. This forms two well holes which are filled with concrete below water line and left open from there to the roadway. Spaces are also left from 2 feet above the crown of the arches to within 4½ feet of the top of the tower. Above the roadway the tower consists of three columns having an oblong section; they are united at the top by arches having a span of 33¾ feet. Each arch is formed by the intersection of two arcs of circles having a radius of 48 1-6 feet. Below the water the masonry is largely limestone, except the facing of the two upper courses, which is granite; the backing from high water to the roadway is granite, which constitutes all the remainder of the tower. At the towers the height of the roadway is 119¼ feet, the top of the towers being 272 feet from the water. The height from the bottom of the foundation to the top is, in the Brooklyn tower, 316 feet, and in the other 349 feet. At high water mark the towers measure 141 by 59 feet, at the roadway 131 by 48, and at the base of the cornice 126 by 43. The greatest pressure at any point is in the tower masonry at the base of the central shaft at the roadway, where each square foot supports about 26 tons.

ANCHORAGE

At a distance of 930 feet from each tower is an anchorage which rests on timber grillage, and in which the ends of the four cables are anchored. Each anchorage weighs 60,000 tons and is built solid, with the exception of tunnels or openings for the passage of the cables. Near the outside lower angle of each anchorage are four anchor plates (one for each end of each cable), which are held down by the dead weight of masonry piled upon them. Each platê weighs 23 tons, and in shape resembles an enormous wheel having a hub and sixteen spokes. The connection between the cable wires and the plates is made with eyebars, which start in double sets from each plate, one curving over the other, and are vertical for a distance of about 25 feet, when they curve about 90 degrees on a circle having a radius of 49½ feet. The bars have an average length of 12½ feet. The first three sets have a section of 7 by 3 inches, the next three 8 by 3, the next three 9 by 3 inches; the tenth set is double in number and each bar is 1½ by 9 inches in section. Piercing the center of the anchor plates are two parallel sets of apertures, each containing nine holes. A bar is passed through each hole and a 7-inch pin run through the eyes or holes in the end of each bar. These bolts bear firmly against the under side of the anchor plate, and serve to distribute the strain to every part of the plate. The next series of bars is attached to these by a bolt 5 feet in length and 5 inches in diameter. In this manner the succeeding bars are united, forming a chain having very long links connected to each other by bolts passing through the eyes. At each knuckle of the chains a large block of granite was placed with a heavy cast iron plate inserted as a bearing for the heads of the links. The bars in the last link are increased in number to 38, and are arranged in four courses, one above the other. The wires of the cable are divided into 19 strands and each strand is fastened around a grooved eye-piece which is held between two of the anchor bars.

CABLES

The first work connected with cable making was the passing of a rope from one anchorage to the other over the towers. By August, 1876, an endless rope had been placed from a driving engine at the Brooklyn anchorage to and around sheaves at the New York anchorage.

The first operation, preliminary to placing the cables in place, was that of adjusting four wires, one for each cable, to be used as guides in obtaining an exactly uniform deflection of all the others. Four wires of uniform size and weight were selected. These were adjusted to a tangent line for the land spans, whose position had been calculated, and to a level line at the lowest point of the curve for the center of the span. Allowances were made for the temperature prevailing at the time.

STRENGTH OF CABLES

The cables were made of galvanized steel wires, No. 8, Birmingham gauge. The strength of the cables per square inch of solid section is 160,000 pounds. Each cable is composed of 19 strands, each of which contains 278 wires. The last wire of the cables was run over October 5, 1878. At a distance of 21½ feet from the anchor bars heavy clamps were put on the cables to draw them to a cylindrical form. This was made necessary as the anchor bars spread so as to cover a space 5 feet square. The cables were finally wrapped with galvanized iron wire, the finished diameter being 15¾ inches.

On top of the towers the cables rest in saddles which furnish a bearing with easy vertical curves. In plan they are rectangular, 13 by 4 1-12 feet, and have an extreme height at the center of 4½ feet and a thickness of 4 inches. Each cable passes over the center of its saddle in a groove 19½ inches wide by 17½ inches deep. The saddles rest on steel rollers, which in turn rest on planed plates. This permits the cables to move freely backward and forward, and to accommodate themselves to any unequal loading, and also to adapt themselves to changes in temperature.

Passing over the towers alongside of the cables are 100 steel wire rope stays, arranged 25 to each cable, and secured at each end to the trusses carrying the floor system. The longest extend to a distance of about 400 feet each side of the towers, and are spaced 15 feet apart at the trusses.

SUSPENDED STRUCTURE

The floor system consists of six longitudinal trusses connected by floor beams, the whole being hung from the cables by suspender ropes. The suspender ropes are of twisted galvanized steel wire, and are from 1⅝ to 1¾ inches in diameter. Each is capable of sustaining about 50 tons, or five times the load it will ever be subjected to. As the floor system is in a continuous line from the top of the anchorages, and as the cables leave the anchorages a few feet below, the floor beams rest on the cables until the latter rise above the grade. The beams are here laid on posts resting on the cables, which vary in height to suit the distances, and are braced by plate brackets. The lower end of each post is bolted to the upper half of a strap encircling the cable. The whole number of suspender ropes is 1,520, and the posts number 280. The floor beams were made in half lengths, and when riveted together at the center formed a continuous beam 86 feet long. They are 32 inches deep, 9⅝ inches wide, and each weighs 4 tons. Each has two top and two bottom chords so united as to form a triangular, latticed girder. The chords are of steel channel bars. The beams are spaced 7½ feet between centers, and between each pair is placed an I-beam, which rests on the bottom truss chords, so that the planking is supported at every 3¾ feet. The work of placing the floor beams was begun at the towers, and carried each way at the same time, in order to load the cables uniformly.

PROMENADE AND ROADWAY

The bridge is divided by six longitudinal trusses into five passage ways, the trusses being of the following heights, measured from the top of the floor beams: The two outside ones 7½ feet, and the four intervening ones 15 feet 7½ inches. Across the central opening is a system of light beams supporting the promenade, which is 12 feet above the floor beams. The roadways at the outside are 18¾ feet wide in the clear, and although only designed for vehicles, each now has a trolley track. The two remaining divisions are 12 2-3 feet wide in the clear, and are used for passenger cars. As the foot passenger approaches the towers he ascends a few steps, the walk dividing and passing through each of the tower arches on a flooring laid on the beams over the car tracks.

VIBRATION

To prevent horizontal vibrations and to resist the force of the wind, there are wind braces placed beneath the floor beams. These are steel wire ropes from 2 to 3 inches in diameter, and are anchored at the four facing corners of the towers to eye bolts set in the masonry. From the corners to which they are attached they pass diagonally across the floor beams to the opposite side of the bridge, where they are secured. The longest ones reach about half way across. Similar braces are provided on the short spans. As a further precaution, and particularly to secure stability at the center of the span, where the braces are of little effect, the outside cables are drawn in a short distance toward the center. To allow for expansion and contraction of the trusses, slip joints are formed between the towers and anchorages and in the main span. The aggregate weight of the suspended structure, including cables, trusses, suspenders, braces, timber flooring, and rails, is 14,680 tons; the estimated transitory load is 3,100 tons, making the total weight of the superstructure 17,780 tons.

APPROACHES

The Brooklyn approach is 971 feet long on the center line, and is 100 feet wide throughout. It spans several streets by plate girders, and has one curve at about 200 feet from Sands street. The New York approach is 1,562½ feet long, begins at grade at Park Row, and rises 3.25 feet per hundred to the rear of the anchorage. It is 100 feet wide for about 500 feet of the distance, and 85 for the remainder. At Franklin Square is an opening measuring 210 feet on one side and 170 on the other, which is spanned by a bridge. The other streets are crossed by semi-circular brick arches. Both approaches consist of arches resting on massive piers, the fronts being entirely of granite. The cornice over the arches has a dentil course below, surmounted by a heavy projecting coping course. The whole is capped by an ornamental granite parapet. The arches are used as stores and warehouses.

OPERATION OF CARS

When the bridge was opened the cars were moved by an endless cable operated by engines located beneath the Brooklyn approach. This service soon proved to be inadequate, and the third-rail electric system was introduced and is now in effect. As a further improvement, and in order to accommodate the travel using the elevated roads of Brooklyn, connection was made with these roads so that the passage of the bridge could be made without change. In addition to this a trolley track was laid along each roadway in order that all the trolley lines in the Borough could cross the bridge without interruption. All these changes made necessary the complete re-designing and re-construction of the Brooklyn approaches, and also the changing of the station at the western end.

COST

The financial condition of the bridge on March 31, 1883, shortly before it was opened to traffic, was stated as follows:

Cash received from New York, ...	$4,871,900.00
Cash received from Brooklyn, ...	9,423,692.73
Cash received from rents, interest, sale of material, &c., ...	391,463.93
Total, ...	$14,687,056.66
There is still due from the City of New York,	216,666.66
And from Brooklyn, ...	433,333.34
Total cost of bridge, ...	$15,337,056.66

ADMINISTRATIVE INTEGRITY

During the period occupied by its erection New York was in the clutches of the Tweed ring, an audacious and unscrupulous gang of thieves. Yet, when the accounts were finally audited, every dollar of the appropriations was found to have been expended in wages or material, and its actual face value was represented in the completed structure. The ring had proposed otherwise and the belief was general that the bridge treasury had been looted. Mayor William C. Havemeyer appointed a committee to investigate the matter. Abram S. Hewitt was a member of that committee. In speaking of the results of this inquiry, Mr. Hewitt said:

MR. HEWITT'S TESTIMONY

"The duty was performed without fear or favor. The methods by which the ring proposed to benefit themselves were clear enough, but its members fled before they succeeded in reimbursing themselves for the preliminary expenses which they had defrayed. With their flight a new era commenced, and during the three years I acted as a trustee I am sure that no fraud was committed, and that none was possible. Since that time the board has been controlled by trustees, some of whom are thorough experts in bridge building, and the others men of such high character that the suggestion of malpractice is improbable to absurdity.

"The bridge has not only been honestly built, but it may be safely asserted that it could not now be duplicated at the same cost. Much money might, however, have been saved if the work had not been delayed through lack of means and unnecessary obstacles interposed by mistaken public officials. Measured by its capacity and the limitations imposed on its construction by its relation to the interests of traffic and navigation, it is the cheapest structure ever erected by the genius of man."

SUCCESS OF THE BRIDGE

In a certain sense this bridge was an experiment. That it would largely eliminate the East River as an obstacle to travel to and from Brooklyn, and that it would place the outlying districts of that city at the door of New York, were facts known and appreciated by its promoters; but whether the people would avail themselves of the increased facilities afforded was a matter of freely expressed doubts. To convince oneself that the bridge has more than fulfilled all the expectations of its projectors, it is only necessary to view the vast multitudes that are continuously passing across it. But the real work it has accomplished can best be ascertained by an examination of the sections of Brooklyn, formerly waste spaces, that are now covered with the homes of people, a large portion of whom resort daily to New York.

We have extended our notes on the Brooklyn Bridge to considerable length because of its vast importance in providing easy transit between sections of the city that were separated by a natural barrier, because it was the first municipal undertaking on the line of rapid transit, and because the bridge is beautiful to a

WILLIAMSBURGH BRIDGE.

degree as well as useful. It is said to be the most inspiring example of suspended bridge construction in the world. It is doubtful whether it will be duplicated anywhere in the future. Its lofty towers and its graceful span are visible to everyone who enters our harbor. It is a notable monument to the genius of the engineers who planned it and to the public spirit of those citizens who, with untiring zeal in the face of great obstacles, so worked that it was carried to completion. It typified union between nearby centers of unrelated population. It has led to the conception of that political union which has made New York the second city on the globe. It brought the men of both sections into collaboration for transportation facilities of far wider scope and usefulness. ITS IMPORTANCE

WILLIAMSBURGH BRIDGE.

A second suspension bridge over the East River was begun in 1896 and formally opened in December, 1903. It spans the river between the foot of Delancey street, Manhattan, and the foot of South Fifth and South Sixth streets, Brooklyn, and has a total length, from the entrance at street grade in Manhattan to the entrance in Brooklyn, of 7,200 feet. Through its entire length it has a clear width of 118 feet, and provides for two elevated railway tracks, four street railway tracks, two 18-foot roadways, two footpaths, and two bicycle paths. It is very remarkable in its capacity to carry traffic. CAPACITY

The foundation piers, two for each tower, were sunk to bed rock, about 70 feet below mean high water, by means of timber caissons similar to those used in the old bridge, but different in one essential point. The entire caisson was stiffened with a series of massive plate-steel riveted trusses, eight in all, which extended entirely across it from wall to wall. The working chamber was also strengthened with two solid bulkheads built across it. Level with the bottom of the walls was a framework of 16-inch timbers bolted to the side walls with tie rods. At each intersection vertical posts reached from this frame to the roof, and the whole system was tied together and stiffened against lateral distortion by diagonal struts and tie rods. The object of this bracing and truss work was not merely to enable the roof to carry the superincumbent load of masonry, but to enable the whole caisson to endure without distortion the heavy transverse strains to which it would be subjected should it become "hung" upon any projecting point of the uneven rock bottom. Each caisson was built upon launching ways and floated to its destination. CAISSONS

The piers are built of limestone up to low water level, above which they consist of a granite facing with a limestone backing. They are finished with two heavy coping courses of simple and pleasing design, and one pedestal course of granite blocks.

ANCHORAGE The anchorages measure 182 feet in width, 158 feet in depth, and 120 feet from the foundation to the coping. Forty feet of the mass is below the street level, above which it rises some 80 feet. The total pull of the four cables is 20,250 tons. The anchorage could only be moved by being rotated upon its "toe" as an axis, or by sliding bodily forward. To resist rotation the masonry is massed at the rear, most of it being directly above the anchor plates to which the cables are secured, the forward half being of hollow construction. Sliding is resisted by the mass of earth at the toe and by the frictional resistance between the masonry itself and the earth upon which it rests; this is also increased by the stepping of the bottom of the foundation.

TOWERS At each corner of each of the tower foundations, or piers, is a large block of dressed granite upon each of which rests a casting forming the base of a leg, or column, of the tower. Each half of each tower is composed of four columns which are 8 feet square at the bottom and taper to a square of 4 feet at a height of 20 feet, the latter section being then maintained throughout their full height. The columns are 310 feet in height, and are built up of two thicknesses of plate riveted together. The base is stiffened by diaphragms, but in the upper 4-foot section there are eight built-up Z-bars, two on each inside face of the column. All the columns are vertical up to the level of the roadway, above which they have a batter toward each other of 14 feet in a height of 215 feet. The four columns are strongly united by bracing, and just below the floor a system of lattice bracing is placed entirely around each tower and also between the towers. Above the roadway the towers are tied together by latticed and diagonal members. The saddle castings upon which the cables rest are located immediately above the legs of the towers, the weight being distributed and the structure stiffened at this point by a system of deep girders.

CABLES Each of the four cables consists of 37 strands of No. 8 wire, and each strand is made up of 281 wires, so that in each cable there are 10,397 wires. The specifications required a tensile strength of 200,000 pounds per square inch of section, and an elongation of at least 5 per cent. in a length of 8 inches. Instead of wrapping the cables with wire in order to protect them from the atmosphere, as was done with the Brooklyn Bridge cables, they were enclosed in 1-16-inch sheet steel which reaches from one suspender band to another. The suspenders, which are 20 feet apart, are steel wire rope; they are attached to the stiffening trusses at their point of intersection with the floor beams.

SADDLES

The saddles weigh over 32 tons each. The cable rests in a groove struck in a plane parallel with the axis of the bridge and on a radius of 21 feet 6½ inches. The saddle is supported upon 22 steel channel beams, and movement of the saddle is provided for by 40 steel rollers placed between the saddle casting and the beams.

SUSPENDED STRUCTURES

In order to compensate for the vertical distortion produced by unequal loading, and to distribute such loads, it was necessary to stiffen the floor system. In the old bridge this was accomplished by four longitudinal trusses; but in this case there are only two trusses, each 40 feet deep, which extend entirely across the bridge. The bottom chord is built into the floor system and is of the same depth. The floor of the bridge is composed of a series of transverse plate girders, 5 feet in depth, which extend all the way across. These are spaced 20 feet apart, and are bridged longitudinally by lines of plate-steel stringers. There are 20 of these lines of stringers which extend through the structure from end to end. The roadways are carried by the overhanging ends of the floor beams. The central portion of the floor beams is supported at two points from overhead trusses, which are built in between opposite panel-points of the upper chords of the stiffening trusses. This construction reduces the weight and admits of the use of much shallower floor beams than would otherwise be necessary. Wind pressure is resisted by a horizontal truss between the top chords of the stiffening trusses, and by the manner in which the longitudinal stringers are riveted intercostally between the floor beams; the tensional stresses, due to a wind blowing across the bridge, are resisted in the leeward half of the floor by the stringers and the bottom chord of the stiffening truss, and the compressive stresses are similarly provided for by the stringers and bottom chord of the windward half of the floor system.

THE TRUSSED STRUCTURE

The suspended portion of the structure occupies only that portion lying between the towers, the land part of the cables carrying no load whatever. Between the anchorages and towers are parallel-chord trusses with their centers resting upon steel piers. The main trusses are not provided with slip-joints, as are those of the Brooklyn Bridge, but are continuous from anchorage to anchorage; neither are they rigidly united to the towers or anchorages. They are furnished with roller bearings at the anchorages and with rocker bearings at the main towers; this construction permits of their free expansion from the center toward each anchorage.

The bridge was designed by L. L. Buck, whose work in renewing the original Roebling suspension bridge at Niagara had already attracted attention.

COST The contract prices for the bridge were as follows:

New York tower foundation, ...	$373,463
Brooklyn tower foundation, ...	485,082
Anchorages, ...	1,570,000
Towers and shore spans, ...	1,221,726
Cables and suspenders, ...	1,398,000
Approaches, ...	2,411,000
Main span suspended system, ...	1,123,400

The total estimated cost of the bridge, including land and stations, is $20,000,000.

MANHATTAN BRIDGE

SIZE The new Manhattan Bridge, the foundations and piers of which have been completed, will extend from near the intersection of the Bowery and Canal Street in New York, to Willoughby Street, between Prince and Gold Streets, in Brooklyn. It will be the longest of the bridges across the East River, measuring about 10,000 feet between terminals. The floor of the bridge will be 120 feet wide over all; the center span will be 1,470 feet from center to center of the towers, and each land span will be 725 feet in length. The two steel towers will be 400 feet above high water.

The proposition to use steel eye-bars for this bridge was rejected by the Commissioner of Bridges in 1904, and it was decided to return to the wire cable type. The arrangement of spans, capacity and loadings proposed for the eye-bar bridge and recommended by the commission of engineers appointed during the preceding year was, however, retained in the new wire cable design. The specifications for the cables and suspenders called for an ultimate strength of not less than 215,000 pounds per square inch before galvanizing, and an elongation of not less than 2 per cent. in 12 inches of observed length.

TOWERS The principal novelty in the design is found in the towers. Each is composed of four columns standing in a transverse plane, the columns being in the same vertical planes as the chain cables. A side view of the columns shows that, from their greatest width of 22 feet at the platform, they taper to 14 feet where they are supported upon a steel pin 2 feet in diameter, which rests upon a cast-steel footing. This construction distributes the load evenly over the masonry pier. In theory the towers are free to rock upon these pin bearings, but a movement of a few inches at their tops, caused by live load or temperature changes, would be taken care of by the elasticity of the towers themselves.

The anchorages will be formed with arches for street traffic, and will be provided with stairways and elevators, so that access can be had to the roadway from these points. The large interior space will be utilized as an assembling hall.

The estimated cost of the tower and anchorage piers is about $3,000,000, and of the superstructure $10,000,000. These figures do not include land damages, or stations. The bridge was designed by Gustave Lindenthal, working in connection with H. Hornbostel as consulting architect. COST

BLACKWELL'S ISLAND BRIDGE.

In 1884 a franchise was granted for the bridging of the East River at Blackwell's Island, but no steps toward actual construction were taken until 1898, when the Commissioner of Bridges prepared plans. These provided for a bridge having its western terminus on the block bounded by Fifty-ninth and Sixtieth streets and Avenues A and B, and its eastern terminus in Long Island City. Work was commenced in 1901, and was carried forward so slowly that in 1902 only about $42,000 had been expended. The plans were then revised, the changes affecting the superstructure chiefly, although provision was made for elevators to the roadway from the island. These called for two cantilever bridges having the following spans: A shore span on the Manhattan side, 469½ feet in length; a river span of 1,182 feet; a central span across the island of 630 feet; a second river span of 984, and a shore span of 459 feet on Long Island. The length of the bridge, including approaches, will be 7,636 feet. DESIGN

The towers will rest upon masonry piers which will extend up to the roadway. Each tower will consist of two steel legs of box section, spaced 93 feet from center to center at the base and 60 feet at the top, transversely of the bridge. The height between the chords at the towers will be 185 feet. The superstructure will be made up of two lines of trusses placed 60 feet from center to center. The top chord, being the tension member, will consist of eye- TOWERS bars of nickel steel having a tensile strength of 90,000 pounds per square inch and an elongation of 18 per cent. in 8 inches. The bottom chord will be of standard box construction. The roadway will be carried on transverse floor beams which will extend beyond the trusses a sufficient distance to provide a line of trolley cars at each side. The central portion of the bridge will be two-decked, the upper floor having two elevated railway tracks and two footwalks, each 11 feet wide. Beneath this will be two more trolley tracks, between which will be a roadway with a clear width of 36 feet.

The estimated cost of the bridge, including land damages, is $12,548,500. It is expected to be finished in 1906.

The three bridges last described will open sections of Brooklyn that cannot be conveniently reached by the Brooklyn Bridge. They will connect with the elevated system of that Borough, and thereby serve the territory to the north-east of that covered by the old bridge. In addition they will do much toward relieving the crowded condition of the old bridge, since the termini of two of them in New York are in the districts that supply most of the traffic for that bridge.

KIOSK — N. Y. SUBWAY

CHAPTER V

TUNNELS

HUDSON RIVER TUNNEL.

Greater problems than those involved in the making of an easy way across from Manhattan Island to Brooklyn were involved in the proposition to provide transit facilities to the section of New Jersey opposite New York City. The Hudson is a full mile wide. Up and down the river vessels of all sorts are constantly plying. They must have an unobstructed passage, not only at the center of the stream, but at all points between the banks. From time to time proposals were advanced to build a bridge over the river. To this moment no individual or interest has made progress in that direction. Ferryboats are still carrying passengers and teams over it. Freight is transported largely in cars placed on floats and towed by steam vessels. Some barges, large enough to take on board passenger coaches, are used to facilitate transit with New England connections.

THE NORTH RIVER PROBLEM

In 1871 an individual who was neither a citizen of New York nor connected with the business of New York; who was not even an engineer, although he had been concerned in railroad construction, conceived the idea of making a tunnel under the river. He had come from the Pacific coast via Omaha, and had seen there work going on building piers for a great railroad bridge over the Missouri. This was done by setting up iron cylinders at points suitable for piers. In order to sink these to bedrock they were so made that compressed air could be pumped into them, and workmen and materials could be taken into them through so-called air locks at the top. The water having been driven out at the bottom by air pressure, the men were able to remove earth, and drop the cylinders by degrees until rock was reached. The structure was then filled with concrete masonry, and sure foundations provided for the superstructure.

D. C. HASKIN

Seeing this work, this man of engineering turn and enterprise, of long foresight and undaunted courage, conceived the idea that the iron cylinders, fitted

PNEUMATIC TUNNELING

with air locks, could be placed horizontally, starting out below water-level from a shaft provided for the purpose; that the earth could be excavated in front, the compressed air providing a safe place for the workmen; that successive rings of iron could be added to the cylinder, and so a tunnel constructed from shore to shore of any river or arm of the sea. Having reached his conception he cast about for a place of importance to begin work, and very naturally decided that the best location would be under the Hudson at New York. He did not live to see his great project completed; but it may be doubted whether the actual fact would have added to the certitude of his mind. He was one of those men whose faith in their ideas, wild though they may seem to others, is absolute.

So while the work of sinking the piers for the Brooklyn bridge was under way, and no step had yet been taken to string cables across the East River, he set to work to solve the problem of transit to New Jersey on a different and more venturesome line, declaring to his friends that tunnels, not bridges, were practical, and that in the long run the world would so decide. And so convinced was he of the merit of his proposed enterprise that he would not seek state or municipal aid, or the aid of the great railroads centering in Jersey City, but would do it all himself, out of his own means and the means of friends who might have faith in the enormous values he proposed to create. It is almost unnecessary to say that he died in proverty. He was blind in his latter days, yet his courage never failed. To the end he believed that he had pointed the way, shown others how a great work should be done, and that he would be called a great benefactor long after his critics were forgotten.

NATURAL CONDITIONS

The originality of Mr. Haskin's plan was not more conspicuous than its extreme simplicity. The silt forming the bed of the Hudson is a deposit due to the washing away of the rocks of the upper river. When dry it is an impalpable powder, and when saturated with water it is as difficult to control as any water-bearing sand. But between these two conditions, that of extreme dryness and wetness, is a stage in which the silt assumes almost the consistency and characteristics of clay. When carrying a certain of degree of moisture, it will stand up like clay, and may be handled in the same way. This fact was taken advantage of, and because of it the first part of the work was done successfully. The scheme was to maintain within the heading an air pressure as nearly equal as possible to the hydrostatic head. In this way it was thought that the silt, having just the right amount of moisture, would form a barrier or partition that would effectually prevent the entrance of water and permit the heading to be worked.

The result proved the soundness of this reasoning. The heading was advanced without support of any description and the tunnel advanced without resort to timbering.

WORK STARTED

In November, 1874, work was begun by sinking a shaft on the New Jersey side 83 feet back from the bulkhead wall. This shaft was circular in plan, 30 feet inside and 38 feet outside diameter, the brickwork being 4 feet thick at the bottom and 2½ at the top. The bottom of the shaft was sunk to a depth of 54 feet below mean high water. Upon each of the east and west sides was built a false piece, 26 feet wide by 24 feet high, having an elliptical form, and which was finally to be removed to permit the passage of the tunnel. In the east side of the shaft, above the false piece, was an opening to receive an air-lock. The lock was 6 feet in diameter by 15 feet in length, and was provided with a door in each end in the usual manner. The so-called temporary entrance was then begun. This consisted of a series of 11 rings, formed of plates 2 feet wide. Each ring was 18 inches larger than the one preceding it and the largest was 20 feet in diameter. As the tops of these rings were in the same horizontal line, their bottoms formed steps leading up to the lock, the chamber forming a cone having its upper side at right angles to the diameter. From the base of this cone two tunnels were started, it having been decided to build two parallel single-track tunnels instead of one large one.

METHOD OF OPERATING

The north tunnel was first begun. As the largest ring of the chamber was not large enough to embrace both tunnels, it was necessary to extend the sides and inverts beyond the ring. Plate by plate an iron ring or shell was built, of a size equal to the exterior of the north tunnel, and brickwork was laid in this 2 feet thick. The regular work of tunnel building was then begun. Silt was removed until the top center plate of a new ring could be put in and bolted to the one behind. Then a plate was inserted at each side and bolted to the center plate and to the ring already in place. When four rings of plates had been put in and braced, the heading was cleaned out and the masonry laid, thus completing a section of 10 feet. The plates were of ¼-inch boiler iron 2½ feet wide by 3½ feet long, and were flanged with angle iron on the four sides. The heading was cut into steps, upon which the men stood while shoveling, and was entirely exposed, no attempt being made to sheath any part of it. The air pressure was kept about equal to the hydrostatic head, and increased from 18 pounds at first to 36 at a distance of 1,800 feet from the shaft. The tunnel was 16 feet wide by 18 feet high inside.

AIR PRESSURE

Early in the work it was found that no fixed rule could be adopted to govern the pressure of air, and that a pressure that served well one day would not be suitable the next. This was due to two causes. The excavated chamber, ready for the masonry, was about 23 feet in diameter, and the difference in water pressure between the top and bottom was, therefore, about 11 pounds per square inch. This was a disadvantage, and, in combination with the constantly changing nature of the material passed through, rendered it difficult to decide upon the air pressure that should be carried. Experience soon showed that a little less than the hydrostatic pressure at the axis of the tunnel was the most desirable under ordinary conditions. Even under these circumstances air would escape at the roof while water was weeping through at the bottom. It was more desirable to keep the silt at the top in perfect condition than at the bottom, for the reason that an excessive air pressure meant the forcing out of the water at the crown, thereby drying the silt and causing it to fall in lumps sometimes of considerable size. This was more to be dreaded than the weeping in of water at the invert, since the falling of a mass from the roof might open a pocket that would permit the air to rush out in such volume as to cause flooding. Leaks in the crown and top sides were detected by passing a candle over the surface, the flame being blown into a hole by the escaping air; larger openings could be detected by the sound of the outrushing air. Wet silt applied to the spot in right quantity remedied the trouble.

REMOVING TEMPORARY ENTRANCE

After the north tunnel had been finished to a distance of over a quarter of a mile the south one was started, and after this had been advanced some distance the two headings were closed with timber bulkheads, and the work of removing the temporary entrance was started. This entrance had been built through made ground, mostly of cinders, which had been disturbed by the sinking of the shaft and had given trouble during the placing of the air-lock by flowing down the side of the shaft. The first operations were directed toward the removal of the last or largest ring. The two plates adjoining the center one were taken down and the silt dug out, so that when the plates were re-inserted they were on the curve to be formed for the new work, the object being to construct a bridle, as it were, to cover both tunnels with one span or arch and leave a large chamber. This became known as the "working" chamber. In this way four rings were removed and the masonry built, after which the plates in the roof of the remaining rings were taken down, their place being supplied by the hood forming the crown of the new work. This hood reached from the completed work to the shaft, which it joined 3 feet above the lock, and then extended down each side and against the shaft as close as it could be fitted.

On the morning of July 21, 1880, a blow-out occurred at this point, the air escaping up along the side of the shaft. The falling earth and plates so wedged the inner lock door that it could not be opened to allow the men to escape and 20 were drowned. At the inquest that followed, the engineers employed upon the tunnel were vastly relieved when Mr. Haskin stated that he, and he alone, was responsible for the plans and for their execution. The accident itself injured the undertaking from a financial standpoint. ACCIDENT

After the accident the tunnel was re-opened by means of a caisson that was sunk within a cofferdam, the latter being employed to confine the loose material. The caisson was 41½ by 24 feet 10 inches. After it had reached the proper level it was united with the tunnels and shaft, and the interior lined with masonry. The work was now the same as before the accident, with the exception that the temporary entrance had been replaced by a substantial chamber of brick, and additional facilities had been made for entering the work.

When building the tunnel proper it was found that the shell was at times forced out of line by the weight of silt resting upon it, making it difficult to maintain an accurate grade. The difficulty was overcome by the introduction of a "pilot." This was a tube of boiler iron, 6 feet in diameter and of a length sufficient to project a few feet into the undisturbed silt of the heading and also a few feet into the completed work. It thus formed a rigid hub, supported at each end, from which, as a foundation, braces radiated to support the plates. The pilot was built of flanged plates, all of the same size, so that those at the near end could be taken down and carried forward as the work advanced. PILOT

In view of the fact that other tunnels are building or to be built across the Hudson, it may not be amiss to dwell briefly upon some of the peculiar characteristics of the silt which forms the bed of the river. When it carries the proper degree of moisture it forms a compact, dense, tenacious mass, having such cohesion that it retains a given shape for an extended period of time. In this state it may be handled much as ordinary putty. It is not dirty, in the usual sense of that word; a little water quickly relieves the hands of its presence, and the flesh has a soft, almost oily, feeling afterward. Its most important feature in relation to tunneling operations, and one directly the outcome of its cohesiveness when of the proper degree of saturation, is that both air and water pass through it very slowly. When well mixed with a sufficient volume of water, it flows as freely PROPERTIES OF SILT as quicksand and is much more troublesome to control. It was found impossible to force the hand, either clenched or open, to any considerable depth into the exposed silt at the heading. The steps cut in the face of the heading retained their sharp outlines quite long enough to permit the placing of plates in the upper portion of a ring and excavating a new series of steps. It is impossible for an air pocket to remain in moist silt, because the gradually closing silt is bound to force the air out. These properties of silt make it a most reliable material through which to build a tunnel, since, once constructed, it may be safely assumed that the structure will remain in place indefinitely. Piles may be driven to almost any depth in silt, provided the blows are rapidly delivered and that the operation is continuous; and again if a pile be sunk too far it may be drawn up to the desired level, where it will remain firmly planted after the silt has had time to settle around it. Constant and uniform pressure has little or no effect upon this material, but a shock or jar disturbs it and partially or wholly destroys its grip. It was for this reason principally that the engineers of the Pennsylvania Tunnels decided to anchor the tubes by means of screw piles, as they feared the disturbing effects of heavy trains.

STARTING NEW YORK END

The shaft method of reaching grade, as adopted at the western end, had proved costly and troublesome, and therefore the chief engineer of the work at this time, S. H. Finch, decided to start the tunnels at the New York end by means of a timber caisson, which measured 48 by 29½ feet in plan. When the caisson had been sunk to a depth of 56 feet below mean high water it was almost wholly embedded in sand. Holes were bored through the west side of the caisson on the line of the outside of the tunnels. After the circle of holes had been nearly finished the upper part was cut out and a roof plate put in and held by braces. Others were inserted at the sides and in advance of this, until, at a distance of 12 feet from the caisson, a bulkhead of iron plates was started at the top and built down. In building the next section the same method was pursued, but the plates of the first bulkhead were always kept at a higher level than the bottom of those in advance, in order to prevent the entrance of water. As soon as it had been lined with iron the section was cleaned out and the brickwork laid. An idea of how this job was viewed by the technical press may be formed by the following extract, which was published after the tunnels had been carried forward some distance:

TUNNELING THROUGH SAND

"The fact that the caisson was embedded in sand led to the belief, among many engineers of high standing, that an outlet could not be obtained and the tunnel started by the system of working by compressed air. It has become unsafe to pronounce an unfavorable opinion in regard to any particular piece of work connected with the tunnel. In more than one instance obstacles which seemed to present an insurmountable barrier to all future progress have been met and conquered, and the work has gone forward. New devices and plans have kept pace with new difficulties. At a first glance the sand above mentioned seemed to contain all the characteristics requisite for a first-class insurmountable obstacle. Upon the least reduction of the air-pressure this material would follow the water into the caisson; the smallest opening afforded a ready passage. The water and sand could be kept quiet as far down as the air-pressure was carried, and no farther; and if a trench were dug the upward pressure, due to the difference between the air-pressure and head of water, or depth of excavation, would fill the trench with sand and water faster than it could be taken out, and the adjacent material would be in no better condition than at first."

THE DIFFICULTIES

This was the first and has remained the only instance of the building of a sub-aqueous tunnel through sand and gravel without the aid of a shield. It is safe to predict that it will never again be attempted, but as a specimen of what can be accomplished under the most discouraging surroundings it deserves record.

ENGLISH CONTRACTORS

In 1888 the firm of S. Pearson & Son, of England, assumed the contract, with Sir John Fowler and Sir Benjamin Baker, who had just finished the Forth Bridge, the greatest cantilever ever erected, as consulting engineers. The plans were immediately changed and the shield method substituted. The next most important change made was the use of heavy cast-iron plates in place of masonry. The light boiler plates used in the early work were never considered as being an integral and permanent part of the cylinder; they only served to keep the silt out until the masonry had been laid, after which their existence was a matter of no moment. Lack of funds forced the stoppage of work, and, although spasmodic attempts were made from time to time to resume operations, nothing of a serious nature was done until the early part of 1902.

NEW COMPANY IN CONTROL

The New York & New Jersey Railroad Company acquired the franchise and property of the old company in that year. The north tunnel has been opened from shore to shore and operations have been begun on the approaches. The plates in the south tunnel, which had been reduced in diameter to 15 feet 3 inches, were 6½ feet long, 2 feet wide, 1 7-16 inches thick, 8 inches deep through the

CHANGE OF PLAN

webs, and had flanges $1\frac{1}{2}$ inches thick. The sides of each plate were accurately faced, the long ones being in a plane at right angles with the axis of the tunnel and the short ones on a radius, so that they fitted together with great nicety. With these plates it was impossible to distort the circular section of the tunnel, and with the shield it was easy to follow the exact grade and alignment. The change in diameter was decided upon because the large size is not necessary for trolley service. The original plan was to use the tunnel for regular railway service. The same plan would have been adopted with the north tunnel but for the fact that the heading, when the present management assumed control, was at the lowest point below the surface of the river, and had but a few feet of silt overhead. Under these circumstances it was not thought expedient to make the change. The general method of working does not differ from that usually followed, and therefore needs no special description.

The charter of the company made no provision for connecting tunnels or roadways within the city. Application was made to the Rapid Transit Commission for authority to cross the city to Fourth avenue, and also by Sixth avenue to Thirty-third street. These applications were granted.

FRANCHISE BY RAPID TRANSIT COMMISSION

Beginning when these extensions shall have been finished, and ending in twenty-five years from the completion of the railroad under the Hudson, the company is to pay 50 cents per linear foot of single track and of station platform for the first 10 years, and $1 per annum per linear foot during the next 15 years. A further annual sum is to be paid of 3 per cent. of the gross receipts for the first 10 years and 5 per cent. afterward. The gross receipts are estimated by agreement at $300,000 a year for the first 10 years. After that the gross receipts are to be determined upon the basis of the information then available as to actual traffic returns, and fixed by agreement or by arbitration.

RENTALS

The rental payable to the city, in accordance with the statute, is to be readjusted at the end of the period of 25 years above mentioned, and thereafter at intervals of 25 years. If the city and the company shall not agree upon the rates at the time of such readjustment, they are to be determined by the Supreme Court of this State.

The tunnel entrances are to be constructed entirely through private property, unless the Board shall approve of an exit or exits situated within the streets; this will do away with the use of kiosks in the streets. An important clause in the franchise is the following:

"As soon as the railroad is completed, the Tunnel Company is to file with the

Board a statement of the cost of construction of the portions which the city has the right to acquire; and if those statements are disapproved by the Board, the whole subject of cost is to be submitted to arbitration forthwith. In this manner the actual cost of construction will be determined at the time, instead of being left to be determined under great difficulties many years afterwards." COST

The franchise contains provisions regarding the disposition of gas, water pipes, sewers and the like. The Tunnel Company agrees not to interfere with the construction of any rapid transit or street railroad over, along or under any portion of the streets occupied by it, provided they do not actually interfere with its structure.

In January of the present year the Hudson Company was incorporated, with a capital of $21,000,000, to take over and eventually operate the tunnels now under construction under the Hudson. These comprise the tunnel just described, and one to be built from Church and Cortlandt Streets in New York to Exchange Place in Jersey City, and by tunnel under Jersey City and Hoboken, with the depots of the Delaware, Lackawanna & Western, Erie, Pennsylvania and Jersey Central Railroads. OPERATING COMPANY FORMED

HUDSON & MANHATTAN RAILROAD TUNNEL.

This is the line to be built from Cortlandt street, New York, to Jersey City, referred to above. The franchise granted by the Rapid Transit Commission provides for the construction of two tracks under Cortlandt street, to Church, to Fulton and thence to the State boundary line in the Hudson. Provision is also made for a subway for foot passengers from Church street station under Dey street and Broadway to John street to connect with the present subway. The payments by the company to the city for the first 25 years are as follows:

"A charge of $100 per annum for the right to enter the city, including the approaches from the west to the pier line. TERMS OF FRANCHISE

"A charge for the right within the pier line, and for the underground portions of streets, and for the passenger subway under Dey street and Broadway, at the rate of 50 cents per linear foot of single track or subway per annum for the first 10 years, and $1 per annum per linear foot during the next 15 years.

"A charge for the underground portions of Cortlandt, Dey and Fulton streets near the terminal station, and where the company's tunnel construction comes within 16 feet 8 inches of the surface, at the rate of 40 cents per superficial square foot per annum for the first 10 years, and 80 cents per annum per superficial square foot for the next 15 years.

"A further annual sum for tunnel rights under the street of 3 per cent. of the gross receipts of the New York portion of the railroad for 10 years, and 5 per cent. for the next 15 years. Such gross receipts are fixed for the first 25 years at $300,000 per annum, whether in fact such gross receipts shall be more or less."

The franchise is granted in perpetuity. In regard to this the Committee of the Board on Contracts said:

READJUSTMENT

"The tunnel authorized by this franchise, at the west, ends at the boundary line between the States of New York and New Jersey; and from that line west the tunnel must be continued under the authority of the State of New Jersey. It is obvious that the New York grant is susceptible of use only in connection with the New Jersey part of the tunnel under the Hudson River. If the New York grant were limited, then at the end of the limited term the grant would be of no use or advantage to the city. A readjustment of rental charges at 25 year intervals will, in cases like this, give the city all the practical advantages of a limitation of the life of the grant."

The tunnels along the water front of Jersey City connecting the railroad depots will be two-track, as will also be the tunnels in New York, while the river will be crossed in each case by twin tunnels. The Hudson Companies are working in harmony with the railroads and with the Public Service Corporation of New Jersey, which controls the surface transportation facilities of Jersey City, Newark and other districts.

PENNSYLVANIA RAILROAD TUNNELS.

Of more importance than the original enterprise of Mr. Haskin, extended as it has been by the company that now holds the franchise, is the great work being pressed forward by the Pennsylvania Railroad in order to provide terminals in the heart of New York City, and make connections with other systems.

ROUTE OF TUNNEL

Its new roadway, devised for this purpose, will leave the main line a short distance east of Newark, N. J., and pass across the Hackensack Meadows to the west face of Bergen Hill. From this point the road will be entirely in tunnel under Bergen Hill, the North River, the Island of Manhattan, and the East River, reaching the surface about a mile east of the latter in Long Island City.

The road will be double-tracked across the Meadows, and will pass under the North River in two parallel, single-track tunnels. These will be spaced 37 feet between centers, and at intervals of 300 feet will be connected by passageways that will ordinarily be closed by doors to prevent the air passing from one tunnel to the other. Under Manhattan Island the tubular construction will cease, and the two tracks will diverge into two tunnels, with three tracks each—the main line and two sidings. These large tunnels will extend for about 1,000 feet, when they will unite into a four-track, single-arch tunnel, extending for a distance of 605 feet to the western end of a station or depot. The station will be 260 feet wide from Tenth to Ninth avenues, on the line of Thirty-second and Thirty-third streets; then about 560 feet wide to Seventh avenue. Its area will be about 27 acres, and it will contain about 16 miles of track. The lower level of the station will be devoted to the tracks; an intermediate level will contain waiting and baggage rooms, ticket offices, etc.

EASTERN DIVISION

The eastern division, beginning at Seventh avenue, will comprise two lines of triple-track arched tunnels, one underneath Thirty-second and the other underneath Thirty-third street. These will be continued for 1,600 feet, when each set of three tracks will unite into a double-track arched tunnel for a distance of 2,400 feet. The East River will be crossed by four single-track tubes, coming to the surface at Thompson avenue, Long Island City. At this point there will be a terminal yard, where cars will be stored, and where the motive power will be changed to electricity or steam, according to the direction in which the train is traveling. Electric power only will be used in the tunnels.

CONNECTIONS

Connection will be made from this yard, by bridge and railroad, with the Long Island system and, via Hell Gate, with the New York, New Haven & Hartford Railroad on the north shore of Long Island Sound. A large freight terminal is being built at Greenville, N. J., from which cars will be transferred to Bay Ridge, L. I., and will then be taken to the Hell Gate Bridge by means of a connecting railroad. The total length of railway to be constructed in New York is 4.2 miles; and the total length of main track, exclusive of side tracks or track in the station, will be 22.6 miles. The distance from the surface of the ground at Twelfth avenue to the base of the rail will be 65 feet, and at Fifth avenue 75 feet.

FOURTH AVENUE STATION

The franchise provides also for a station at Fourth avenue and Thirty-third street, but this does "not include any right to connect at this point the tracks of the railway of the tunnel company with the tracks of any other railroad, for the continuous operation of trains over such tracks of the tunnel company and of any other railroad."

The undertaking is divided into two parts, and is being carried forward by two distinct companies. That portion lying in New Jersey, west of the State boundary line, which is about midway of the North River, is being built by the Pennsylvania, New Jersey & New York Railroad, while that portion east of the boundary and lying in New York is being constructed by the Pennsylvania, New York & Long Island Railroad. The eastern section is under the direction of Alfred Noble and the western under Charles M. Jacobs, chief engineers.

CAST-IRON SCREW PILES

The sub-aqueous portions of the work are being built by means of shields in the usual manner. All of the tunnels under the two rivers will be lined with cast-iron plates. In the North River tunnels a novel engineering feature has been introduced. The silt forming the bed is sufficiently firm to preserve the tunnel in perfect alignment, but it was thought that if the heavy motors are allowed to bear directly upon the shell their weight, and particularly the shock due to movement, may produce settlements, or set up stresses, that would result in fracture and consequent leakage. This difficulty will be overcome by the introduction of cast-iron piles placed beneath the center of the inverts, at every 15 feet, and extended, if necessary, to a depth of 150 feet. The tops of the piles are to be filled with concrete to a depth of 15 feet. The load will be distributed by a system of stringers capping the piles and carrying the rails. Should there be any movement of the piles, under the loads carried, it will not affect the tubes, which will serve their proper purpose as enveloping casings. After a certain length of shell has been completed it will be bulkheaded, placed under air pressure, and the piles screwed down from the interior. The piles are 27 inches in outside diameter, the screws being cast upon a shell 1¼ inches in thickness, and are made in sections 7 feet long. The screw, formed upon the lowest section, is 4 feet 8 inches in diameter. After one section has been screwed down another will be bolted to it, the process continuing until firm material has been reached. Grout under heavy pressure will be forced around the outside of the shell in both soft material and rock, and each tunnel will be lined with concrete.

CROSS SECTION

The tunnel is of new design in its cross section. The track is to be laid in a trough slightly greater in width than the widest car, the sides of which extend nearly up to the window sills. Sidewalks will be formed upon each side at the top. Within the sides there will be conduits for telegraph and telephone wires, with high and low tension circuits. By the terms of the franchise the company pays the city $200 a year for the privilege of passing beneath the two rivers. Concerning this requirement, the committee appointed by the Rapid Transit Board to carry on preliminary negotiations with the railroad company said:

FRANCHISE

"The annual payment of $200 for the routes under the North and East Rivers outside of pier head-lines is more than nominal, though it is not important. It may be said in general that anyone who bridges a navigable river, or tunnels it so as to bring the opposite banks into easy communication without interference with navigation, confers great benefits upon the communities upon both sides of the river. Nevertheless, it is not practicable to certainly forecast the future, and your committee has, therefore, deemed it wise to affirm the principle of compensation, although making the rate for the first period of 25 years so small as not to be a material burden to the Pennsylvania Company."

For passing under the docks and bulkheads the payment is to be $0.50 per annum for the first 10 years and $1 for the next 15 years, for each linear foot of single track. The same rate is required for passing under the streets, with the exception of Thirty-second and Thirty-third streets, between Seventh and Ninth avenues. For the latter privilege the company will pay $14,000 per annum for the first 10 years and $28,000 for the next 15 years.

For the station at Thirty-third street and Fourth avenue the payment will be $14,000 a year for the first 10 and $28,000 for the next 15 years.

For the privilege of its main station the company will pay $36,000 per annum for 25 years, after which the compensation is to be readjusted. These annual payments cease if the company buys, for the sum of $788,600, that portion of Thirty-second street used by it. The franchise allows five years for the completion of the work.

In regard to the rental for the space within pier lines and streets, at so great a depth as not to interfere with underground structures or future rapid transit railroads, the committee said:

PRINCIPLE INVOLVED

"The Pennsylvania Company claimed, and not without reason, that its enterprise involved a large investment and serious risk; that it would bring enormous advantage to the city; that it would promptly and greatly increase the assessed valuations within a considerable area of the city, from which, in the increase of taxes, the city would derive a large and immediate increase in revenue; that the underground portions of the streets, nowhere approaching within 19 feet of the surface, had no present value; that the city itself made no use of such portions of its streets and might never use them; that, with unimportant exceptions, the city had never derived and may never derive revenue from them; that in foreign cities, and in other American cities, like rights had been accorded without compensation; that, in the city of Washington, the Pennsylvania Company had itself recently received such a right without rental, and that for the very enterprise now proposed the Pennsylvania Company has secured in Jersey City a right without rental. On these and other grounds the Pennsylvania Company claimed that the city ought not to require the payment of rental for the use of such underground portions of streets and dock property.

FRANCHISE VALUABLE

"Nevertheless, your committee was of the opinion that the franchise sought was in itself very valuable; that, although the enterprise would secure to the city highly important advantages, it was equally true that the advantages were mutual. Heretofore it has been usual in this city, as in other large American cities, to grant free of rental to railroad corporations traversing large sections of the country and which cannot be classed as urban, rights of way, over, on, or under any streets. But conceding that such a liberal policy in the past has benefited cities and helped to build them up with marvelous rapidity, it is also true that the railroad corporations themselves have been benefited in equal, and oftentimes in far greater measure. It would have been better for the cities,

RATE LAW DETERMINED

and more in consonance with sound policy in dealing with public property, that municipal authorities should have better appreciated the future value of their franchises. Your committee insisted that in this case a departure from the rule heretofore too generally prevailing must be made, and that in fixing the rental it ought to be assumed that, as the franchise was valuable to the company, and as it granted use of city property, the company should pay a fair rental. The committee was without precedent in determining the precise amount, but finally concluded that the best theory to adopt was that of an annual payment for trackage, and to fix the rate at one dollar per foot."

BALANCE OF VALUES

The report concludes with the following pertinent remarks:

"It is estimated that in the city of New York there are elevated, surface and steam railroads aggregating nearly 1,500 miles of single track. While it is not the purpose of your committee to imply that every mile of them is equal in franchise value to each mile of the Pennsylvania tracks now to be authorized, your committee is decidedly of the opinion that very many miles, and especially those of some of the steam railroads, have now a corresponding franchise value, and that if there had been a reasonable appreciation of the future value of all these railroad franchises (elevated, surface, and steam) by the municipal authorities when they were granted, the city would at the present time enjoy, and in the future continue to enjoy, a fair proportion of the pecuniary benefit which now goes wholly to the railroads; not solely as the result of their operation, but, in very great measure, of the continuous development of the city."

PERMANENT CONTROL

When this franchise was under consideration, the Pennsylvania Railroad firmly insisted upon the granting of certain privileges which it considered of vital importance to its plans. In building and developing its terminal, and in providing the necessary connections with existing steam railroads, it would spend from $35,000,000 to $50,000,000. The company expected to provide all the needed capital solely from its own resources. In time the business would assume proportions of great magnitude, and the city would be sure to derive its share of the benefits accruing therefrom. The company was, therefore, fixed in its determination to abandon the project if it were not assured of the permanent control of the improvements it was prepared to create. Without a grant in perpetuity the railroad might, at the expiration of its franchise, be deprived of all the results of its work. These considerations led to the changing of the rapid transit act so as to provide for grants of this character.

AMENDMENT TO CHARTER

On March 24, 1902, Mayor Seth Low sent to the Governor a bill entitled, "An act to amend the Greater New York Charter by adding a section in relation to franchises of tunnel corporations, for constructing and operating railroads to connect with other railroads, and form thereby a continuous line between points within and points without the City of New York." The following paragraphs from Mayor Low's memorandum on this bill are interesting:

"While the bill provides that a franchise may be granted in perpetuity for such a purpose, it carefully guards the right of the city to readjust the terms upon which the franchise shall be enjoyed, at intervals of not more than 25 years. The city is thus assured of the periodic opportunity to profit by any increase in the value of the franchise such as time may easily bring. The city is also assured of the right and opportunity to attach such conditions to the grant as public interests may require."

"Under these circumstances, I am of the opinion that a perpetual franchise in such a case may properly be granted; for the city is not deprived of the opportunity to profit by its increase in value. It is only deprived of the opportunity of using the franchise itself at the expiration of a limited grant. Inasmuch as the project in contemplation involves a tunnel under the North River for its completion, which tunnel lies outside of the city's control entirely; and inasmuch as that portion of the enterprise which the city does control is so vital to the Pennsylvania Railroad Company that it cannot afford to enter upon the undertaking except upon the grant of a franchise in perpetuity, I am of the opinion that this is a case in which good judgment justifies an exception to the general rule.

BASIC PRINCIPLE

"In this connection, it may not be amiss if I say that the provisions in the Greater New York Charter of 1897, limiting the power to grant franchises to a grant for a term of years, which were the basis of the provisions of the present charter, were inserted at my suggestion, when a member of the first charter commission. It is also interesting to point out that the provision for a periodic opportunity for a readjustment of the terms of any franchises that may be granted, under Section 32 of the Rapid Transit Law, was also inserted at my instance, when I was a member of the Rapid Transit Board. It will not therefore be contended, I am sure, that I have ever been careless of the city's interests in these regards. The basic principle of the ground lease, which I have often urged as a model for the city in its dealings with its franchises, is the opportunity which such a lease affords for a periodic adjustment of the terms between the owner and the lessee. If this privilege is retained, it becomes to a certain extent a matter of discretion as to whether a franchise should be granted in perpetuity or not. I freely admit that I prefer grants for a limited period; but even so good a rule as this may sometimes suffer an exception in the public interest."

LAW ENACTED

The Governor sent to the Legislature an emergency message in behalf of the immediate enactment of the bill. It became a law; and established beyond question the power of the Board to grant such franchises as that desired by the Pennsylvania Company. This new legislation and the grants to the Pennsylvania and to the New Jersey tunnel companies have tended to establish the policy that, for all transportation purposes, the streets of the city, whether on the surface or below the surface, shall be dealt with in the first instance by the Rapid Transit Commission.

That Commission has consistently and effectively sought to guard against improvident grants of transportation franchises to private corporations. Whether railroad construction and operation be municipal or under control of private corporations, it has held that no railroad use of streets shall obstruct future rapid transit or other profitable use of the streets for transportation purposes; that the city shall receive compensation for the use of streets, and that the terms of such compensation shall be readjusted at reasonably brief intervals. If the Rapid Transit Commission had rendered no other service to the city than to promote and determine this policy, it deserves very high appreciation from the citizens of to-day and those who will come hereafter.

USEFULNESS

The stupendous work undertaken by the Pennsylvania Railroad will be useful in our city in a remarkable degree. The city will no longer be insular, so far as passenger transportation is concerned. It will have direct communication under the East and North rivers. This will serve greatly the convenience of people who are journeying to or from distant points, and also the convenience of the greater multitudes who go and come from their homes in the country or by the sea.

FUTURE EFFECTS

And this must follow. There are other railways that serve our city. For each of these new conditions will be created by the enterprise of the Pennsylvania people. It would be going far to say that these other systems must emulate in full the enterprise of that great railroad. But certainly they will be stirred to do what they can. And so we may expect more than one system of railway tunnels under the Hudson, and we may expect great improvements in the approaches from the north. Otherwise it will be said in the future that the Pennsylvania Railroad had the courage to provide not only for its own proper traffic, but also in such way as to gather to itself traffic that belongs normally to others—that in fact it found great opportunities in the failures of rival lines. Some of these other lines command enormous resources. The real traffic of some of them is greater than that of the Pennsylvania. Surely it behooves them to look to the future.

CHAPTER VI.

ELEVATED RAILROADS.

NEW YORK.

RAPID TRANSIT SCHEMES

The present generation can have but a vague conception of the many and varied schemes that have been brought forward to solve the rapid transit problem. Thirty years ago, in 1875, the city took official cognizance of the question, and the first Rapid Transit Commission came into being. Before and after that time private enterprises were advocated, plans innumerable were drawn, legislation was obtained, capital was subscribed; yet only one undertaking became an accomplished fact. Some of the more prominent of these schemes are mentioned in the following chapters; but in a cursory way, since they are interesting only as incidents having an influence, but not a permanent place, in the final solution of the problem.

Dealing with the subject in January, 1874, the *Railroad Gazette* said: "The number of people in New York who think they know how to build a rapid transit railroad is, we believe quite as large as those who are sure they could edit a newspaper or keep a hotel. It is amusing to hear some of these assert, in the most dogmatic way, principles about which the most experienced engineer would hesitate to give an opinion. The whole subject has been up for discussion twenty years or more, and makes its appearance annually in the State Legislature. No systematic effort, so far as we know, has thus far been made to collect accurate information, and the public mind is in a state of chaos regarding the whole subject."

GRAVITY OF SITUATION

That the gravity of the situation was appreciated is shown by the following further quotation from the same paper: "It is not necessary to say anything here of the importance, in many different ways, of rapid transit to New York. It would widen her borders immensely; and population that belongs to her, instead of being driven across two rivers, would find convenient and in every way desirable homes to the northward in Westchester County. It is the one possible remedy for the overcrowding which has imposed so many social, moral and political evils upon the city. This overcrowding is likely to grow worse in degree and in consequences, unless some means shall be provided for supplying frequent, rapid, and cheap means of traveling between those parts of the city where business is done and districts nearby, now thinly peopled."

ELEVATED LINES

The undertaking that formed the exception referred to was the inception of elevated railroads. The four lines, constructed prior to 1880, constituted the only method of rapid communication between the northern and southern sections of the city, until the opening of the subway last year.

NEW YORK ELEVATED ROAD

The first line to be put in practical operation was popularly known as the Greenwich street elevated, although its corporate name was the New York Elevated Railroad. The plan of this road originated with C. T. Harvey. A company was organized, and in April, 1867, a charter was granted by the Legislature, empowering the company to construct an experimental line. Section 2 of the act was as follows:

GENERAL DESIGN

"The railway hereby authorized shall be operated exclusively by means of propelling cables attached to stationary engines placed beneath or beyond the surface of any street through which such railway may pass, and shall be concealed from view so far as the same may be detrimental to the ordinary uses of such streets. The structure shall consist of a single track, upon which the cars are to be moved in contrary directions upon opposite sides of the street, which track shall not exceed 5 feet in width between center of rails, and shall be supported by a series of iron columns, not exceeding 18 inches in diameter at the surface of the pavement, or equivalent space if in an elliptical form, which columns shall be placed at intervals of not less than 20 feet, except at street crossings or sidings, along the curbstone line between the sidewalk and carriageway, and attached at their upper extremities to the track aforesaid, so that the center of the track shall be perpendicular to the center of the columns, and at a distance of not less than 14 feet above the surface of the pavement. Wherever deemed necessary to prevent oscillation of the track aforesaid, a second series of columns may be extended on the building side of the sidewalk, at intervals of not less than 20 feet, which shall not be more than 9 inches in diameter at surface of pavement, and shall be so placed as not to obstruct any existing door or window without consent of the owner; and from the upper extremity of which braces or girders may be extended to the first series of columns mentioned for the purposes aforesaid."

EXPERIMENTAL SECTION

In July, 1868, an experimental section was built from the Battery to Dey street, along Greenwich, a distance of about one-half mile.

In the editorial correspondence to the *Journal* of the Franklin Institute, dated New York, December, 1867, we find the following, under the caption, "West Side and Yonkers Patent Railway," which describes how this road should be constructed and operated:

DESCRIPTION OF ROAD

"The experimental half mile authorized by act of legislature last winter is nearly completed. The line starts corner of Greenwich street and the Battery, and is now finished up to Rector street, a distance of some 1,500 feet. If the present experiment proves a success, the line will be continued this winter up Ninth avenue to the Hudson River Railroad depot, corner of Thirtieth street, with the eventual idea of extension to the village of Yonkers, on the Hudson, *via* King's Bridge. Should results warrant the further introduction of this system, a middle route up Broadway, as also an east side one as far as New Rochelle, on the Sound, are embodied in the schemes of the projectors.

CONSTRUCTION

"The mode of construction is simple and elegant, being unobstructive and open. The supporting principle, following the line of the curbstone, consists of single, wrought-iron columns, as made under the patent of the Phœnix Iron Company of Philadelphia, about 14 feet high, with the segments spread out in a graceful curve, to which the cross-heads for supporting the rail girders are attached. These are four-segment, 8-inch columns, with a thickness of metal of $\frac{3}{8}$ of an inch. They will be spaced 25 feet apart from center to center, as near as may be, thus necessitating simple girders to span the interval. These girders are composed of 8-inch deck beams in pairs, packed with a timber scantling, to which the rails are spiked, thus acting as an absorbent and cushion for the shocks of the traveling load. Beyond their fastening on the cross-heads of the columns, nothing more is required but simple stay-rods to prevent the spreading of the rails and girders.

The foundations are made stable by spreading out the segments at the base of the columns in a similar manner as noted above. A heavy casting, with the necessary lugs and ribs upon it, is made to fit the under surface of the segments thus swelled out, to which they are securely bolted. This casting, by means of its broad, flat base, is in turn bolted to a very heavy under-casting, secured to a well-bedded masonry pier 10 feet deep, by means of long bolts running the whole length of the masonry and firmly anchored therein. Between the rail girders a small covered square trough, with a slot on its upper side, is placed, returning under the street in the axis of the roadway, and of course through the masonry piers, into which it is carefully built."

A more interesting part of this description is the following:

METHOD OF OPERATING

"The motive power will consist of stationary engines at every half mile, under the sidewalk; each one operating a large single drum 6 feet in diameter, ingeniously contrived to accommodate two ropes of contiguous sections. The sections being so short, steel-wire ropes of but ½ inch in diameter will be used, thus obviating what has always been considered an insurmountable difficulty. The cars pass from one section to another by means of their own momentum. The gap thus caused is not over 20 feet, so that at a speed of 10 miles an hour the resistance to progression must be inappreciably small. At proper intervals, the rope will be attached to what you may call "universal trucks," about 2 feet long. They are universal in the sense that no matter what position they may assume, friction rollers will always be presented to roll upon. Upside down or sideways, they will roll; in addition to which the attachment of the rope is by means of swivel joints, so that no kink or twist can arise. A strong finger, as it were, projects above the slot mentioned in connection with the middle box in which it runs. To this the car is attached.

"The construction of the cars becomes, perhaps, the vital point in this scheme; but so far as competent engineering judgment can discern, no mechanical device has been neglected that promised to insure success. Experimenting alone will tell the tale.

"The difficulty is just here—a rope is running, say at a speed of 10 miles an hour, with nothing visible but the little fingers of the trucks. To these fingers the cars must be attached and detached, without slackening the rope and without producing a shock on the car or its passengers; it must slow up in stopping and gradually get headway in starting. It would hardly do to jump at once to full speed; it would rack everything to pieces. The slowing up after detachment will be a matter easily regulated by the brakes; but how to store up sufficient momentum to get under headway before making fast is the crucial point beyond which all other difficulties are but trifles."

This was to be accomplished in the following way:

CABLES

"The first experimental car will be about 30 feet long, with a barrel placed immediately below the floor, running the full length of the car, surrounded by a stiff spiral spring. Secondary springs of india rubber are attached to the spiral spring and the body of the car, running in an oblique direction. The shock of contact will be taken up on the springs, which force is stored up by another set of springs, to be used in starting the car for the next station. Attached to the spiral, and sliding on the barrel, the immediate attachment is effected by means of a lever operated by the attendant in charge of the car."

N. Y. ELEVATED RAILROAD CO.

Mistakes of a serious nature had been made both in the design of the structure and the method of propelling the trains. The columns were much too light for the service, and considerable experimenting was done before a satisfactory support was obtained. Moving the cars by a system of endless cables, as prescribed by law, proved to be a total failure. The result was that those who had contributed financially to the undertaking lost all confidence; the road was placed in the hands of trustees, and finally sold under foreclosure of mortgages held by various parties. The property and franchise were taken over by the New York Elevated Railroad Company, a corporation organized with a capital of $10,000,000.

STEAM AS PROPELLING POWER

In the meantime, legislation had been obtained permitting the use of steam as the propelling power. The new owners immediately removed the cables, and introduced light four-wheeled locomotives. Tests with the new engines were so successful that the company began the regular carriage of passengers April 20, 1871. After the installation of the engines the road became genuinely successful. At the beginning of 1874 the equipment comprised 4 engines and 10 cars; each of the latter seating 48 passengers and weighing 11,000 pounds. The quickest running time for the four miles of road then in operation was 18 minutes. From April 20, 1871, to January 2, 1872, 54,968 passengers were carried; in 1872 there were 242,190 passengers; and in 1873, 723,253 passengers. Up to the first of 1874 not a passenger had been injured. In those days the company refused to take more passengers than it could seat.

GILBERT ELEVATED RAILROAD

In 1871 a new road was chartered by the Legislature. The Gilbert Elevated Railroad proposed to erect a pneumatic tube, supported from heavy arches above the street. It was claimed that this road would be practically noiseless and the trains out of sight. As this plan was found to be impracticable and entirely too expensive, it was decided to build the tube without a top, and operate a steam road in the trough thus formed. Finally the trough was also abandoned, and the plan resolved itself into a simple elevated steam road. These alterations caused much opposition and extended litigation.

According to Wilson's History of New York, the Rapid Transit Commission of 1875* reported, in December of that year, "that their work was at an end, and that the task of building the roads upon the assigned streets—Ninth, Sixth, Third and Second avenues—had been awarded to the Gilbert road and to the New York road, the corporation then operating the little elevated road on Greenwich street.'

In 1876 the New York road had extended its line to Fifty-ninth street, and was running "40 through trains each day."

In the spring of 1877 a controlling interest in this road was obtained by Cyrus W. Field, who exhibited the same zeal in pushing it to final completion that had marked his connection with the Atlantic cable.

LEGAL TROUBLE

In those days the companies were almost constantly obstructed by suits brought by abutting property owners. In 1877 a single track and several sidings had been built from the Battery to Central Park, but it was impossible to complete the system because of legal proceedings. The same cause stopped work on the east side. In September of that year the Court of Appeals, by unanimous decision, declared that both companies were legal organizations, having proper authority to build the structures they had undertaken when stopped; and all injunctions were dissolved.

After this, work was rushed on both lines, and on June 5, 1878, the Sixth avenue road was opened from Rector street to the Park. In the intervening time it had passed into the control of the Metropolitan Elevated Company. In 1879 the two companies were consolidated under the control of the Manhattan Railway Company.

In August, 1878, the Third avenue line was opened to Forty-second street, and two years later the Second avenue line to Sixty-seventh street. In 1880 the roads on both sides of the city had reached the Harlem. Later the Third avenue line crossed the river and was carried to Bronx Park.

INTER-BOROUGH RAPID TRANSIT CO.

On January 1, 1903, the Interborough Rapid Transit Company leased the Manhattan Railway Company for 999 years, beginning April 1, 1903; the lessee guaranteeing dividends of 6 per cent. per annum, and an additional amount, if earned, of 1 per cent. until January 1, 1906; and after that date dividends of 7 per cent. upon the par value of stock outstanding. At the present time, therefore, the Interborough Rapid Transit Company controls the entire elevated system, as well as the underground roads now finished.

---

*A more extended account of the work of this commission is presented in another chapter.

The elevated roads certainly provided rapid transit facilities between the congested southern portion of New York and the districts to the north for many years. In sparsely inhabited regions such roads will undoubtedly be found useful in the future, but their field is limited.

TWENTY-THIRD STREET STATION — N. Y. SUBWAY

CHAPTER VII.

RAPID TRANSIT COMMISSION OF 1875.

A law enacted in 1875 authorized the Mayor of New York City to appoint a Board of Rapid Transit Commissioners to decide whether the city actually needed rapid transit, to select the route or routes, and, if found expedient, to organize a company to build the lines. Mayor William H. Wickham appointed the following commissioners: Joseph Seligman, Lewis B. Brown, Cornelius H. Delamater, Jordan L. Mott and Charles J. Canda. COMMISSION APPOINTED

This Board had power to locate "such railway or railways over, under, through, or across the streets, avenues, places, or lands, except Broadway and Fifth avenue below Fifty-ninth street, and Fourth avenue above Forty-second street, and except such portions of streets and avenues as are legally designated for the main line of or occupied by an elevated or underground railway in actual operation." The Board was to decide the first question within 30 days after its organization, and the second within the next 60 days.

At that time the only facilities the City of New York had for the transportation of passengers north and south were the Broadway omnibuses and the horse car lines on the avenues and along the docks, and the section of the New York Elevated Railroad, along Greenwich street and Ninth avenue, from the Battery to the Park.

The Gilbert Elevated Railway Company had been incorporated, and had the privilege of building an elevated road along Sixth avenue; but the structure, required by the terms of the charter, was so costly that the company had not been able to procure the necessary capital. That company held the opinion that if the Commission would permit them to construct a less expensive road, they would be able to complete the work. The two companies entered into amicable arrangements to construct certain portions of their lines, which were located in common, by a union of their funds. To further this object the Commission located routes for each company; one from the Battery to the Harlem River, through Third avenue and the Bowery, for the New York Elevated, and EARLY RAILWAYS the other from the Battery to the Harlem, by way of Second avenue, for the Gilbert Company.

The Commission was satisfied with these two companies. In its communication to the Mayor under date of September 6, 1875, it says:

"Having investigated the plans by which the two companies propose to raise capital, and having ourselves personally conferred with and interrogated the gentlemen whose names were put forward as furnishing the financial guaranty, we were satisfied that the location, upon their chartered routes, of rapid transit roads under this act, would, humanly speaking, render success certain."

COMMISSION ORGANIZES CORPORATION

Doubts as to the exact meaning of certain sections of the act influenced the Commission to organize a corporation "as the law allows us to do, to render assurance doubly sure that our labors will result in rapid transit actually." The corporation was known as the Manhattan Railway Company, and was capitalized at $2,000,000. The corporation was organized for the purpose of constructing, maintaining, and operating steam railways for the transportation of passengers, mails, or freight, wholly within the city of New York. The routes selected were practically identical with the present Second, Third, Sixth and Ninth avenue lines. The articles of association defined the type of elevated road to be built, the time for the erection of the several portions, and the rates of fares. Books were opened October 29, 1875, and the entire capital stock was subscribed for. The work of this commission was finished with the granting of franchises for building roads to the Harlem River along the routes just named. In 1879 the Manhattan Railway Company acquired control of the other two companies, and thereby the control of the elevated railroad service of New York.

TUNNELS NOT SERIOUSLY CONSIDERED

Although tunnel projects were at that time very numerous, the Commission did not at any time seriously consider the subway question as in any way likely to meet the demands for better transit accommodations. The engineering difficulties and the financial uncertainties involved were held to bar such projects. At that period underground works of the kind were in their infancy. The great sub-surface lines of to-day did not then exist, excepting two tunnels under the Thames. But London had already foreseen that the only practical solution of rapid transit, in thickly populated cities having narrow streets, involves the use of tunnels. Upon the completion of the Tower Subway, in 1869, this method was widely heralded as being the only one capable of solving the street traffic problems of a crowded city.

The next fifteen years witnessed a change of opinion in New York. The Commission of 1891 advocated a tunnel scheme, and the absolute exclusion of further elevated structures from narrow streets. Its work merged into that of the present Rapid Transit Commission.

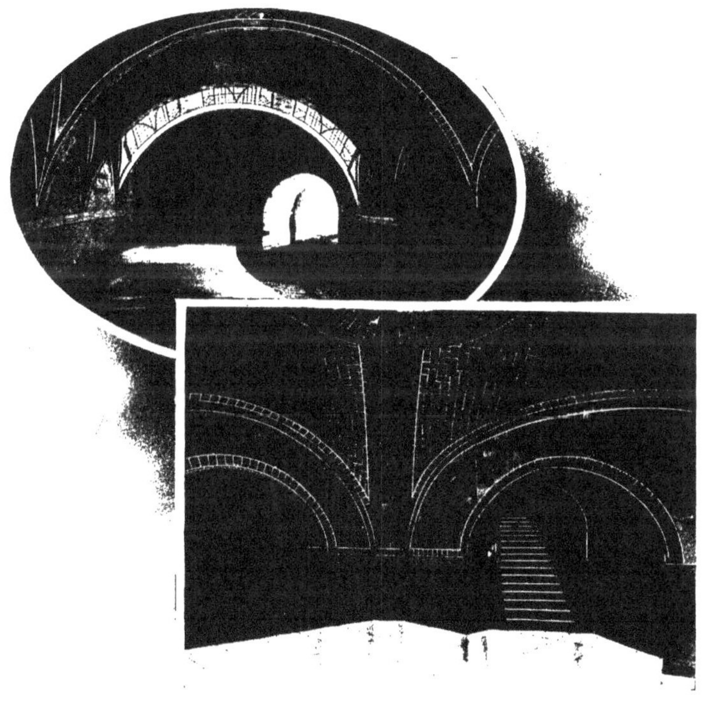

CITY HALL STATION—NEW YORK SUBWAY.

CHAPTER VIII.

COMMISSION OF 1891.

ORGANIZATION COMMISSION OF 1891

The rapid transit act of 1891 provided for the continuance in office of William Steinway, John H. Starin, Samuel Spencer, John H. Inman and Eugene L. Bushe, who had been appointed commissioners by Mayor Grant in 1890 under the Act of 1875. The commissioners were required, if, after investigation, they deemed the construction of a rapid transit railroad necessary, *first,* to adopt the routes and general plan of construction for such railroad; *second,* to obtain the consent to the construction and operation of such railroad by the local authorities and the property holders affected, or, if the consent of the property holders should be withheld, then the consent of the General Term of the Supreme Court; *third,* to adopt detailed plans for the construction and operation of such road; and, *lastly,* to sell the right to construct and operate such railroad to a corporation to be formed under the terms of the Act, for such a period of time as they should deem advisable and upon such terms as they should be able to exact.

This Board made a careful examination of the entire question with the assistance of William E. Worthen and Wm. Barclay Parsons, whom it had appointed its engineers. After holding a number of public hearings the unanimous conclusion was reached that not only were additional transit facilities needed, but that such facilities could only be obtained in an adequate manner by the construction of underground roads.

LOCATION OF ROUTES

It was appreciated that any system devised with a view to permanency and the capacity requisite for the future, would be costly; and the route, in order to give relief where most needed and to command the necessary traffic to make the line remunerative, should be along main arteries of travel. Statistics established the fact that the existing north and south lines of transit nearest the center of the city absorbed the greatest travel, and that the relative pressure upon them was in proportion to their proximity to Broadway.

These considerations required the location of the lower part of the route on or near that thoroughfare, the continuation of the line north of Fourteenth street to be made by diverging lines to the east and west. Since an elevated structure on Broadway below Thirty-third street was prohibited by the statute, it became necessary to plan a subway.

BROADWAY SELECTED

Two types of tunnel were considered, namely, one for a double-deck tunnel with two tracks upon each deck, and the other for four tracks on a single level. After a thorough discussion of the advantages and disadvantages of both plans, it was decided to build all the tracks on the same level. The route selected extended from the Battery under Broadway to Fifty-ninth street, and thence north, on the west side of the city, to the city line. At Fourteenth street the line turned and passed under Fourth and Madison avenues to the Grand Central; thence under Madison avenue north to the Twenty-third and Twenty-fourth Wards. Loops were to be built at the Battery, City Hall park, and Fourteenth street. From Morris street to Vesey there were to be three tracks, and from Vesey to One-hundred-and-ninetieth street, on the west side, four tracks, and the remainder of the distance two tracks. On the east side, from Fourteenth street to the Harlem River, there were to be four tracks, and thence to the city limits two tracks.

A line under Broadway having been decided upon, the question was narrowed to the character of the structure and its distance below the surface, whether it should be deep or shallow; whether, in providing for four tracks, the entire width of the street, or only a portion, should be used; and whether the surface of the street and existing pipes should be disturbed. Although the impression had prevailed that a rock tunnel could be driven the entire distance, borings made by the Commission showed that a large portion would be in sand.

TUNNEL PLANS

As finally drawn, the plans called for a tunnel not less than 11½ feet in clear height and 11 feet in width for each track. The roof of the tunnel was to be as near the surface of the street as the pipes and underground structures would permit. The Government Ship Canal and the Harlem River were to be crossed by double-track draw bridges not less than 50 feet in the clear above mean high water mark, with clear spans of not less than 125 feet between center piers and bulkhead line.

The stations were to be provided with ample elevator service wherever the platforms were 20 feet or more below the curb line. The road was to be operated with electricity or other power not requiring combustion in the tunnel.

The plans were approved by the Board of Aldermen, the Department of Public Parks, and by the Commissioner of Street Improvements of the Twenty-third and Twenty-fourth Wards, as required by the terms of the Act. All the necessary consents were obtained, including a majority of the property owners along Broadway.

But, after all this had been accomplished, it was found that capitalists could not be induced to invest in the enterprise. The undertaking was upon such a vast scale, and the prospective revenue so doubtful, that hopes of carrying the scheme to completion were hardly entertained at all.

BID RECEIVED

In the fall of 1892 the Commission advertised for bids for the franchise, and on December 30 met in the City Hall. But one bid was received, that of $1,000 from William N. Amory, who deposited ten per cent. of the amount, or $100 cash, as required by law. If the Board accepted this offer, it became its duty to notify the bidder to make the final deposit of $1,000,000 within five days. This amount was required in order to insure the completion of the road along the lines laid down, the protection of the city and of property holders. The records show that Mr. Amory refused to make any statement to the Board regarding his ability to deposit the million dollars, and at the meeting held January 3, 1893, Mr. Bowers, counsel for the Commission, said: "If you satisfy this Commission, by the production of your securities to-day, or, for that matter, to-morrow, that you are ready to build this road and carry out the scheme, there will be no difficulty about your getting the franchise." No explanation being presented, the Board refused to accept the proposition.

Previous to this important negotiations were held with the Manhattan Railway Company looking to the granting of franchises permitting the company to extend their elevated lines and to build additional ones. Just after the first meeting in January the Manhattan Company withdrew all the proposals they had made.

At a meeting on January 17 it was decided, since a satisfactory bidder could not be obtained, to hold the franchise in abeyance. It was voted also that "the Commission will, at any time, upon information that a proposed purchaser is ready to make a deposit with the Comptroller sufficient to justify the belief that the road will be built in accordance with the plans and specifications therefor, again offer said franchise at public auction, in accordance with the terms of the statute."

ELEVATED ROADS FOR TEMPORARY RELIEF

At this meeting the Commission decided, further, that it was its duty to provide elevated roads as a temporary relief, and to provide further relief by "granting additional facilities to the existing elevated railways," which were to be extended on both the east and west sides of town.

Three days later an application was received from the Manhattan Elevated Railway Company for permission to build new lines and extend its old lines, the total length of the extension being about 38 miles. These covered the whole city like a network. The Commission refused some of these and substituted others.

At subsequent meetings questions arose whether other privileges should be given to the Manhattan Company, or whether the new lines at least should be disposed of at public auction. At the meeting on March 11 Mr. Starin said: "My point is: Why are you going to give all these privileges to the Manhattan system? Are you going to give them all these privileges, or put them up at auction? If it is desirable to give everything, there is an end of rapid transit for all time. You cannot think of having two rapid transits in the city of New York."

OFFER TO MANHATTAN COMPANY

In April Mr. Starin offered to vote in favor of granting the franchise to the Manhattan Company, provided it be compelled to pay 5 per cent. on the net receipts of its entire system; to maintain a fare of 5 cents from the Battery to the city line; and to pay all expenses of the Commission up to the day of the execution of the contract. A motion to this effect was approved, as was one to grant franchises to the company for the extensions needed. A copy of these resolutions was sent to the officials of the elevated road, who replied that they were willing to pay 5 per cent. on the net income of the new lines other than third track, or 3 per cent. on the income of the entire system.

The Commission stipulated that the net earnings should be ascertained by deducting all operating expenses and taxes from the gross earnings. As generally understood, earnings of this character are usually found by deducting only the operating expenses, and not the taxes, from the gross earnings. This made a material difference in the amount to be paid by the company.

NET EARNINGS

The following tables show the amount that would have been received by the city under the proposition of the Commission and also under that of the company:

The gross earnings of the Manhattan Company for 1892 were		$10,835,978
Deductions		
Operating expenses	$5,375,349	
Taxes	479,864	
		5,855,213
Net earnings as determined		$4,980,765
Compensation proposed by the Commission, 5 per cent. upon net earnings		249,038

The counter-proposition made by the company was to pay 3 per cent. upon the amount found after deducting from the gross earnings, not only all the operating expenses and taxes, but also the interest upon bonds, as follows:

Gross earnings		$10,835,978
Deductions		
Operating expenses	$5,375,349	
Taxes	479,864	
Interest on bonds	1,919,052	
		7,774,265
		$3,061,713

Three per cent. on the above, as proposed by the company, would be $91,851. In 1892 the difference between the two propositions would have made a loss to the city of $157,187.

COST OF OPERATING SURFACE AND ELEVATED ROADS

The average cost of operating street surface railroads in New York is 72 per cent. of the gross receipts, and yet such roads are required to pay the city 3 per cent. annually of their gross receipts, for the first five years, and 5 per cent. of the gross receipts thereafter. At that time the operating expenses of the Manhattan Company were about 50 per cent. of the gross receipts, so that the compensation proposed by the Commission was equal to but 2½ per cent. of the gross receipts, or less than one-half the ordinary tax regularly paid by the street railroads.

In a statement before the Commission, made by John H. Starin, we find the following:

"The tax upon street surface roads amounts to one-quarter of a cent for each passenger carried. The Commissioners' proposition would tax the Manhattan Company only one-ninth of a cent for each passenger carried.

MANHATTAN PROPOSITION ANALYZED

"The Manhattan Company's proposition contemplates but one-twenty-fourth of a cent for each passenger carried. Yet it costs nearly 50 per cent. more to transport a passenger on the surface roads than it does on the elevated.

"Is that company harshly dealt with when it is asked to pay less than one-half as much as street railroads pay? Or should the Commissioners accede to the demands of the company that the city accept one-sixth of the tax heretofore, in other cases, found just and equitable, for the most valuable passenger traffic franchise in the world?

EARNINGS OF MANHATTAN

"In proof of the contention that the payment of the tax proposed by the Commissioners would result in no hardship to the Manhattan Company, it may be stated that the company, had it paid such tax in 1892, besides every other expense incurred by it, would have earned a clear profit of more than $2,800,000, equal to 9 37/100 per cent., upon the company's capital stock of $30,000,000.

"The bonded indebtedness of the company is $40,000,000. The total of stock and bonds is, therefore, $70,000,000. It is certain that were the elevated roads bonded or stocked for an amount equal only to their exact cost, they could have carried last year the 214,000,000 passengers actually carried for a fare of 3 cents each, and after payment of all expenses would have earned nearly 6 per cent. dividends upon the actual cost of the roads."

The president of the Manhattan Railway Company, in a letter dated May 25, 1893, refused the proposition of the Commission and withdrew the proposal made by his own company. It is impossible to conceive the reasons that prompted the directors of the Manhattan Company to decline a franchise that would have placed in their control, for an indefinite period, the rapid transit facilities of the city.

In order to understand the condition of affairs at that time, it is necessary to explain that the law creating the Board of Rapid Transit Commissioners provided that a franchise could not be granted without the unanimous consent of the members. New York city at that time was in sore need of increased rapid transit facilities, and there were thousands of citizens who would have welcomed any addition to the transportation methods, no matter at what cost to the city. The temptation to yield to this pressure on the part of the people was very great.

COMMISSION RESIGNS

A resolution introduced in June, 1893, proposed to give the franchises to the Manhattan Company on a 4 per cent. basis. This motion had the support of four of the members of the Commission, Mr. Starin alone voting against it, and it was lost because of the unanimous clause in the statute. After the meeting Messrs. Steinway, Bushe, Spencer and Inman resigned, but, with the exception of Mr. Spencer, were immediately reappointed by Mayor Gilroy. D. F. Porter was appointed in place of Mr. Spencer. The proposed franchises were of the most extended and far-reaching character, covering many of the principal streets and avenues of the then city of New York. It seems not too much to say that, but for the vote of Mr. Starin, and the determined stand he took all through the discussions with the elevated railroad officers, the construction of subways in New York would have been indefinitely postponed.

SERVICES OF MR. STARIN

Another service to the city, the value of which it is difficult to estimate, was rendered by Mr. Starin when the elevated railway company made application for authority to build an elevated line on the Boulevard, now upper Broadway. Such a structure would have ruined what is now recognized as one of the finest thoroughfares in the world. Against this proposal Mr. Starin interposed opposition, and was again successful.

On August 15, 1893, Geo. J. Gould, president of the Manhattan Company, wrote to the Commission that, "owing to the present disturbed financial condition of the country, it is not considered wise to assume large contracts." The Commission thereupon abandoned all negotiations with the elevated road, and concluded to lay out independent elevated lines and offer them for sale. The Commission was engaged upon that work when the present Commission, created by the Act of 1894, came into existence. On May 24, 1894, the Commission voted to pass its records, property, etc., over to its successor.

Not all of the achievements of the Commission of 1891 were of a negative kind. The studies made by the engineering staff under the direction of William Barclay Parsons were of the greatest value to the next Board. The examinations made by him furnished accurate data with regard to the nature of the material through which a subway would have to pass, both on the east and west sides of the city. The study of the physical conditions peculiar to New York, and of the work that had been done along similar lines abroad, had a marked influence upon the decision taken by the present Commission.

CHAPTER IX

THE CHAMBER OF COMMERCE.

While the Rapid Transit Commission of 1894 was vainly striving to perfect a plan that would give the people the transit facilities they so sorely needed, the Chamber of Commerce was giving attention to the same problem. Members of the Chamber were familiar with the work that had been done, and were convinced that the remedy must be sought along different lines. The work so done resulted in the framing of a bill that was passed by the Legislature in May, 1894. Under that act, and amendments, the present subway was constructed.

At a meeting of the Chamber, held February 1, 1894, William D. Sloane offered the following resolution:

RAPID TRANSIT COMMITTEE APPOINTED

"Resolved, That the president be authorized and requested to appoint a committee of five to examine the subject of rapid transit, and report what action, if any, on the part of the Chamber of Commerce, it is advisable to take for the purpose of aiding in the solution of this important problem.

"Resolved, further, That this meeting be adjourned until Thursday, February 15, at half-past twelve o'clock, for the purpose of receiving and taking action upon the report of the committee to be appointed under the provisions of the above resolution."

The following committee was appointed:

Alexander E. Orr — Cornelius N. Bliss
John A. Stewart — J. Edward Simmons
John Harsen Rhoades.

A portion of the report presented at the later meeting was as follows:

REPORT OF COMMITTEE

"In view of the present needs and the probabilities—not to speak of the possibilities—of the future of this city as the commercial metropolis of the United States, New York requires, and should have, the very best system of rapid transit that the legislative and municipal authorities of the state and city can authorize, and engineering and mechanical skill, and money within reasonable bounds, can provide.

"Her geographical position is such that growth can only be made in one direction—towards the north—and it does not require elaborate argument to prove that in order to insure the comfort and happiness of the people, as well as continuous prosperity and development, there must be an efficient, convenient, and safe system of rapid transit between the business and residential divisions of the city, which, of necessity, will always be widely apart from each other.

ELEVATED RAILROADS NOT RAPID TRANSIT

"The ways and means of communication that have heretofore been provided are now found to be entirely inadequate. It is true that the surface roads were a great improvement on the old style omnibus, and the elevated roads, in many ways, an improvement on the surface roads; and it is acknowledged that the city has derived very great benefit through their construction and operation; but it is also true, and a truth that must not longer be overlooked, that they cannot, in any practical sense, be said to be systems of rapid transit, or meet the needs, nor can they be made to meet the needs, that are daily becoming more and more apparent, and that should not be longer ignored.

"It is evident to all who study the question in the light of to-day that if in the past there had been intelligent appreciation of the possibilities of New York, and that growth could only be made in one direction, suitable provision would have been made for rapid transit when streets and avenues were being located and land was comparatively cheap. In that case, the problem that now confronts us could have been easily solved. But there was no such appreciation; and ten or twenty years hence the same criticism will apply to us if, suffering as we now are because of past thoughtlessness, and as we shall continue to suffer with increasing intensity as we grow in years and population, we fail, even at this late date, to provide for present and prospective relief. The growth of New York has no more culminated to-day than it had a decade ago, and your committee hazards the opinion that, with ordinary forethought on the part of her citizens and the taking advantage of opportunities as they arise, it is impossible to say with any degree of certainty when, in the future, the culminating point will be reached.

MUNICIPAL CREDIT FOR BUILDING ROAD

"For reasons that need not be stated in this report, your committee cannot advocate the building of any system of rapid transit by the city of New York; but, under certain safeguards to be provided by legislation, it urges upon the Chamber the propriety of recommending that a single exception be made to the admirable law which restricts municipal credit being lent to promote private enterprises.

"For the reasons stated above, effective rapid transit construction must now prove a very costly undertaking, and does not present to capital—which is always more or less timid—sufficient inducements to attract the large sums necessary to insure a complete system of rapid transit development. This is why the Rapid Transit Commission has been unsuccessful in inducing private enterprise to accept any plan that they have recommended in the past two years, nor will they be successful for many years to come, in the opinion of your committee, unless in some legitimate way private enterprise is stimulated.

PRIVATE CAPITAL WILL NOT UNDERTAKE WORK

"A corporation organized for the purpose of rapid transit construction could not expect to obtain the necessary capital upon a better basis than six per cent. interest per annum, while money borrowed upon the credit of the city of New York could be obtained for three per cent. Hence it is evident that the revenue necessary to protect the fixed charges on capital borrowed in the ordinary manner must be double the amount of that needed to provide for the fixed charges on capital borrowed upon the city's credit. If, therefore, the city should agree to lend its credit to such corporation to the extent of two-thirds of the cost of the completed system, with the view of minimizing the volume of fixed charges, the needed stimulus referred to above would be presented and a large margin of safety secured."

The report then referred to the building of the Union and Central Pacific Railroads, both of which were private enterprises. The completion of these roads was deemed essential to national development, and the credit of the Federal Government was lent to provide, in part, for their construction, and a second mortgage, subject to a prior lien of equal amount, was taken as security for the credit so advanced. Although this was a departure from conservative principles, the result proved the wisdom of the course, for hundreds of millions of dollars' worth of wealth were added to the resources of the whole country.

The report set forth further the following:

ADVANTAGES OF RAPID TRANSIT

"Aside from the advantages of comfort and convenience to the people, New York would gain immensely in revenue through rapid transit contact with the yet undeveloped portions of the city lying to the north. It is a well known fact that in four years after the elevated roads had been permanently established one ward alone (the Nineteenth) increased in taxable value more than fifty millions of dollars, a sum many times greater than the cost of their construction, and there is no reason to doubt that similar experiences will follow rapid transit development.

"It is not proposed, however, that the city should lend its credit for the whole amount needed, or take undue risk. The transaction should be based upon business principles of equity and safety. Not more than two-thirds of the cost of construction should be the maximum credit granted, secured by a first lien upon the completed structure, its franchise and equipment.

"Your committee realizes the gravity of the action it proposes the Chamber shall take in urging an exception to a wisely enacted law, but the whole question is of such paramount importance, and further delay is so dangerous, that exceptional measures are necessary to insure success. If the following resolution, which is presented for the consideration of the Chamber, shall be adopted, your committee asks to be continued:

CITY TO LEND ITS CREDIT

"'Resolved, That the Chamber of Commerce of the State of New York requests the proper authorities of the city, the Legislature of the State, the Constitutional Convention, and the Rapid Transit Commission to take such action as may be necessary to enable the City of New York to lend its credit to corporate enterprise for the construction of a rapid transit system in the said city, upon such terms and conditions as the Legislature may impose; provided, however, that the loan of such credit shall be restricted to such one purpose; and, provided further, that such loan shall not exceed in amount two-thirds the cost of construction, and be a first lien upon the property; and, provided further, that the aggregate amount of the credit to be so loaned shall not exceed the sum of thirty millions of dollars.'"

It will be observed that the resolution proposed that the city should lend its credit to a private corporation which should build the road, and, presumably, own and control it; the city having no financial interest in it after the amount borrowed had been repaid. The resolution did not look to municipal ownership, control or operation.

In the discussion following the presentation of the report, Morris K. Jesup said:

A GRAVE QUESTION

"We all agree, at least I do, with that part of the report which sets forth the importance of rapid transit in this city. It is a grave question in my mind, and I have thought a good deal about it, as to whether we ought to set the example of asking the voters of this State to undo such a wise provision as now exists with reference to the city's being empowered to lend its credit to private enterprises. I am free to say that, so far as my own mind is concerned, it is not made up as yet; and before entering into a discussion of the matter, as I think it ought to be discussed, we should have a larger attendance than we have here to-day, so that if we do decide that it is best to adopt the recommendations of the committee, it shall be done after a very careful and serious consideration of the whole matter. I therefore move that the report be printed; that a copy be sent to each member of the Chamber, and that final action be postponed until the next regular meeting of the Chamber, to be held two weeks hence."

Jacob H. Schiff said in part:

IMPORTANCE OF RAPID TRANSIT

"If we do not get rapid transit sooner or later—we may not see it, but coming generations will feel it—we shall lose our importance as a commercial metropolis. Such things work slowly, but they work surely; and I cannot see why, in a matter that is just as important to the city of New York as the supply of its water or the supply of anything it needs for its daily wants, the citizens of New York should not put their hands in their pockets and tax themselves at as low a rate as possible, instead of taxing themselves at as high a rate as possible, which they will have to do if private capital builds the road. It will not cost six per cent., but will probably cost ten or twelve per cent., to get private capital to build that road; for, in all probability, five per cent. bonds will have to be issued, which will be sold, say at 80, and stock will be issued, which will be thrown in as a bonus, and on which in years to come some ten per cent. dividends will be paid; so that it will not cost six per cent. to the city of New York to build this road, but ten or twelve per cent., and every man, woman, and child in the city of New York will have to pay a part of it. * * * I am heartily in favor of the report of the committee and hope it will pass."

Abram S. Hewitt said:

LEGISLATION UNPRECEDENTED

"Mr. President and gentlemen, I suppose there is no one in this room who does not concur fully with the statement of the committee that rapid transit is indispensable for the present comfort and future growth of this city. The committee, however, proposes a new departure—legislation without precedent, so far as I now recall, in the history of the United States, or the State of New York, or the city of New York. They propose that the credit of the city of New York shall be loaned to a private company for the construction of a work of a public nature, but to be owned and administered by private individuals. * * * The constitution of the State of New York absolutely prohibits the loaning of the public credit of the state, or of any city or municipality in the state, in aid of any private enterprise. It does not prohibit, however, the construction of public works by municipalities, to be owned by them in such ways as they may see fit, except that they must not issue bonds beyond ten per cent. of the assessed valuation. That is the only limitation.

ERIE CANAL

"When the State of New York was confronted by a greater problem than this, the greatest that has ever presented itself to a civilized community on this side of the Atlantic—the construction of the Erie Canal, upon which has been built up the superstructure of the whole state, its prosperity, commercial, agricultural and otherwise—the state took it in hand; became the owner, borrowed the money, paid for the work, and, perhaps unfortunately, retained the administration of the property after it was constructed.

CROTON AQUEDUCT

"The city of New York has pursued the same system. The Croton Aqueduct was constructed by the public, at its own cost, and administered by its own officers. In no instance has the city of New York gone into partnership with a private company. In no instance has the government of the United States ever done such a thing."

Mr. Hewitt stated that the loaning of the public credit, in the case of the Union and Central Pacific Railroads, was an illustration of the danger of any connection between the state and private enterprises. While that great enterprise returned more than it cost in increased value of the property of the country, it is also true that "every dollar of the money advanced by the government in aid of that enterprise was misapplied by the people who had charge of the enterprise." The money was not used for the construction of the road, but was put into private pockets.

"Gentlemen, bear with me, because I am going to point out what I conceive to be the danger of a departure from well-recognized principles of action. This committee who have brought in this report are among the ablest and most reputable men in this Chamber. In their own spheres of action there are no men whom we would follow more willingly and even blindly to a conclusion; but able and intelligent as they are, I doubt whether they have given that attention to the underlying principle in their report which it would receive from the hands of statesmen. In the only departure which I have ever known the city of New York to make from the sound principle of having no connection whatever with private enterprises, the scandal was equally great.

BROOKLYN BRIDGE

"The Brooklyn Bridge was originally a private corporation with private stockholders. The city of New York never loaned its credit to the Brooklyn Bridge, not a penny, but what it did was to subscribe for a portion of the stock.

The city of Brooklyn did the same thing. The administration of the work was in the hands of private stockholders, and it terminated in a scandal; and the result was that the city of New York and the city of Brooklyn were compelled to do—what they ought to have done in the first place, or to have done nothing—they were compelled to buy out the private stockholders and become the sole owners of the work. Now I think these illustrations are sufficient to point out to the members of the Chamber the danger of any proposition which shall look to a partnership between the city of New York and any private company for any purpose whatever, however urgent. * * * The scandal of the Brooklyn Bridge led to the inhibition which is now in the Constitution against allowing any credit of the city to private enterprise. It was not in the original Constitution of 1846, but was inserted by amendment in order to avoid just such propositions as the one this committee have submitted to this Chamber.

BROOKLYN BRIDGE SCANDAL

"Now I like to get up and down town in comfort, and I confess I am unable to do so at present; but I am not willing to do so at the expense of what I regard as the fundamental principles by which governments of great communities like New York should be conducted. You may get temporary relief, but you will have set a precedent that is so dangerous that you will have speculators, men who are seeking to carry on enterprises for their own profit, appearing before the legislature and coming to the city of New York, and you will be entreated to lend the public credit for the execution of works which in themselves would be desirable, but which, if the public became interested in them, would become abuses and scandals.

DANGEROUS FOR CITY TO LEND ITS CREDIT

"Nor is there the slightest necessity for such a course in this case; and this is a point which I beg gentlemen to consider most carefully. Mr. Schiff has been good enough to allude to the fact that while I was mayor I gave some attention to this question of rapid transit. I may say to you, gentlemen, and Mr. President, that I gave all the attention that it was possible for me to give, with such abilities as I may happen to possess, to the solution of the question. I had consultations with the most experienced and able engineers. I consulted with the ablest lawyers in the city.

"The conclusion was:

"First, that as the Constitution stood, and as the law stands, it was competent for the legislature of the State of New York to authorize the city of New York to construct the work.

CONCLUSIONS OF MR. HEWITT

"Second, it was concluded that to get rapid transit the underground system must be adopted; that it was impossible to get real rapid transit with an overhead railway.

"Third, that the city of New York could borrow the money and provide the capital—as all the committee agree, and as Mr. Schiff has told us—at a cost not exceeding three per cent.

CITY OWNERSHIP NOT FAVORED

"And lastly, that the danger and abuse that might come from the construction of the work by city officials and the operation of the railway afterwards by public officers, could be avoided by the simple process of making a lease to a responsible corporation who would have the expenditure of the money in construction, under the supervision of city officers, and who would be sure to make it as light as possible, because they would have to pay interest on every dollar that was expended."

The following further remarks of Mr. Hewitt were prophetic:

"It was thought that that could be made to work out in practice, and the draft of a law was made and sent to the legislature, and I regret to say not a man in the legislature could be found to advocate it, and it was finally introduced as a personal favor by a member of the legislature who was willing to do me a kindly service. It was referred to the committee and never reported back; and the reason was that there was no money for any private individual behind that act. Nobody could make a cent out of it.

PROPHETIC REMARKS OF MR. HEWITT

"But this would have happened if it had been enacted: The work would have been constructed; the money furnished by the bonds of the city of New York at three per cent.; and it would have been leased, as I had reason to think, although I am not at liberty to mention names, by a responsible corporation, at five per cent., and the difference of two per cent. would have retired the bonds in thirty-three years, and the city of New York would be the absolute owners, free and clear of all indebtedness, of this great enterprise, which is as essential to its prosperity as is the Croton Aqueduct. It would have been conducted on exactly the principles on which the Croton Aqueduct has been conducted. Now this committee, whom I respect very much, come to this body and recommend a departure from this sound principle.

"I agree with Mr. Jesup in what he has said, that such a proposition as this needs to be most carefully considered, and I trust, therefore, that his motion that it be laid upon the table and that it be printed and sent to the members of the body for consideration, will be carried; because it will be a very serious thing indeed if this Chamber, which is supposed to represent the commercial intelligence of New York, shall commit itself to propositions, or legislation, that have been condemned not only by the judgment of the greatest statesmen of this country, but by the experience of every state and city that has attempted to become a partner with private individuals in the construction and management of public enterprises."

It was voted to defer further consideration of the question until the next regular meeting, March 1, 1894.

At that meeting Mr. Hewitt offered the following resolutions as a substitute for those presented by the committee:

CITY CREDIT TO BE ADVANCED

"Resolved, That, in the judgment of the Chamber of Commerce of the State of New York, additional rapid transit facilities are so necessary to the growth and prosperity of the city of New York that the use of its credit would be justifiable, in case it is not found possible, after careful investigation and liberal concessions in regard to taxation and right of way, to secure the construction of a proper system of rapid transit by private enterprise.

CITY TO OWN RAPID TRANSIT SYSTEM

"Resolved, That in case the credit of the city is used, the ownership of the rapid transit system should be vested in the city, but its construction and operation should be entrusted to such responsible corporation now existing or hereafter to be formed, as may be willing to pay, in addition to the interest on the city bonds, the largest annual rental, such excess to be used as a sinking fund to retire the bonds of the city, and when the bonds are so retired, the lease to be terminated.

"Resolved, That thereafter the lease should be sold to the highest bidder, upon such terms as may be prescribed by the city authorities, for periods not exceeding thirty years, in the same general manner as the ferries are now sold, with the stipulation that the successful bidder shall purchase from the previous lessee the rolling stock and other personal property at its fair valuation, to be determined by arbitration.

CONTROL OF SYSTEM

"Resolved, That proper safeguards and conditions ought to be provided by appropriate legislation in reference to the issue of the city bonds and the construction and operation of the rapid transit system, under the general supervision of a board of engineers, so as to insure economy of cost and adequate accommodations for the public use, and that the committee be continued, with power to add to their number, to confer and co-operate with the authorities of the city, in reference to the general plan and the needed legislation."

Mr. Hewitt said also that he had had opportunities to take the opinions of the best engineers and most competent authorities upon the subject of rapid transit, and that he had never known anyone who had studied the question to reach any other conclusion than that the system must be of an underground character; that a system upon masonry arches, like Berlin, would be enormously expensive and an injury to the general aspect of the city; and that the improvements made during the last six years in regard to lighting, ventilation and motive power have removed objections that formerly held good concerning underground roads. Continuing, he said:

MUST BE AN UNDERGROUND ROAD

"Conceding, then, that we must have a new system, and that it must be an underground system, the question comes as to how its construction can be secured. There are only three methods: either by private capital, or by an association of private capital with the city, or by the city itself. Those are the three alternatives.

"The method of construction by private capital was the one arrived at by the Rapid Transit Commission, and I wish to say, in justice to that Commission, that they gave a most exhaustive and intelligent examination to the whole question, and I have no doubt they conceded, in the plan which they devised and which was offered at public auction to the bidders, all that they thought the public would grant in the way of immunity from taxation and privileges to use the streets. As you know, that plan failed. There was no bidder. I think that fact demonstrates the conclusion that it is idle to expect that private capital, unassisted in the same way, will undertake the construction of this very important and very expensive work."

Mr. Hewitt explained that the second method—by association of private capital with the city—would require a change in the Constitution of the State, and that the safeguards now thrown around the lending of the credit of municipalities of the state were none too strong. Any proposition looking to a change should be most carefully considered. In the present case it should first be shown that the work could not be done in any other way. He continued:

CREDIT OF THE CITY

"The advocates of this proposition have made no demonstration, and they cannot make the demonstration; for the very simple reason that if this work could be secured by the use of the credit of the city of New York to the extent of two-thirds of its cost, certainly it could be secured by the use of the credit of the city of New York to the extent of its entire cost; and the step from two-thirds to three-thirds is a very small one indeed, when you get over the idea that the city's credit may be used. It is a very small one, indeed, in reference to the fundamental fact, that in the case where the city's credit is loaned to a private corporation the work becomes the private property of that corporation; whereas, in the other case, by the advance of a very much smaller additional amount, the work becomes the property of the city, subject to its control and management; and if it be profitable, as I believe it will be at the end of thirty years, then the gains will flow into the city's treasury instead of into the treasury of a private corporation.

ADMINISTRATION NOT TO BE IN HANDS OF CITY

"It has been objected to the undertaking of this work by the city and on account of the city that there would be scandals involved in the expenditure of this large amount of money by the city authorities, and that the administration of such a work by the city authorities after it was constructed would result in an intolerable abuse, and would practically turn over the city of New York to the politicians and their followers. This objection would be an absolutely conclusive one to my mind, and I suppose to the mind of everybody else, if it were necessary that either the construction or administration of the work should reside in the hands of the city officials. There is no such necessity. The construction of this work, and its administration after it is constructed, can be put up at public auction to the highest bidder, upon the simple condition that the bidder shall be responsible; and, secondly, that he shall pay the interest upon the city bonds and give reasonable security of his ability to do so; and, thirdly, such further sum as in competition he may bid in addition to the rate of interest upon the city bonds. This mode of construction insures the most absolute economy. That is to say, the economy of a private owner in the building of the work, because the lessee will have to pay a rental upon the cost of the work, and he will therefore keep the cost of the work down to a minimum. In regard to the administration of the work, it will be conducted just as other railway corporations are conducted. Competent men will be employed—not politicians—because the lessee will find that his profit depends upon the economy with which the work is operated."

Mr. Hewitt did not believe that the road should be operated by a commission in behalf of the city. He cited the case of the Croton Aqueduct, from which great abuses had arisen, and added:

NEITHER CONSTRUCTION NOR ADMINISTRATION TO BE CONFIDED TO A COMMISSION

"With this experience before us I do think that we ought not to confide either the construction of this work or its administration to any commission. I think the only path of safety is to lease it, as the ferries are leased, and as many other public works are leased, to private individuals, but keeping sure that at the end of a reasonable term the property shall revert to the city, to be again leased, either at lower rates of fare, which will contribute enormously to the prosperity and growth of this city, and to the advantage of its working classes, or yielding a larger revenue to the city treasury, to be used in the reduction of the rate of taxation.

"You will see from what I have said that I am in favor, therefore, of the use of the city's credit for the construction of this work."

VIEWS OF MR. INMAN

John H. Inman, a member of the Rapid Transit Commission of 1891-4, said: "In regard to the rapid transit scheme proposed by Mr. Hewitt, there is no assurance that a responsible bid by a responsible corporation will be made to lease and operate it on the lines indicated by him. A million dollar guarantee (the amount named by Mr. Hewitt) would be insufficient. Of course, anyone who had a million dollars would be willing to put up that amount for the opportunity of saying at the end of five years (which time it would take to construct the road) whether they would take the lease or forfeit the guarantee, as by that time (that is to say, after the road was constructed) the practicability of an underground rapid transit system would be demonstrated, and if successful, the parties putting up the million dollars would have a great big thing in being able to control this system and its earnings for thirty years. Whereas, on the other hand, if for any reason the underground system should be a failure, the party putting up the money risks only the million dollars, while the city must stand the real loss. * * * I am very much in favor of Mr. Hewitt's scheme, and will do my best towards carrying it out; but it is in the air, in my opinion. I am as fond of Mr. Hewitt as any man present, but I must say that I do not think there is anything tangible about his scheme. It proposes to spend $40,000,000 to $60,000,000 of the city's money, and he only names a guarantee of a million dollars for faithfully executing the work, and for guaranteeing to carry out the terms of the lease for a period of thirty years, which, in my opinion, is entirely inadequate. Upon a responsible guarantee I would say go ahead."

MR. ORR'S REMARKS

Alexander E. Orr said: "The question that the Chamber is now called upon to decide is simply this: Shall we urge that a single exception be made in behalf of rapid transit construction, to an admirable law (viz., that which forbids any city in this State lending its credit to promote private interests,) so that private enterprise may be stimulated into providing for a great public need, or shall we recommend, irrespective of consequences, a strict adherence to the statute? That is the question.

"I am free to say that I should hold the same opinion that I did when we went before the Board of Aldermen and advocated the building of our rapid transit system by the city, provided we had men at the helm of our municipal affairs that we could trust; but as that is not now the case, nor is there any prospect that we soon shall have, I could not and I would not, as a member of this committee, put myself on record as advising the Chamber to recommend that the city should build this much needed system of rapid transit, which, as far as the light we have had on the subject leads us to believe, would be an expenditure of some fifty millions of dollars, at least, to be controlled by the power which controls the municipal government of the city of New York."

SUBSTITUTE RESOLUTIONS ADOPTED

On motion the substitute resolutions offered by Mr. Hewitt were adopted. The President of the Chamber, Charles Stewart Smith, and Abram S. Hewitt were added to the committee.

At the regular monthly meeting of the Chamber on April 5 the committee on rapid transit submitted a copy of the bill which it had prepared and caused to be introduced into the legislature. The following is a synopsis of the bill which was drafted by Henry R. Beekman:

The bill provides for a new Board of Rapid Transit Commissioners, consisting of the Mayor, the Comptroller, the President of the Chamber of Commerce, *ex-officio*, and five others named in the bill. The Board may fill vacancies.

BILL PREPARED EY THE CHAMBER

Aside from this, the scheme of the bill is to extend the powers of the Board of Rapid Transit Commissioners, under the act of 1891, so as to confer upon said Board the right, if in its judgment it is found desirable, of providing for the construction and operation of rapid transit roads for and on account of the city. The existing powers, therefore, which by law are now vested in the Board of Rapid Transit Commissioners are still retained.

OUTLINE OF BILL

If the Board shall determine that it is expedient that a rapid transit road should be constructed at the expense of the city, it is authorized to use any plan which has been heretofore adopted by the old rapid transit commissioners, and which has received the constitutional consent of the legal authorities and the property owners, or of the General Term of the Supreme Court, in case the property owners shall have refused their consent; or it may proceed to devise and adopt new routes and plans which must, in turn, be submitted to the Common Council and to the property owners, or to the General Term of the Supreme Court, for the requisite approvals.

When the plans are finally adopted and consented to, the Board is authorized to advertise for proposals for the construction and operation of the road. Power is given to the commissioners, if they see fit to do so, to make one or several contracts for the construction of the entire system, or parts of a system, of rapid transit. The commissioners are authorized to reject all the bids and re-advertise, or they may accept any bid that, in their judgment, will best promote the public interest.

BIDDER TO CONSTRUCT AND OPERATE ROAD

The successful bidder is then required to enter into a contract for the construction of the road, and also to equip, maintain, and operate the same for a term of years to be specified in the contract, not less than thirty-five nor more than fifty years.

The annual rental to be paid by the contractor to the city must be an amount, to be fixed by the commissioners, not less than the interest on the bonds issued by the city to pay for the construction of the road, and an additional sum, not less than one per cent., upon the amount of said bonds. In order to secure the city, the contractor is required to enter into a bond with sureties which shall be satisfactory to the commissioners. He is also required to make a deposit of one million dollars with the Comptroller of the city, which sum is to be repaid to him, with interest at the same rate as that paid by the city upon the bonds issued under this act, as soon as the road has been constructed, equipped and the operation of the same commenced to the satisfaction of the Board.

BONDS TO BE ISSUED

For the purpose of paying the cost of construction the city is authorized to issue its bonds, principal and interest payable in gold coin, to an amount not exceeding fifty millions of dollars. The road itself, upon being constructed, immediately becomes the property of the city for which it is constructed. The rolling stock and other equipment of the road is to be the property of the contractor, provided by him at his own expense.

As a substitute for the security of one million dollars, when repaid, the city is to have a first lien upon the rolling stock and equipment. Power is also given to the Board to enter into any agreement that may be considered wise in reference to renewals of the lease, or the purchase by the city of the rolling stock and equipment at a valuation, if the lease is not renewed, and the property of the contractor, embracing his interest in the franchise and the equipment of the road, is to be exempt from taxation.

RENEWAL OF LEASE

The contract is also to provide the rates of fare to be charged and the character of service to be furnished. The rentals received are to be paid into the sinking fund for the redemption of the city debt.

Sections 39 to 63, both inclusive, relate exclusively to judicial proceedings for the appointment of commissioners of appraisal and the conduct of such proceedings, where the Board of Rapid Transit Commissioners shall find it necessary to condemn any property in order to provide for the construction of such road.

The bill also contains a provision that where in the existing law a vote of four members of the Board is required, the number shall be increased to six. This is in effect giving the same veto power to two members of the Board that the existing law now provides for; the present Board consisting of five persons, and the Board provided for in the act consisting of eight persons.

The bill also terminates the offices of the present commissioners of rapid transit, and requires them to transfer and deliver to the new Board all the records, maps, plans and other property relating to their work. Provision is also made for the payment of the expenses and compensation of the out-going commissioners. This was considered just. It was necessary to make provision for it in the act, in view of the fact that the payment of the compensation of the commissioners under the present law is dependent upon their making a successful sale of a franchise for rapid transit, which has not yet been done. Provision is also made for the payment of the expenses of the new Board of Rapid Transit Commissioners, and also a reasonable compensation to the members thereof, other than the Mayor and Comptroller, which compensation is to be ascertained and determined in the manner provided for in the existing law; that is, by the General Term of the Supreme Court, but it is to be paid to them from time to time.

OLD COMMISSION TO DELIVER RECORDS TO NEW

The persons named in the bill as passed were: William Steinway, Seth Low, John Claflin, Alexander E. Orr and John H. Starin.

It will be seen from the foregoing that the Chamber of Commerce took up the discussion of rapid transit problems at its meeting on February 1, 1894; that a sub-committee was appointed to examine the subject and report what action it was advisable to take; that this committee reported at the adjourned meeting on February 15; that at a meeting, held on March 1, resolutions offered by Mr. Hewitt were adopted, and that at the next regular meeting, April 5, the committee reported that a bill had been prepared and caused to be introduced into the Legislature. The bill so prepared passed the Legislature and was signed by the Governor May 22, 1894.

RESULTS The Chamber of Commerce worked two months upon problems that had engaged earnest attention for a quarter of a century. It found the correct solution. That it did so was due to the clear judgment of Mr. Hewitt, a man singularly well equipped both as a successful merchant and trained in the affairs of state. The Chamber has not forgotten the man or his service.

ELEVATED STRUCTURE—N. Y. SUBWAY.

CHAPTER X.

ABRAM STEVENS HEWITT.

On the 5th of April, 1900, the Chamber of Commerce held a meeting at which Alexander E. Orr, President of the Rapid Transit Commission, reported the signing of the contract for the construction of the subway.

That act marked the beginning of the end of an undertaking that had been vainly attempted for a period of twenty-five years. Just six years before (1894), the Chamber of Commerce had discovered the key to the solution of the problem of rapid transit with municipal ownership, and through the efforts of its members had prepared the way leading to successful achievement. It had drawn the bill that had become the Rapid Transit Act of May, 1894, and under that law the work had been commenced and would be carried to final completion. After giving a brief history of the efforts made to secure this great boon, Mr. Orr said the result was due mainly to the active influence of the Chamber and the genius and foresight of Abram S. Hewitt, who had brought to the task a wide experience in civic affairs and an intimate knowledge of the requirements of the case.

At that meeting the following resolutions were adopted:

MEDAL TO MR. HEWITT

Resolved, That a gold medal* be struck in recognition of the eminent services of the Hon. Abram S. Hewitt in the cause of civic rapid transit under municipal ownership, and that it be presented to him by the President, with the assurances of the admiration, respect, and affectionate regard of his fellow members of the Chamber of Commerce of the State of New York.

Resolved, That a committee of five be appointed by the President, of whom the President shall be Chairman, to carry out the provisions of the foregoing resolution.

The committee was constituted as follows: William E. Dodge, Alexander E. Orr, Charles S. Smith, Seth Low, and the President as chairman. A medal was

* Following the frontispiece is an engraving of this medal.

designed under the direction of the committee and executed by O. Roty, of Paris. It carried the following inscription:

Ingenio svo vrbis benefactor et rei pvblicæ conservator
Abram Stevens Hewitt,
Aetat svae LXXVIII

Translated this reads:

By his genius, benefactor of the City, and conservator of the public property. Age 78 years.

On the obverse:

The Chamber of Commerce of State of New York.
Rapid Transit,
MDCCCC.

At the monthly meeting of the Chamber held October 3, 1901, the medal was formally presented to Mr. Hewitt by the President.

In reply Mr. Hewitt said in part:

MR. HEWITT'S REMARKS

"The present honor would, perhaps, have been deferred until the completion of the rapid transit system, with which this occasion will imperishably link my name. Time, however, moves with relentless tread, and when a man reaches his eightieth year, it may well be supposed, as doubtless it was by the Chamber, that whatever recognition it desired to make during my lifetime should be quickly done. I regard it, and my family will always look upon it, as the seal of your approbation upon my public career.

"I am not the author of the idea of rapid transit in this city. It is an old story, but the circumstances probably ought to be recalled on the present occasion, even at the risk of being somewhat tedious, in order that your records may show how it has come to pass that the Chamber of Commerce is so thoroughly identified with this great enterprise.

N. Y. CITY CENTRAL UNDERGROUND CO.

"For many years prior to my election as Mayor in 1886, I had given careful study to the means of communication in the city of New York, and had been connected in various ways with the changes required from year to year since 1850, when I was concerned in the manufacture of the first tram rails for street railroads in this country. For a time the demand for increased move-

MARBLE STATUE BY WM. COUPER IN CHAMBER OF COMMERCE.

ment of passengers was met by the construction of these tramroads on the leading avenues of the city. The growth of business, however, made it apparent that some better mode of transit should be devised in the near future; and at various times propositions were made for building railways overhead and underneath the surface of the streets. In 1868 the legislature granted a charter to the New York City Central Underground Company, with ample powers as to route, capital, and facilities for construction. Under this charter, however, it was found impossible to raise the money required for the construction of the road.

N. Y. CITY RAPID TRANSIT CO.

"In 1872, therefore, the legislature incorporated the New York City Rapid Transit Company, authorizing Cornelius Vanderbilt and his associates to construct and operate an underground railway, which would have connected the City Hall with the Grand Central Station. This corporation was duly organized, and the necessary surveys and plans were made for the construction of the railroad. Unfortunately, however, the criticism which this grant produced in the newspapers and elsewhere brought Commodore Vanderbilt to the conclusion that he would not construct the proposed underground railway, and to this decision the members of his family, who succeeded in the management of the New York Central Railway, uniformly adhered, although they, as well as he, always insisted that the extension at that time ought to have been made, and would probably be profitable, at least to the New York Central Railroad.

OTHER LEGISLATIVE GRANTS

"Various other grants were made by the legislature. It was found, however, that capital could not be secured by any of these companies, and hence the undertakings were practically abandoned as early as 1875. In that year what is known as the Rapid Transit Act was adopted, under which the elevated railroads were constructed. The completion of these railroads relieved the congestion of travel to such an extent that no substantial complaint existed until about the year 1884, when the pressure for an underground railroad system reappeared, and the subject occupied much public attention and very general discussion, which I followed with great interest. It was evident to me that underground rapid transit could not be secured by the investment of private capital, but in some way or other its construction was dependent upon the use of the credit of the city of New York. It was also apparent to me that if such credit were used, the property must belong to the city. Inasmuch as it would not be safe for the city to undertake the construction itself, the intervention of a contracting company appeared to be indispensable. To secure the city against loss, this company must necessarily be required to give a sufficient bond for the completion of the work, and be willing to enter into a contract for its continued operation under a rental which would pay the interest upon the bonds issued by the city for the construction, and provide a sinking fund sufficient for the payment of the bonds at or before maturity. It also seemed to be indispensable that the leasing company should invest, in the rolling stock and in the real estate required for its power houses and other buildings, an amount of money sufficiently large to indemnify the city against loss in case the lessees should fail in their undertaking to build and operate the railroad.

MAYOR'S MESSAGE OF 1888

"These views were communicated to the Common Council in the Mayor's message of January, 1888. They did not receive the approval of the Common Council. In this communication it was suggested that the New York Central Railroad Company might be induced to undertake the construction and operation of the underground road. On consultation with the officers of that company I found that their co-operation could not be secured. Hence in drawing the act, which was submitted to the legislature, it was made general in its character, and provision was made for competition on the part of any and all responsible individuals or corporations who might be disposed to undertake the work. The act thus drawn was submitted to the legislature in 1888. The prejudice against the scheme was so great, however, that it was difficult to find any member of the legislature who would be responsible for the introduction of a bill, which was opposed, not only by the Common Council of the city, but by the political organization which controlled the politics of the city.

N. Y. CENTRAL NOT INTERESTED

"The Mayor appeared, however, before the committee of the legislature and made a very elaborate argument as to the necessity for increased rapid transit facilities, and of the mode under which he proposed to secure them at an early date. The committee declined to report the bill back to the Senate, and so far as the session of 1888 was concerned the proposition entirely failed.

RAPID TRANSIT COMMISSION OF 1891

"Nothing further was done in this business until 1891, when the pressure of travel had become so excessive that some action was demanded by public opinion. The result was the passage of Chapter 4 of the Laws of 1891, under which the Rapid Transit Commission of that year was appointed, and in October, 1891, reported a plan of rapid transit, mostly underground, which, in accordance with the provisions of the statute, was approved by the Board of Aldermen, by the

Department of Public Parks, by the Commissioner of Street Improvements of the Twenty-third and Twenty-fourth Wards, and by the Supreme Court.

"Bids were then invited for the construction of this work by private capital, as required by the provisions of the Act of 1891. The attempt thus to secure the construction of the line failed for want of responsible bidders, and the whole scheme was practically abandoned."

Mr. Hewitt then briefly outlined the work of the Chamber that led to the passage of the Act of 1894, under the provisions of which the present Rapid Transit Commission was organized. The only amendment of any importance made in the legislature was that which required a referendum to the people. The address then continued:

RAPID TRANSIT SYSTEM

"It is by no means certain that the contracting company will, for a considerable time, be able to realize any profit from the operations of the railroad, although the outlook is now much more favorable than at the time when the contract was made. The estimate of the profit which was to be made by the contractors out of the enterprise was purely conjectural, but it is generally agreed by competent men familiar with great public works that the terms of the contract are unusually favorable to the city. One thing is certain: that the rapid transit system adopted by the Commission will be fully completed and put in operation without involving any additional taxation whatever, and at the end of fifty years it will be the absolutely unencumbered property of the city. Compared with other enterprises in other cities, it must be conceded that the arrangement made for the construction of this work is the most favorable that has ever been devised or accomplished.

RESULTS DUE TO CHAMBER OF COMMERCE

"In achieving this result the Chamber of Commerce has been the prime mover, and I think it is not too much to say that in the future its successful intervention will be regarded as one of the most creditable achievements in its long and honorable history, identified, as it was and is, with the construction of the Erie Canal and of the great system of water supply which has made it possible for more than three millions of people to dwell together in health and comfort.

"If by the continued efforts of the Chamber of Commerce we can secure a municipal government which will enable great public works to be undertaken and carried to completion with the same economy and honesty as have characterized the execution of the Erie Canal, the Croton Water Works, and the Rapid Transit System, no reasonable limits can be assigned to the future growth of this city in prosperity and grandeur.

"In conclusion I take this occasion to thank the members of the Chamber for the confidence which they have uniformly manifested in my efforts to serve the public, and I am particularly grateful to Mr. Alexander E. Orr, Mr. Charles Stewart Smith and Mr. William E. Dodge for the gracious remarks which they were good enough to make at the time when the Chamber voted to bestow upon me this medal. It will be treasured by my children as the most precious possession which will descend to them, and be regarded by them, as it is by me, as the crowning honor of a long career, which, by the action of the Chamber of Commerce, is brought to a happy ending."

STATUE OF MR. HEWITT

The Chamber of Commerce having so honored Mr. Hewitt in the closing days of his long and useful career, did not forget him when less than fifteen months later he passed to the greater reward which lies beyond the grave. At he meeting following his death the Chamber directed that a statue of him should be made and placed in the corridor near the north end of its assembly chamber. It is the first time in its long history that such an honor has been rendered to any member of the body. It will be long before a like honor can be so appropriately awarded to any other member.

This statue was unveiled at a special meeting on the 11th of May, 1905. The address made at that time before the Chamber by Charles Stewart Smith, in the presence of Mr. Hewitt's widow and other members of his family, was an impressive and affectionate tribute to his character, his intellectual endowments, and his services to the city, the State, and the nation. The statue will give evidence, so long as the Chamber lasts, that whether or no it is true that republics are ungrateful, the Chamber of Commerce seeks to cultivate the highest ideals of citizenship by generous recognition of those of its members who have best illustrated such ideals.

CHAPTER XI.

COMMISSION OF 1894.

PERSONNEL OF 1894 COMMISSION

The Act of 1894 was signed by Governor Flower on May 22, of that year. It substituted a new rapid transit commission for that created by the Act of 1891, and provided that it should be composed of the Mayor, Comptroller and the President of the Chamber of Commerce, and of William Steinway, Seth Low, John Claflin, Alexander E. Orr, and John H. Starin. While it left unmodified the provisions of the Act of 1891, authorizing the Board to grant additional franchises to existing railroads, it provided that the Board should either adopt the plans prepared by the preceding Board, or adopt new plans and obtain the consents of the local authorities and of the property holders, or the substituted consent of the Supreme Court. It required that, after either re-adopting the old plans or making new ones and obtaining the consents, the Board at the next general election should submit to the qualified electors of the city "the question whether such railway or railways shall be constructed by the city and at the public expense." The act provided that if such question were decided in the negative at the election, the Board should proceed to sell the franchise to construct and operate such railroad to some private corporation as prescribed by the Act of 1891.

POPULAR VOTE TO BE TAKEN

The vital portions of the law depended upon the vote being cast in favor of municipal construction of the road. The new provisions were to the effect that if the question were determined in the affirmative at the election, the rapid transit railroad should be constructed at the public expense, and should be and remain the absolute property of the city, and that the Rapid Transit Commission should either provide for the construction of the railroad according to the routes, plans, and specifications adopted prior to the election, or "should change and modify the said routes, plans, and specifications" or adopt other and new routes, plans, and specifications, as they might see fit.

CONTRACTOR'S OBLIGATION

The act further provided that, after establishing the routes and plans for the railroad and obtaining the consents, the Board should, after advertising for

MORRIS K. JESUP.

proposals, enter into a contract with some person, firm, or corporation for the construction of the road for the city and at its expense. The contractor was to be required to operate the road, as the lessee of the city, for a term of not less than thirty-five nor more than fifty years, to be specified in the contract, at an annual rental sufficient to pay the interest upon the bonds to be issued by the city to raise the money necessary to build the road, and one per cent. in addition thereto. The equipment was to be supplied by the contractor at his own expense. As security for the performance of the entire contract, the contractor was to furnish a bond to the city in an amount to be determined by the Board; the city was to have a lien upon the equipment furnished by the contractor; and the contractor was also to deposit the sum of $1,000,000 with the Comptroller, which was, however, to be returned when the railroad was constructed and equipped. The details of construction and operation were left to the discretion of the Board, with the injunction that such matters should be provided for in the contract. The Board was also to supervise the construction and operation of the road. The equipment of the road was to be exempted from taxation.

The city was to issue its bonds to raise the funds necessary for the enterprise, but the total issue should not exceed $50,000,000.

ORGANIZATION OF COMMISSION

The new Rapid Transit Commission held its first meeting June 8, 1894, and organized by the election of Alexander E. Orr as president. At the same meeting Mr. Orr, who had been elected President of the Chamber of Commerce, and had thus become an *ex-officio* member of the Board, as well as being named by the statute an individual member thereof, resigned the individual appointment, and John H. Inman was elected to fill the vacancy thereby created. Subsequently Mr. Starin was elected vice-president. Wm. Barclay Parsons was appointed chief engineer, and Henry R. Beekman and Albert B. Boardman counsel.

The Board soon became convinced that several sections of the Act of 1894 required amendment, partly to eliminate certain provisions which were not in the original draft as prepared by the committee of the Chamber of Commerce, and partly to provide for various contingencies which had not been foreseen when the bill was prepared, including the plan to build pipe galleries along a portion of the route.

AMENDMENTS TO ACT

The amended statute was passed in 1895. It provided that the city should extinguish all easements of abutting property holders that might be affected by the construction of the road, thus guaranteeing the contractor against the class of litigation which had proved so serious to the elevated railroads, and authorized the city to expend the additional sum of $5,000,000 for that purpose.

The Board could permit the contractor to postpone the construction of any part of the railroad as planned until such time as, in the judgment of the Board, the interest of the city demanded.

A vote of six members of the Board was sufficient for the granting of additional franchises to existing railroads; the former act required a unanimous vote. But the act provided that any such grant should require the corporation receiving it to make proper compensation to the city, and that such compensation should be subject to re-adjustment at the expiration of successive periods to be fixed by the Board, none of which should exceed 35 years.

PEOPLE VOTE FOR MUNICIPAL CONSTRUCTION

After careful consideration of the situation the Board decided that an effective solution of the rapid transit problem could only be obtained by the construction of underground railways; and that the routes and plans adopted by the former Commission were not satisfactory if the railroad was to be constructed by the city within the limit of cost prescribed by the statute. But it was found that, under the statute, the question of municipal construction could not be submitted to popular vote until after the Board had either re-adopted the routes and plans of the former Commission, or had adopted new routes and plans and procured the necessary consents. The latter method would have taken so much time that it would have been impossible to have submitted the question to vote at the general election in the fall of 1894. The Board learned, however, that it could provisionally re-adopt the routes and plans of its predecessors and, if the vote proved favorable to municipal construction, could alter the plans or adopt entirely new ones. Before the election the Board issued a statement explaining the situation and announcing their intention, in case of an affirmative decision, to consider the question of routes and plans *de novo*. The result of the election showed an overwhelming majority in favor of municipal construction.

ELM STREET ROUTE

The Board discussed early the advisability of adopting the Elm street route, but the general opinion of the members was that the commercial advantages of a line under Broadway would more than offset the difficulties and expense of building a road beneath its surface. It was felt that the cost of construction on the Broadway route would be less then than at any future time, and that, sooner or later, a Broadway line must be provided. Therefore the route adopted by the former Board was thought to be the best, provided a branch could be selected in extension of the East-Side line to the north, as a substitute for the Madison avenue line recommended by the earlier Commission, which had been rendered unavailable by the Act of 1892. It was thought that it would be possible to extend the Fourth avenue route north from Fortieth street under the Grand Central Station, and under Fourth avenue to Ninety-seventh street, where it would become an elevated structure to be erected on either side of the Harlem railroad and then to and across the Harlem River.

PRELIMINARY STUDIES

Concerning the nature of construction, the Board believed that the plans adopted by the former Commission were wise; except that it was desirable to increase the width of the road as a measure of safety, and to omit the requirement that the work under Broadway should be done without disturbing the surface. This preliminary study included the making of maps showing all the underground pipes and conduits, and the foundations and vaults of all the buildings along the proposed routes. In addition a thorough examination of the subsoil was made.

PIPE GALLERIES

The Board came to the conclusion that it would be advisable to construct pipe galleries on either side of the road along certain sections. While it was known that these would encroach upon private vaults and would add materially to the cost, the opinion was held that, as there must be a costly re-location of the pipes, it would be wiser and less expensive in the end to construct such galleries as a part of the general plan.

BOARD OF ENGINEERS

In forming a tentative plan the Board was not unmindful of the necessity of keeping the cost within the prescribed limit, and, in order to be certain upon this point, the plans were submitted to a committee of experts composed of Abram S. Hewitt, Thomas C. Clarke, Charles Sooysmith, Octave Chanute, and Prof. William H. Burr. The report approved the estimates of the engineer that the construction, if carried to the city line on both the East and West Sides, would cost $50,000,000. It also approved the suggestion of the chief engineer that the subway should be widened from the plans of the previous Commission from 44 to 50 feet for a four-track road, and it also was of the opinion that a separation on Broadway of the local and express lines was practicable and wise.

In answer to the question as to whether any better solution of the problem than had been already brought forward could be suggested, the board of experts advised a change in the route by substituting Elm street, Lafayette Place and Fourth avenue as the route between City Hall Park and Fourteenth street. The board of experts also recommended the construction of four tracks under Fourth avenue to and under the Grand Central Station, and thence under Madison

JOHN CLAFLIN.

avenue to Ninety-seventh street. Other changes of less importance were also suggested.

ROUTES

The Commission was now called upon to choose between the Broadway and Elm street routes. As has been already explained, all of the former Commissions and all of the private companies favored the former route, all holding the opinion that the engineering difficulties and increased cost were more than compensated for by the superior advantages of that location. This was not the first time the Elm street line had been advocated, but it was the first time it had come before a rapid transit commission for serious consideration.

BROADWAY ROUTE

At that time the plan to widen Elm street seemed doomed to indefinite delay. It was, therefore, thought best to adopt the Broadway route. This began at a loop at the Battery, passed under Broadway to Fifty-ninth street; thence under the Boulevard to One-hundred-and-twenty-fourth street; thence by viaduct to One-hundred-and-thirty-fourth street; and thence under the Boulevard and Eleventh avenue to One-hundred-and-eighty-fifth street. Also a loop at City Hall and a connection with the Brooklyn Bridge. A second line diverged from the other at Fourteenth street and ran under Fourth and Park avenues to Ninety-eighth street; thence by viaduct across the Harlem (by bridge), to One-hundred-and-forty-sixth street. There were to be four tracks from Broadway and Park place to One-hundred-and-thirty-fifth street on the West Side; and four tracks on the East Side from Union Square to the Grand Central Station. Elsewhere there were to be two tracks. All tracks were to be on the same level and of standard gauge. Each track was to be allowed 12½ feet in width.

TUNNEL

The entire line was to be in tunnel, with the exception of the viaduct on the Boulevard from One-hundred-and-twenty-fourth to One-hundred-and-thirty-fourth streets, and the east side line from Ninety-eighth street northward. North of the Grand Central Station there were to be two separate tunnels along Fourth avenue as far as Ninety-sixth street. The Harlem was to be crossed by a double-track drawbridge.

BROADWAY ROUTE NOT ALLOWED BY COURT

One of the most interesting and important legal contests in the history of the Commission occurred in 1895. The importance of the decision of the court will be appreciated from the statement that it compelled the Commission to change the route from Broadway to Elm street. The consent of the local authorities to the construction and operation of the road along the lines just mentioned had been obtained; but it was found impossible to get the consent of the property owners, and therefore the substituted consent of the Supreme Court became imperative under the terms of the statute. The Court refused to consider the question at all, and entered an order to that effect in October, 1895. This order was reversed by the Court of Appeals, and the Supreme Court was directed to consider the application upon its merits. The latter Court then appointed Frederic R. Coudert, George Sherman, and William H. Gelshenen Commissioners to take testimony and report whether the road should be built. The testimony was exceedingly thorough, covering every possible aspect of the question.

In March, 1896, the Commission appointed by the Court unanimously reported that the road ought to be built.

ROAD MUST COST LESS THAN $50,000,000

Two months later the matter was argued before the Supreme Court, which unanimously refused to confirm the report of its Commissioners. The opinion was based upon the belief that the road when finished would not furnish an adequate system of rapid transit from one end of the city to the other; that it was doubtful if the road could be built with the money at the command of the city; and it was the opinion of the Court that the expenditure of such a vast sum would do away with the city's power to engage in any other public work, and might possibly so impair its credit that it could not recover in many years. It was plain that the Court would not sanction any road on the Broadway route, nor an underground road on any other route, unless it extended from one end of the city to the other, and it was shown that the total cost would be less than $50,000,000.

RAPID TRANSIT ACT CONSTITUTIONAL

Action was brought in the Supreme Court for the purpose of enjoining the city from using its funds for the construction of the road, upon the ground that the Act of 1894 was unconstitutional in many of its features, and therefore afforded no legal warrant for the proposed expenditure. This action was carried to the Court of Appeals and there decided in favor of the city. As explained in the first report issued by the Rapid Transit Commission, these decisions set at rest the vital question of the constitutionality of the legislation underlying the rapid transit enterprise, and entirely justified the wisdom and foresight with which the scheme had been devised.

The action of the Appellate Division of the Supreme Court, in refusing consent to the construction of the road upon the Broadway route, led to heated discussion of the subject in the press and elsewhere. Persons standing high in the community urged the Board to continue the work, and, if possible, find a solution of the problem committed to it. The report of the Commission says:

OPINION OF COMMISSION

"Although the reasoning of the judges seemed, at first sight, to amount to an absolute prohibition of municipal construction on any terms, yet further consideration led to the conclusion that all hope of a successful issue need not be abandoned. The action of the Court might be construed as being merely a condemnation of the particular plan presented for its consideration; and in so far as the opinions seemed to foreshadow a refusal on the part of the Court to consent to any practicable plan of municipal construction, they were capable of being regarded as so far extra-judicial as not to be binding upon the future action of the Court. The Court, indeed, might be expected, in view of the popular demand for some system of rapid transit, to consider with an open mind any new plan which did not conflict too seriously with the views held by its members, as outlined in the two opinions rendered.

"Urged by these considerations, and by an anxious desire to use every possible effort to carry into effect the important duties with which they were charged, a majority of the members of the Board concluded, after a period of hesitation, to make still another effort to find some solution of the problem before them.

MANHATTAN RAILROAD APPLICATION

"Following closely upon the announcement of the fact that the Rapid Transit Board would continue its efforts to secure the construction of a rapid transit railroad for and at the expense of the city, came an application from the Manhattan Railway Company that the Board would authorize it to build elevated railroads over a number of additional streets.

"This application was vague and indefinite in some respects, and, in still others, it sought privileges which the Board had no power to grant. A communication was sent to the railroad company on August 6, 1896, pointing out these defects and suggesting that an amended application be filed. No reply was returned to this communication, nor did the Board receive any further intimation that the Manhattan Railway Company desired to extend its lines until, after the lapse of eighteen months, it had become evident that the rapid transit railroad was likely to be constructed by the city."

During the year 1896 Mr. Low resigned from the Board, and Mr. Steinway and Mr. Inman died. Woodbury Langdon, George L. Rives, and Charles Stewart Smith were elected in their places.

ELM STREET ROUTE ADOPTED

After due consideration the Board decided to adopt, provisionally, the Elm street route for its main line. In this connection it is interesting to note that

WOODBURY LANGDON

the late Abram S. Hewitt had, in 1888, laid down a route from the Grand Central Station to the City Hall identical with that now to be adopted by the Board. In his message to the Board of Aldermen, in January of that year, he said:

ROUTE FORMERLY PROPOSED BY MR. HEWITT

"It is perfectly feasible, by an underground tunnel beginning in the neighborhood of Fifty-fourth street, to pass under the station and under the present tunnel from Forty-second street to Thirty-second street; and thence along the center of Fourth avenue to Ninth street; thence into Lafayette place; thence under Lafayette place, and thence through a new street, connecting with the Elm street improvement, which has been the subject of much discussion. It will be remembered that Fourth avenue, above Thirty-third street, is 140 feet in width, the additional 40 feet having been provided for the tracks of the railway. In opening the new street from Lafayette place to the City Hall the same width might be adopted. This would enable the four tracks to be constructed in the center of the street through an open cut, for which 50 feet would be required, leaving 90 feet between the two sides, or 45 feet of street and sidewalk on each side. From Lafayette place along Fourth avenue to Thirty-second street the four tracks would be made in a subway. The open-cut portions of the route would, of course, require no provision for ventilation or light.

FOUR TRACKS

"It will be observed that provision has thus been made for four tracks, extending from the Grand Central Station to the terminus of the Brooklyn Bridge. Between the City Hall and the Grand Central Depot two tracks will be used for express trains stopping only at the Grand Central Station. The other two tracks will be used for trains stopping at Grand street, Bleecker street, Astor place, Fourteenth street, Twenty-third street, Thirty-third street and Forty-second street. This train will take intermediate passengers who may desire to catch trains at the Forty-second street station. Two of the tracks will then proceed to the Harlem River, making the necessary stops, and thence under the Harlem will provide frequent transit for the eastern portion of the city and of the annexed district. The other two tracks will turn to the left, under Forty-sixth street, to Broadway, under which they will pass to Fifty-ninth street, at which point the Boulevard is reached. Here four tracks should be laid in an open cut extending in time as far as may be desirable. Two of these tracks will be used for through trains and two for local distribution."

On January 14, 1897, a resolution was adopted establishing the present route and plan as follows:

Beginning at the intersection of Broadway and Park row, under Park row to Center street, to New Elm street, to Lafayette place, and thence under Fourth and Park avenues to Forty-second street, to Broadway, to Fifty-ninth street, and thence under the Boulevard to One-hundred-and-twenty-fourth street; thence by viaduct to One-hundred-and-thirty-fourth street; thence under the Boulevard and Eleventh avenue to One-hundred-and-ninetieth street, and thence under or over private property, as may be most convenient, to the southeast end of Ellwood street, and thence over Ellwood street to Kingsbridge avenue or Broadway; thence to Riverside avenue to a point within 500 feet of the present Kingsbridge station of the New York & Putnam Railroad.

PRESENT ROUTE ADOPTED

This route included a loop at City Hall Park and suitable tracks and connections to the Post Office. There were also to be tracks and connections with the yard and tracks of the Grand Central Station.

The second route diverged from the first at One-hundred-and-third street and the Boulevard and thence to One-hundred-and-fourth street; thence under Central Park West and Central Park to the intersection of Lenox avenue and One-hundred-and-tenth street; thence under Lenox avenue to One-hundred-and-fortieth street; to and under the Harlem River and private property to East One-hundred-and-forty-ninth street at its intersection with River avenue; thence under East One-hundred-and-forty-ninth street to a point near its intersection with Third avenue; thence to Westchester avenue, and thence by viaduct along Westchester avenue to the Southern Boulevard; thence to the Boston Road, and thence over the Boston Road to Bronx Park.

The general plan of construction was as follows:

For the route under Park row and City Hall park, two parallel tracks; from the City Hall loop to One-hundred-and-third street, four parallel tracks; north of One-hundred-and-third street both routes to have two tracks.

PLAN OF CONSTRUCTION

All tracks were to be on the same level, except that "wherever required by special necessities of surface or sub-surface structures, or other special or local necessities, and for the purpose of avoiding grade crossings at the southerly end of Center street and the One-hundred-and-tenth street junction, any one or more of the tracks may be depressed below the level of the other tracks to a depth of not more than 20 feet."

The tracks were to be of standard gauge, and for each track there was to be 12½ feet width of tunnel. Wherever the tracks changed from tunnel to viaduct or the reverse, the change was to be made so as to occupy or obstruct the use of the surface of the street to the least possible extent consistent with the proper gradient for the tracks. The roof of the tunnel was to be as near the surface of the street as street conditions and grades would permit.

WIDTH OF TUNNELS

The maximum widths of the tunnels were to be as follows: Under Park row and the City Hall loop, 38 feet; from the loop to the commencement of Elm street, 50 feet; from there to Lafayette place, 68 feet; to One-hundred-and-third street, 50 feet; for both routes north, 25 feet; the tunnel under the river and its approaches to be 35 feet.

Wherever necessary for the support of the street surface, the roof of the tunnel was to be of steel or iron girders with brick or concrete arches supported by iron or steel columns and masonry walls, or a masonry arch. Viaducts were to be built with a width of 12½ feet for each track, and with an additional width of 3 feet on each side for outside footways. The viaducts were to be built of metal or masonry, or both.

The stations and station approaches were to be at the intersection of the streets, and located under or over the streets, or on private property, as required by the situation. Along the Boulevard openings were to be provided in the surface of the street for the purpose of ventilation and light; no opening to exceed 20 feet in width by 50 feet in length.

METHOD OF OPERATION

The general mode of operation required was by electricity, or some other power not requiring combustion within the tunnels or on the viaducts; the motors to be capable of moving trains at a speed of not less than 40 miles an hour for long distances, exclusive of stops. The manner of construction was to be by tunneling or open excavation.

It was believed that this scheme of construction would meet the requirements of the Supreme Court, and for the following reasons which were presented in the first report of the Board:

"In the first place, the road was estimated to cost about $35,000,000, and that this estimate was correct time has conclusively proved. In the second place, it ran from the City Hall—or near the southerly end of Manhattan Island—to Kingsbridge as the terminus of one branch, and to Bronx Park as the terminus of the other. At Kingsbridge a physical connection with the New York Central lines to Yonkers, and beyond, was easy. At Bronx Park the northerly limits of the city were nearly reached; and if the Court had insisted on a further exten-

Photo by Hollinger & Co., N. Y.

SETH LOW.

sion here, it would have cost little, comparatively, to extend the line still farther by an elevated structure through the Park.

"The necessity of avoiding Broadway, below Thirty-fourth street, so as to meet the views of the Court, compelled the use of Fourth avenue and Elm street for the main stem, and the introduction of an awkward alignment from Fourth avenue to the westward along Forty-second street to Broadway.

AN EAST SIDE LINE TOO EXPENSIVE

"It was thought impossible in this scheme to provide for a line on the East Side from the Grand Central Station to the Harlem. The cost of such a line would have brought the total expense up to figures that the Supreme Court was not expected to sanction, even if the West-Side line had been made only a two-track road. A four-track road, carried as far north as possible, was regarded by the Board as essential to real rapid transit. A two-track road forbids the use of express trains, and necessarily reduces the speed of all trains to the speed of the slowest. Upon the fullest consideration, therefore, the Board determined to abandon an East-Side line, and to provide for a four-track service to the neighborhood of One-hundredth street; and from that point to send off an easterly branch which should follow the line, not of Fourth, but of Lenox avenue, and from the termination of that street should cross the Harlem.

"This route appeared to the Board the best that could at that time be devised to meet the conditions imposed; and it seemed probable that, if the system proved a success, additional lines might subsequently be built that would supply some rather obvious defects in the plan adopted. Moreover, the Board believed that the section of the city east of Central Park was already better provided with transit facilities than most other quarters.

ROAD TO BE IN TUNNEL

"In one very important particular the plan of 1897 involved an important departure from the plan of 1895. The entire line of the road on Manhattan Island was to be in tunnel, except for the short distance between Fort George and Kingsbridge. In the Borough of the Bronx the road was to be in tunnel from the Harlem River to a point on Westchester avenue some distance east of Third avenue. The Board was not willing to gain in cheapness by sacrificing important streets to elevated railways.

"It has already been pointed out that the southerly terminus of the route thus adopted was at Park row, and this fact is also to be explained by that statement that, although the Board was of the opinion that the route ought to be extended along Broadway to South Ferry, it was unwilling, in view of *dicta* contained in the opinions of the Appellate Division, to risk a condemnation of its entire plan, unless the owners of property upon that portion of Broadway affected by its route should, by consenting to the construction of the railroad, render unnecessary a recourse to the courts."

EXTENSION TO BATTERY PLACE

As soon as the intention of the Board became known there ensued an agitation among the property owners along lower Broadway in favor of the extension of the road to the Battery. In a few weeks a petition was presented to the Board, signed by a majority, in value, of all the property owners, asking for the extension of the road. The Board therefore adopted a resolution on April 1, 1897, providing for a two-track extension to Battery place, with a loop under Battery Park, Whitehall and State streets. Afterward this extension was abandoned, for the time being, owing to the refusal of the Park Commissioners to grant consent to its construction.

BOND OF $15,000,000

The approval of property owners having been refused, application was again made to the Supreme Court and a commission was appointed in July, 1897. This commission reported unanimously in favor of the plans. A majority of the Court was in favor of the motion, but, as the opinion said, to give "some assurance that the powers of the Rapid Transit Commissioners in respect to security should be exercised so as to protect the interests of the city in a substantial manner," exacted, as a condition precedent to the entry of an order confirming the report, a requirement that the Rapid Transit Board should file a stipulation that, upon awarding any contract for the construction and operation of the railroad, "the penalty of the bond specified in section 34 of the rapid transit act will be fixed at not less than $15,000,000."

BOND EXCESSIVE

It needed no extended acquaintance with the subject to perceive that, if the Court persisted in exacting a literal compliance with these conditions, its action would amount to an absolute veto of the entire plan of municipal construction and ownership. The Board appointed a sub-committee to ascertain if such a bond could be obtained and to report what security in money, bonds, or otherwise could probably be obtained from responsible bidders.

The Greater New York Charter went into effect January 1, 1898. The charter compelled the city to assume the indebtedness of all the consolidated territory, with the result that the debt incurring capacity of the new city was reduced to a very narrow limit. But this proved to be only temporary, since the increase in the assessed valuations of property in the county of New York, which was shortly made in order to equalize its value with the assessed valuations in other portions of the city, resulted in giving such a margin as would suffice for the construction of the rapid transit railroad without intrenching upon the ten per cent. limitation imposed by the charter. Another result of the consolidation was a tendency to array the influence of Kings and Richmond counties, and a portion of Queens, against the plans. At that time it seemed that the endeavors of the Board would be defeated or at least doomed to indefinite postponement.

The Manhattan Railway Company now made public its intention to extend its system of elevated railways as soon as it could obtain permission from the Board, or from the Legislature to do so.

APPLICATION OF ELEVATED COMPANY

The Metropolitan Street Railway Company withdrew from the contest by announcing to the Board that, as matters then stood, it could not be expected to compete for the contract to construct and operate the proposed road. The position assumed by the Elevated Company made it certain to the Board that not only the Metropolitan Company but other responsible bidders would hesitate before making proposals for the contract to build and operate the road. In July, 1896, the Elevated Company presented an application to the Board. This application is reviewed in the report of the sub-committee appointed by the Board in the following language:

APPLICATION REVIEWED BY BOARD

"The application of the Elevated Railway Company was expressly conditioned upon its receiving immunity from claims for damages; it asked for grants of street surface franchises; it asked for franchises including 30 miles of new route, besides additional facilities upon existing routes, but did not pledge the company to any actual extension of its system or other relief within any given period of time, and it made no offer of any rental. The answer of the Board pointed out that the application was not in a form which permitted definite acceptance; that the Board had no power under the law to assure to a private corporation building an elevated railroad immunity from damages; that under the statute rental must be paid on extensions; and that the Board was expressly forbidden by the statute to grant any right to construct a railroad on the surface of a street. It was further pointed out that the granting of any application not limited in time would be, in substance, to give an option to the Elevated Railway Company to extend or improve its system whenever it should become ready to do so, without imposing upon it any corresponding obligation, thus suspending meantime the practical possibility of relief from any other quarter.

Photo by Falk, N. Y.

CHARLES STEWART SMITH

ELEVATED ASKED TO AMEND APPLICATION

"The Board concluded its communication by expressing the hope that the Elevated Railroad Company, in view of the exceptional privileges which it had received from the city, and the exceptional advantages which it then enjoyed for the extension of rapid transit facilities, would promptly amend its application so that the Board could lawfully deal with it; and the Board promised that, upon receiving such an application, it would reach a determination upon it without delay. To this communication, made nearly eighteen months ago, no answer has been received."

The sub-committee inquired into the possibility of securing a bond of $15,000,000, as required by the decision of court. The report states that: "It is not possible for the Board, until it shall have power to propose a contract, to reach a definite conclusion as to what amount of bond ought to be exacted from the successful bidder." At that time the terms of the contract had not been fixed, and upon them much depended; moreover, the length of the lease, character of the requirements for operation, and the probable value of the equipment to be furnished by the contractor, were all elements demanding consideration. Therefore, the committee said:

"If a bond for $15,000,000 be required in the technical form prescribed by section 34, the requirements will, in the opinion of your committee, operate as a substantial prohibition of the enterprise.

CITY AMPLY PROTECTED

"In the opinion of your committee, it was not the intention of the people of the city, or of the Legislature, that the Board should attempt the impossibility of eliminating all risk to the city in carrying out the rapid transit plan. Any future construction involving expenditure of money inevitably involves risk. Municipal construction was not justified, and could not, under the constitution, be justified for the purpose of making money. Its constitutional justification lay in the great public necessity of the city. * * * But it must be remembered that the rental to be paid is the full amount of the interest which the city is to pay upon its bonds, and that, in addition, there is to be paid at least one per cent. per annum, with a conditional deduction for the first five or ten years. This one per cent. is in effect a sinking fund, the result of which will ultimately be to give, without expense to the city, the rapid transit road completely constructed, the entire outlay, as well for principal as for interest, being met by the rental payable by the contractor.

"If, however, the Court shall require a stipulation as to security now, the following considerations may be urged: In the first place, it may well be contended that this Board, as a public body, have no right to enter into any contract as to the future exercise of their powers. Even if the Board can with propriety give a stipulation as to their future action, the facts upon which to form a sound business judgment as to the amount of security to be exacted are as yet not fully known—particularly as the form of contract to be proposed to bidders cannot be settled in advance of the formal consent of the Court. In any case, a joint and several bond for $15,000,000, running for the whole term of the lease, and on which the sureties must justify in $30,000,000, is practically prohibitive, because satisfactory sureties could not probably be found. Even if found, the expense and difficulty of obtaining such surety would operate to limit competition and tend to make the cost of construction larger than it need be, and without any compensating advantages. The attempt to exact too large a bond, continuing long after the road is finished, would only result in defeating the whole scheme of municipal construction and ownership. If the Court will consent to limit its requirements to security for construction—leaving it to the Board to fix the amount of the continuing bond—and will permit the giving of several bonds, such security for a very large amount could be obtained. But even for construction alone, a bond for fifty per cent. of the estimated cost of the work would be unnecessary—especially in view of the requirement of a cash deposit of $1,000,000 and the proposed retention of a large percentage of the cost of the work until the road is fully constructed and equipped—and it is also contrary to the practice prevailing in all city or government work."

LARGE BOND PROHIBITIVE

Acting upon the advice of its committee the Board made application to the Court for the modification of the terms imposed by it. The Court still insisted that the Board must exact a bond for $15,000,000, but it consented that the liability of the sureties as to $14,000,000 thereof should terminate when the road should have been completed and equipped; and that the permanent liability upon the bond might be limited to $1,000,000. These terms, although still severe, were not necessarily prohibitive, and the Board, therefore, entered into the stipulation required by the Court.

BOND REDUCED

Again the matter was taken up with the Manhattan Railway Company, and a sub-committee was appointed to examine the matter. A summary of seven franchises the Board was willing to grant was submitted to the company. The Manhattan officials did not have the plans elaborated, made no estimates of cost, made no suggestions regarding rentals to be paid the city, and continually pleaded for more time for investigation and consideration. They constantly overlooked the fact that the question had been before them for several years, and every conceivable aspect of the rapid transit problem, as far as elevated roads were concerned, had been discussed with the present and former commissioners.

The sub-committee's report concluded as follows:

SEVEN FRANCHISES OFFERED TO THE MANHATTAN

"If the Manhattan Company shall accept the seven franchises thus proposed and carry them out according to their terms, the rapid transit facilities of the city will be materially improved. The rapid transit problem, however, will not be solved. On the contrary, it is our belief that before the periods described in the franchises shall have expired, the necessity will be even clearer than it is now for an additional rapid transit system, having the enormous advantages incidental to a system carried through tunnels constructed on the improved modern method. This will, in our opinion, be the case, notwithstanding the increase of the capacity and traffic of the Manhattan system. If the Manhattan Company shall exercise all the franchises now proposed to be tendered it, it will be able to carry a very much larger number of passengers and to carry the passengers at a materially increased speed. And as our proposition is that the Manhattan Company shall be permitted to take any one or more or all of the franchises, the company is enabled, if it does not see its way to undertake all of these obligations, still to undertake such of them as shall give material relief. If the Manhattan Company shall, pursuant to the statute, accept all the certificates tendered by the Rapid Transit Board, the city and the public will have assurance of a reasonably prompt and material improvement of its transit facilities."

FRANCHISES REFUSED

The Manhattan Company refused to accept any of the franchises. It was unwilling to undertake the work of extending its traffic facilities. Its last opportunity had come and gone. It was controlled apparently by a belief that no solution of rapid transit problems could be obtained without its co-operation, and that in the end privileges would be granted to it on its own terms. A procrastinating policy had been successful with former commissions, and why should it not be in this case?

Photo by Dupont, N. Y.

JOHN H. STARIN

OTHER EFFORTS OF BOARD

Still other attempts were made by the Board to provide rapid transit by enlisting the assistance of those already concerned with railroad transportation within the city. Interviews were had with Cornelius Vanderbilt and with Mr. Depew, president of the New York Central & Hudson River Railroad Company, and with Mr. Clark, president of the New York, New Haven & Hartford Railroad. The Board presented to those gentlemen the advantages which it then believed belonged to the rapid transit plan, and which experience has since demonstrated did in fact so belong, and urged the value of co-operation with the Board. The Board was, however, unable to convince them. Later, like conferences were had with Mr. Whitney and others representing the Metropolitan Street Railway interest, and with capitalists representing other large railroad interests. But until the actual letting of the rapid transit contract in January, 1900, the Board was unable to satisfy any responsible persons in control of railroad interests within the City of New York that they could undertake the rapid transit contract with any fair chance of profit.

KIOSK, BUDAPEST SUBWAY.

CHAPTER XII.

PREPARING THE SUBWAY CONTRACT.

On July 1, 1897, the duty of preparing the contract for the construction and operation of the proposed railroad was submitted to a sub-committee of the Board. The contract was completed March 31, 1898, and sent to the Corporation Counsel for his approval on April 7, of the same year, as required by the act. No attention was paid to the request of the Board until September of the following year, and in the meantime all work toward the construction of the road was brought to a standstill.

CONTRACT SENT TO CORPORATION COUNSEL

The situation at that time was fully explained in a communication by the board to the Legislature. It was stated that, by the terms of the Greater New York Charter, the enlarged city was compelled to assume all the liabilities of all the counties, towns, villages and public corporations embraced in the consolidation. While the amount of this indebtedness was not known precisely, the Comptroller was of the opinion that it was not less than thirteen and a half million dollars in excess of the ten per cent. of the assessed value of the real estate within the city limits. If such were the case it would be impossible to borrow the money required to construct the road. The Rapid Transit Commission was, therefore, constrained to consider carefully the courses open to the city to obtain the relief so long sought and so urgently needed.

Three plans were suggested:

THREE PLANS SUGGESTED

1. To wait until the borrowing capacity of the city became so enlarged by a reduction of the debt, or by an increase of assessed valuations of real estate, or by both, as to enable it to borrow the funds necessary.

2. To obtain legislative authority to issue bonds of the county of New York for the construction of the road.

3. To obtain legislative authority to offer a franchise for the construction and operation of the road to private enterprise.

The net funded debt of the city of New York on January 1, 1899, was $244,-212,835.97; other items brought the total up to $250,928,950.10. The amount was only $1,924,394 less than ten per cent. of the assessed valuation of the real estate of the city. Upon this basis it was manifestly impossible to borrow the amount needed for the construction of the road.

VALUATION OF CITY PROPERTY

But a few days later the Tax Commissioners made public the assessed valuations of real estate for purposes of taxation during the year 1899. These showed an increase of $421,512,876; ten per cent. of which, or $42,151,287.60, represented the amount by which the city's debt-incurring capacity had been increased. But there were other demands for money for important city uses.

The Comptroller was of the opinion that if it should be found desirable to build the road by the use of the municipal credit, the contracts for construction should be so drawn as not to call for the issue of bonds in excess of ten millions of dollars in any one year. The Commission recognized the fact that this could be done by dividing the contract into three sections of $10,000,000 each, one section to be built each year, but considered it their duty to seek an enlargement of their powers so as to permit them to take advantage of the improvement in the city's finances, or to look to other sources for the capital to build the road.

The money could have been raised by issuing bonds of the County of New York, including the Boroughs of Manhattan and the Bronx, as the debt of the county was far below the ten per cent. limit, and as there was nothing in the Constitution prohibiting such a proceeding. Such a course would maintain an essential clause of the act of 1894, namely, municipal ownership with private operation. The road would be an asset of the county. The obligation assumed by the county would not involve the levying of any tax nor impose any burden upon the taxpayers, unless the contractor should default. The Comptroller held the opinion that it would be undesirable to issue such bonds.

TO SELL FRANCHISE TO CONSTRUCT AND OPERATE ROAD

The last possible solution rested in selling a franchise to construct and operate the road, if the statute permitted this to be done. The financial conditions of 1899 were much more favorable to the successful conduct of the enterprise than they were in 1893-4. The pronounced success of the Boston subway served to remove doubts that had existed as to the practicability of such a road, and illustrated the possibility of closely estimating the cost and the probable income. In its appeal to the Legislature the Board says:

"Quite apart from and in addition to the considerations mentioned, is the further consideration that the contemplated rapid transit road, whether built with city money or by private capital, will, at the end of a comparatively short time, become a piece of property whose value it would be difficult to overestimate. It is perfectly safe to say that in the course of fifty years the certain growth of the city's population will so increase the earning capacity of such a road that the value will be far greater than its original cost. The effect of permitting construction by private capital would, therefore, be to surrender to individuals an asset which might be made a valuable addition to the property of the people of the whole city. The former city of New York, in its ownership of markets and docks, exemplified the wisdom of pursuing the plan of municipal ownership. In the surrender of its streets to surface and elevated roads, which are now doing a profitable business on a capitalization far greater than their original cost, it exhibits the results of the opposite course of dealing.

THE SUBWAY JUSTIFIES DEPARTURE FROM SETTLED POLICIES

"The Rapid Transit Board is, however, of the opinion that the proposed underground railway is a work of such peculiar character, and of such exceptional value to the city, that a departure from the settled policy of recent legislation might be justified.

"It is plain that such justification can only be found in the event of the public credit proving unavailable. That such will be the case is not as yet entirely certain. The Board, therefore, recommend that if power is granted them to sell the franchise to construct the road, such power shall be additional to their present powers and not a substitute for them. In this way the Board will be enabled to take advantage of varying conditions as they may arise in the future. If the city authorities shall see their way clear to keep the debt sufficiently within the constitutional limitation, then the Board will be in position to authorize municipal construction; and, on the other hand, if municipal construction shall prove to be constitutionally impracticable within any reasonable time, the Board may be enabled to arrange for construction by private capital.

CONSTRUCTION AND OPERATION BY PRIVATE CAPITAL

"The Board, therefore, ventures to urge that if the Legislature shall determine that it is wise to permit a resort to private capital, the largest measure of authority and discretion compatible with the public interest shall be intrusted to the Board in order that it may frame such a franchise as will certainly attract sufficient private capital and arouse competition. And the Board deems it of special importance, if private enterprise is to be enlisted, that the Board may be authorized, in its discretion, to enter into such a contract with the corporation that shall undertake the work as will exempt it from taxation for some limited period, and will insure it for a period of years, at least, against the possibility of legislative or municipal interference."

PROPOSITION OF METROPOLITAN COMPANY

Before action had been taken upon the bill introduced by the Board to obtain these additional powers, a proposition was received from the Metropolitan Street Railway Company that, if the Board would grant a perpetual franchise to a new corporation to be formed by them, they would build the road and pay the annual sum of 5 per cent. of the gross receipts therefor, "provided that the grantee shall first receive 5 per cent. net upon the cost of construction." While the Board was unanimous in the belief that the benefit of owning the railroad should be preserved to the city, the necessities of the situation imperatively demanded that the construction of a rapid transit system should be obtained in some way. The Board also held the opinion that if it could present as an alternative to the plan of municipal construction "another plan which offered an immediate solution of the difficulty through the medium of a perpetual grant to a private corporation, a clear-cut issue would be presented to the public, and that this would compel the city authorities to come to a decision upon the vital question whether the railroad should be constructed with the city's money and be the city's property, or whether it should be constructed by and belong to a private corporation." In consequence of these considerations, a resolution was adopted "that it is in the public interest that in addition to the powers already possessed by the Board, the Legislature should grant to the Board the power to contract for the construction and operation of the rapid transit railroad by private capital." The introduction of a bill to this effect served to show the intensity of the popular feeling in favor of reserving the ownership of the road by the city. It was made manifest that the public was unalterably against the granting of a perpetual franchise to the Metropolitan Company, or to any other private corporation. The offer of the company was withdrawn.

MAYOR REFUSES TO ACCEPT AMENDMENTS PROPOSED BY BOARD

At the Board meeting of March 11, 1899, it was announced that the Mayor had refused to accept, in behalf of the city, the amendments to the rapid transit acts which had been passed by the Legislature. This was the bill that had been introduced by the Board, but which had been so changed as to seriously interfere with any negotiations the Board might have decided to make with a view to construction of the road by private capital.

In a communication to Mayor Robert A. VanWyck, under date of May 19, 1899, the Commissioners said:

"The Board begs to repeat that its power to carry out the purpose for which it was created now depends practically, first, upon the permission of the Corporation Counsel to make any contract, and, second, upon the assent of the Board of Estimate to a postponement of the making of other contracts involving large municipal debt until a rapid transit contract, actually made, shall assure the carrying out of that great public measure. The Board, therefore, respectfully asks your Honor, and through you the other municipal authorities, whether in these two respects it may be aided to secure prompt and actual construction of the rapid transit road by the city."

NO ACTION BY CITY AUTHORITIES

No answer was received from the Mayor, nor was any action taken by either the Board of Estimate and Apportionment or the Corporation Counsel. The subject was again gone over in a communication to the Board of Estimate and Apportionment in July. The attention of that Board was called to the fact that the debt-incurring power of the city was not less than $40,000,000, a sum amply sufficient to build the rapid transit road; that no contract could be made until the Corporation Counsel acted; that the rapid transit debt of the city could not be technically created until after a contract had been executed; and that until such debt had been created or authorized, other debts might be incurred which would effectually prevent the construction of the road and thus defeat the will of the city as represented by vote of the people. No answer was received to this communication.

It was not until September 20, 1899, eighteen months later, that a letter was received by the Rapid Transit Commission from the Corporation Counsel. He withheld approval of the draft contract "for the reason that, while the approval of the Corporation Counsel was technically merely an approval as to form, it has always been the practice of this Department in such a case not to approve as to form a contract which could not legally be made." He stated that the city was now in a position to undertake the work, and suggested changes in the form.

CORPORATION COUNSEL APPROVES CONTRACT

A revised draft of the contract was approved by the Corporation Counsel October 11, 1899.

The amount of the bond ($14,000,000) was reduced by the Appellate Division of the Supreme Court. The decision rendered on November 10 said:

BOND REDUCED BY COURT

"The Corporation Counsel, on behalf of the city of New York, having joined with the Rapid Transit Commissioners in this application, and the municipal authorities as well as the Rapid Transit Commissioners having represented that in their opinion a bond of $5,000,000 will, in view of the form of the contract and the conditions under which the rapid transit road is now to be constructed, amply protect the city, the Rapid Transit Commissioners are relieved from the stipulation which they gave as a condition upon the confirmation of the report of the Commissioners in approving of the construction of this proposed railway to the extent that a bond of $5,000,000 will be a compliance with the stipulation."

The terms of the contract were, in brief, as follows:

The contractor agrees to construct and equip the railroad upon the routes and in accordance with the general plans of the Commission; to put it in operation; and to use, maintain, and operate it under a lease from the city for the term of 50 years.

TERMS OF CONTRACT

The city agrees to pay $35,000,000 in case the whole of the road is constructed, and other specified sums in case it should determine to construct less than the whole. The city grants to the contractor the right to construct and operate the road "free of all right, claim, or other interference, whether by injunction, suit for damages, or otherwise on the part of any abutting owner or other person."

All the exposed parts of the structure are to be designed, constructed and maintained with a view to the beauty of their appearance as well as to their efficiency, and the work is to be done in substantial manner and in accordance with the specifications embodied in the contract. The contractor is to make all necessary readjustment of pipes, subways, or other sub-surface structures; he must attend to the support, including underpinning wherever necessary, of all buildings, monuments and elevated and surface railways; and the re-construction of street pavements and surfaces. These are declared to be essential parts of the construction of the railway. The contractor must provide a complete equipment for the railroad, including not only cars, but also all engines, electric wires. conduits, power houses, and lighting, signalling, and ventilating apparatus.

RIGHTS OF COMMISSION

The Board reserves the right during the progress of the work to amplify the plans, to add explanatory specifications, and to furnish additional specifications and drawings. It also reserves the right to require additional work to be done, on paying the reasonable value thereof to the contractor, or to require work to be omitted, in which case a reasonable deduction from the contract price is to be made. The contract provides for the thorough inspection by the Board of all materials and work from the beginning of their manufacture or preparation, and all work and materials are subject to the direction and approval of the Chief Engineer of the Board. In case of any dispute as to the obligation of the contractor, the determination of the engineer is to be so far binding that the contractor must, without delay, obey his requirements, leaving open the question as to his right to receive compensation for additional work. In case of dispute as to the value of extra work, an appeal may be taken from the decision of the engineer, either by the Board or the contractor, to a board of arbitration to be composed as provided in detail in the contract.

TIME

The contractor must begin work within 30 days after the execution of the contract, and complete the entire road within 4½ years. If not completed within that time, the city is to deduct from the amount due the contractor 2 per cent. a month until the balances are finally due. In case the contractor shall be delayed by injunction, or by strike, or by any interference of public authority, and cannot make up for the delay so occasioned by quicker work, then the date for completion may be extended by the amount of time of such delay, provided written notice of the delay is given in each case by the contractor to the Board.

TERMINALS AND STATIONS

The contract provides that the city itself shall purchase the real estate for the terminals by condemnation or otherwise, and the contractor is to construct them and receive the cost of such construction, with a profit of 10 per cent. But it is provided that the total amount to be paid by the city for the terminals shall in no case exceed $1,750,000. This amount is to be in addition to the $35,000,000 paid for the cost of construction. It is also provided that the city shall, if necessary, acquire lands for stations and other purposes of the railroad in an amount not exceeding $1,000,000, and that, if the necessary real estate should cost more than that sum, such excess is to be borne by the contractor.

PAYMENTS

The payments to the contractor are to be made monthly upon written requisitions, accompanied by a certificate of the engineer showing the proportion of the whole work actually done. The Board is authorized to fix the amount due at such sum as it may itself determine to be the proper actual relative value of such work and materials, and the amount so certified is to be forthwith paid by the city to the contractor. In case the contractor should be dissatisfied with the determination of the Board, an appeal may be taken to the board of arbitration. When two-thirds of the work in value has been finished, the contractor must begin to provide the equipment, and to have such equipment ready for use three months in advance of the completion of the road.

CONTRACTOR TO PROVIDE EQUIPMENT

It is provided that "The railroad is to be constructed for actual use and operation as an intra-urban railroad of the highest class, adapted to the necessities of the people of the city of New York. . . . The contractor shall construct, complete, and fully equip the railroad in the best manner and according to the best rules and usages of railroad construction, so that the railroad shall be thoroughly fitted for safe, continuous, immediate, and full operation. . . . In the event of any doubt as to the meaning of any portion or portions of the specifications or contract drawings, or of the text of the contract, the same shall be interpreted as calling for the best construction, both as to materials and workmanship, capable of being supplied or applied under the then existing local conditions."

CONTRACTOR TO MAKE GOOD ANY DAMAGE TO BUILDINGS, ETC.

The contractor agrees that the work shall be done without fault or negligence on his part, and that it shall not involve any damage to the foundation walls or other parts of adjacent buildings or structures, and he agrees, at his own expense, to make good any damage which shall be done in the course of construction. He further agrees, during the performance of the work, to maintain safely the traffic on all streets, to take all necessary precautions to place proper safeguards for the prevention of accidents, and to exhibit at night suitable lights.

CONTRACTOR TO LEASE ROAD FOR FIFTY YEARS

The city leases to the contractor the whole railroad for fifty years from the time of completion. The contractor agrees to pay as rental a sum equal to the interest payable by the city upon the bonds issued by it to provide means for construction, and also one per cent. upon the whole amount of such bonds—except that for the first five years the payment is not to be made unless the contractor's profits amount to five per cent. a year—and for the next five years the payment is to be only one-half of one per cent., unless the contractor's profits amount to five per cent. a year. The contractor covenants to operate the road according to the highest standards of railway practice. Local trains are to run at an average speed, stops included, of not less than 14 miles an hour; and express trains at an average speed, including stops, of not less than 30 miles an hour. Between one and five o'clock in the morning trains are to be run, stopping at all stations, at intervals of not more than 15 minutes.

CITY NOT LIABLE FOR ACCIDENTS

The contractor agrees to save the city harmless from all accidents, and to keep the road and equipment in thorough repair, so that at all times and at the termination of the lease the road shall be in thoroughly good and solid condition, and fully equipped for use. Stations and cars are to be kept lighted and heated so that passengers may conveniently read. The waiting rooms are to be kept clean and comfortable; proper seating capacity is to be provided and good drinking water, as also sufficient and suitable water closets, which are to be kept in a thoroughly sanitary condition. All tunnels, stations, and cars are to be thoroughly ventilated with pure air, and all tunnels are to be thoroughly lighted at all times, so as to permit the tracks, walls and roofs to be clearly visible for inspection.

MOTIVE POWER TO BE ELECTRIC OR COMPRESSED AIR

The motive power is to be electricity or compressed air; but it is provided that if, in the future development of the railroad art, any method of generating or transmitting power superior to electricity, and involving no injury to the purity of the atmosphere in the tunnels or cars, shall be discovered to be practicable, then the contractor shall have the right to adopt such method, if approved by the Board, on two months' notice. The contractor must provide rolling stock of the best character known at the time, and the Board reserves the right to make good any neglect on this point of which the contractor may be guilty. The rolling stock is to be adequate to the requirements of the traveling public, and a schedule is to be filed every six months showing in detail all the equipment owned by the contractor.

FARE

The contractor is to charge for a single fare not more than 5 cents; but it is provided that he "may provide additional conveniences for such passengers as shall desire the same upon not to exceed one car upon each train, and may collect from each passenger in such car a reasonable charge for such additional convenience furnished by him, provided that the amount to be charged therefor and the character of such additional conveniences shall, from time to time, be subject to the approval of the Board."

RENEWAL OF LEASE

At the option of the contractor a new lease of the road is to be granted to him for a period of 25 years from the expiration of the lease provided for in the contract. This lease is to be in the same general form, but the rent is to be an amount to be agreed upon, not less than the average amount of the annual rental for the last ten years of the lease. In case of failure to agree upon the rental, it is to be determined, subject to such minimum, by arbitration.

At the final termination of the lease the city is to buy the equipment at a price to be fixed by agreement or arbitration; but at the termination of the lease, even though the price has not been determined on, the equipment is to be turned over to the city for use, subject to the future adjustment of the amount to be paid.

BONDS OF CONTRACTOR

For the construction of the road the contractor must deposit with the Comptroller the sum of $1,000,000 cash. In case of any default on the part of the contractor, and in case the city shall, by reason of such default, incur any expense, the amount of such expense shall be taken from the above sum. Should such a condition arise, the contractor must, within ten days of notice from the Comptroller, restore the deposit to the original amount. For the full and complete performance of the contract, and the construction and operation of the road, a continuing bond of $5,000,000 is required.

In May, 1899, Morris K. Jesup was elected president of the Chamber of Commerce, and thus succeeded Alexander E. Orr as an *ex-officio* member of the Board. At the first meeting of the Board held thereafter John Claflin resigned as a member, and Mr. Orr was immediately re-elected as his successor. At the same meeting Lewis L. Delafield, secretary of the Board, resigned, and shortly after Bion L. Burrows, the present secretary, was appointed.

The organization adopted by the Board for its engineering staff consisted of a chief engineer, Wm. Barclay Parsons; a deputy chief engineer, Geo. S. Rice; six division engineers, five general inspectors, a private secretary, an auditor, and a photographer.

OBSTACLES IN PATH OF COMMISSION

The foregoing fails to convey even a faint conception of the discouraging delays that continually beset all efforts of the Rapid Transit Commission to accomplish the object for which it was created. No sooner was one obstacle surmounted than another, perhaps more formidable, was presented. This constant changing of the aspect of the question made necessary repeated revisions and alterations of the plans, all of which took time. Although there was an imperative demand for rapid transit by the people, who had by a large majority of their votes sanctioned municipal ownership, the city authorities and the courts were indisposed to promote the purpose. Neither the Manhattan nor the

Metropolitan Company seemed at all anxious to provide increased facilities, unless such facilities could be given upon its own terms. It would seem as if the former company had become convinced that no scheme of rapid transit could be carried to successful completion without its assistance, and that if the plans of the Commission could be delayed long enough to thoroughly dishearten the Commission and the people, it would have the opportunity of providing rapid transit according to its own plans and desires.

ENTRANCE, PARIS SUBWAY.

CHAPTER XIII.

CONTRACT AWARDED AND WORK BEGUN.

The legal and financial difficulties which had so long prevented active steps having been overcome during the fall of 1899, the Board decided, in November of that year, to advertise the contract as provided by law. In order not to exceed the limit of the debt-incurring capacity of the city, bids were invited on the basis of dividing the whole route into four sections, the right being reserved by the Board to award contracts for the several sections, beginning with the first, at intervals of not more than one year. The several sections and their lengths were as follows:

ROUTE DIVIDED INTO FOUR SECTIONS

Section 1.—From the southern terminus at the City Hall to and including a station at Fifty-ninth street and Broadway; 5 miles of 4-track subway.

Section 2.—All of the railroad on the north of such station at Fifty-ninth street, to and including a station at the intersection of One-hundred-and-thirty-seventh street and Broadway; and on the East Side from the junction at One-hundred-and-third street and Broadway to and including a station at One-hundred-and-thirty-fifth street and Lenox avenue; 3.43 miles of 2-track subway, and 0.51 miles of 2-track viaduct.

Section 3.—All of the railroad on the West Side north from a station at One-hundred-and-thirty-seventh street to and including a station at Fort George; and on the East Side from a station at One-hundred-and-thirty-fifth street to and including a station at Melrose avenue; 4.32 miles of 2-track subway.

Section 4.—The remainder of the railroad from Fort George to Kingsbridge, and from Melrose avenue to Bronx Park; 5.29 miles of 2-track viaduct.

At noon on January 15, 1900, two bids were opened in the office of the Board, in the presence of all the Commissioners.

The first was that of John B. McDonald, of New York, as follows:

AMOUNTS OF BIDS

If for Section 1, ...	$15,000,000
If for Sections 1 and 2, ...	26,000,000
If for Sections 1, 2 and 3, ...	32,000,000

If for all four sections, ...	$35,000,000
Equipment—estimated at	6,000,000

The second was by Andrew Onderdonk, of New York, as follows:

If for Section 1, ...	$17,000,000
If for Sections 1 and 2, ...	28,000,000
If for Sections 1, 2 and 3, ...	35,500,000
If for all four sections, ...	39,300,000

Percentage—5% on first million after $5,000,000 of gross receipts, and 2½% for each added million thereafter up to a maximum of 15%.

Equipment—estimated at	$6,000,000

After a full investigation of the comparative merits of these two bids, the Board on January 16, all the Commissioners being present, unanimously voted that it would be for the best interests of the city to accept the proposal of Mr. McDonald; and at the same time the Board directed that the President should, in the name of the Board, exercise the option reserved to the city by the contract for the construction and operation of Sections 2, 3 and 4, as well as Section 1. In accordance with this decision, the contract for the whole line was signed and executed February 21, 1900. CONTRACT AWARDED

Even after Mr. McDonald had been notified that his bid had been accepted, it was by no means certain that the contract would be executed by him. He was required to furnish a continuing bond for the payment of rent, etc., in the sum of $1,000,000, and at the same time deposit with the comptroller securities of the value of $1,000,000, which were ultimately to be substituted for the bond of that amount. A construction bond of $5,000,000 was also required.

When the bid was accepted by the city, no provision had been made for the capital necessary to execute the contract. Mr. McDonald's efforts to obtain financial assistance from the surety companies failed. Although the plans had been pronounced feasible, capitalists were timid about investing. This was due, not so much to the magnitude of the sum needed to build the road, as to feelings of uncertainty regarding its earning power when completed. The scheme was regarded as a colossal experiment.

A few days before the expiration of the limit of time, Mr. McDonald sought the assistance of August Belmont. Mr. Belmont took the matter up with the Rapid Transit Commission, to whom he proposed a plan for the incorporation of AUGUST BELMONT a company to obtain the security required, to provide the capital for the undertaking, and to assume control of the entire work. Application was made to the Supreme Court to change the ruling requiring sureties to justify in double the amount of the bond, and to reduce the minimum amount of surety to be taken from $500,000 to $250,000. This application the Court granted.

CONSTRUCTION COMPANY ORGANIZED

The Rapid Transit Subway Construction Company* was organized with a capital of $6,000,000, the incorporators being Charles T. Barney, August Belmont, John B. McDonald, Walter G. Oakman and William A. Read. This corporation executed a bond for $4,000,000, the additional sum of $1,000,000 being furnished by others.

SUBLETTING CONTRACT

Immediately after signing the contract, the contractor sublet the work to fifteen different companies, each of whom executed a bond for faithful performance of the stipulations. In addition the city had a first lien upon the entire equipment of the railroad, so that it was protected in every possible way.

On March 24, 1900, the work of construction of the Rapid Transit Railroad was formally begun in front of the City Hall, the Mayor of the city turning the first spadeful of earth.

WORK DURING 1900

During the year 1900 no work was done on the first section, as the plans were being modified. The loop at this point, as orginally laid out, encircled the Post Office. At the suggestion of the construction company it was finally decided to shorten and simplify the construction at this point by having the loop turn north instead of south of the Post Office, and so arranged that local trains could all be turned around the single track loop thus laid out, passing under the express lines at Park row without crossing at grade; or along Park row to connect with an extension south under Broadway if one should be built. The express tracks under Park row were designed to permit express trains to continue along a possible Broadway extension or be switched back through a "tail track." A station on the loop was located in City Hall Park so as to be conveniently reached from points to the west and south, and relieve the pressure at the Brooklyn Bridge station. Actual construction was begun on this section in March, 1901. During the previous year work had been started on the other sections.

*This was the constructing company. The Interborough Rapid Transit Company, the operating company, was formed in the spring of 1902, the incorporators being: W. H. Baldwin, Jr., C. T. Barney, August Belmont, E. P. Bryan, Andrew Freedman, James Jourdan, G. M. Lane, John B. McDonald, DeLancey Nicoll, W. G. Oakman, John Peirce, W. A. Read, Cornelius Vanderbilt, G. W. Wickersham, and G. W. Young. In January, 1903, this company acquired the elevated railway system from the Manhattan Company by lease for 999 years.

Marking the spot in front of the City Hall where the first excavation was made is a tablet bearing the following inscription:

> "At this place, 24 March, 1900, Hon. Robert A. Van Wyck made the first excavation for the underground railway. Rapid Transit Commission, Alexander E. Orr, President; John H. Starin, Woodbury Langdon, George L. Rives, Charles Stewart Smith, Morris K. Jesup. Robert A. Van Wyck, Mayor; Bird S. Coler, Comptroller. Wm. Barclay Parsons, Chief Engineer. Contractor, John B. McDonald. Rapid Transit Subway Construction Company, August Belmont, president.

TUNNEL APPROACH, 123D ST., N. Y. SUBWAY.

CHAPTER XIV.

ENGINEERING FEATURES OF NEW YORK SUBWAY.*

Before the letting of the contract for the construction of the subway, the Board of Rapid Transit Commissioners had prepared complete plans for a railroad, having Broadway from Forty-second street to the Battery as a portion of the route. The adverse decision of the Appellate Division of the Supreme Court prevented the use of that thoroughfare. The preliminary investigations covered the underground conditions of all that portion of the city traversed by the route in regard to soil, foundations, pipes, sewers, and other sub-surface structures. As a result of these studies the Board reached the following general conclusions:

CONCLUSIONS OF BOARD

First, that, in order to relieve the congestion of travel, there was needed a railway located either directly along or as near as possible to the major lines of travel.

Second, that, in order to bring the extreme limits of the city into closer relations, provision must be made for the running of trains at higher speed than was possible on any existing elevated railway in New York, or in fact on any intra-urban railway in any other city.

Third, that underground construction should only be considered for those portions of the route along important thoroughfares; and,

Fourth, that a route through private property in the lower portion of the city was neither feasible nor economical.

It was evident that these conclusions could only be secured by the adoption of a route near to and parallel with Broadway; that in general it must follow street lines; and that it must be an underground road of four tracks.

SHALLOW EXCAVATION TYPE

The subway is, as far as possible, of the shallow-excavation type; that is, the rail level is as close to the surface of the street as grades and local conditions permit. The design required a flat roof in order to avoid the loss of

* Most of the information in this chapter is from the reports issued by the Rapid Transit Commission.

headroom of an arch, and a re-adjustment of all sewers, pipes, and the like underground structures. This type had been adopted by the Glasgow Central Railway, the Rapid Transit Commission of 1891, the Boston Transit Commission, and in Budapest, Hungary. Heretofore railways of this kind have provided a single service, with all trains stopping at all stations, a limited express service being sometimes obtained by a third track, on which trains could run in the direction of the heaviest travel, and stop at longer intervals than the others. The disadvantages of this system were obvious, and the Board decided that the subway should represent a step in advance. It was therefore determined to construct four tracks over that part of the route where the traffic was greatest, and two and three tracks along the remainder.

ELM STREET

In 1897, when the court decided against the Broadway line, the proceedings relating to the widening of Elm street had been finished, and that route suggested itself as an alternative. In January and February, 1897, plans were adopted by the Board. In order that the cost might not exceed $35,000,000, the southern terminus was fixed at the Post Office, and four tracks were laid along Park row, Center, and Elm streets, Lafayette place, Fourth avenue, Forty-second street, and Broadway to One-hundred-and-fourth street. The line divided at this point, the west side extending to Kingsbridge and the east side to Bronx Park. The route having been decided upon, an investigation was made of the topographical and geological features, the foundations of buildings, sewers, water and gas pipes, conduits, etc. South of Astor place the soil was for the most part coarse sand; to the north it was gneiss rock and gravel. The most serious part of the problem was the handling of the different underground structures. The sewerage system of New York is the "combined" system, by which both house drainage and rainfall are carried away. These, together with the sewers, pipes, and conduits, were almost all near the surface. All of these had to be kept in service and most of them moved to new locations without interruption of their operation.

ROUTES

While the larger portion of the route was placed practically parallel with the street surface, this was not possible in some localities. In order to avoid interference with the Fourth avenue tunnel of the Metropolitan Railway, the subway was divided from Thirty-third street north into two two-track tunnels, one at each side of, but below the street-car tunnel. In order to overcome depressions, viaducts were adopted on the west side between One-hundred-and-twenty-second street and One-hundred-and-thirty-fifth street and north of Fort

Photo by Davis & Sanford, N. Y.

WM. BARCLAY PARSONS,

FORMER CHIEF ENGINEER RAPID TRANSIT COMMISSION.

George, and on the east side north of Third avenue. The length of each type of construction was as follows: Cut-and-cover, 10.46 miles; tunnel, 4.55 miles; viaduct, 5.8 miles.

TYPE OF TUNNEL

The allowed limit of clearance between the street surface and the top of the subway was 30 inches, that being the depth of the yokes of the conduits of the electric railways. The roof was made as thin as possible. To further this aim columns were introduced between each track, so that the roof beams required were only heavy enough to span a single track, an arrangement that would be economical and that, by making the individual members smaller, would façilitate construction. The standard type was a rectangular tunnel consisting of a concrete floor with steel ribs set five feet apart, with arches turned between them. A bed of concrete was first laid down, and on that thin side walls of hollow brick to a height of several feet. On the floor and against the walls was laid a waterproofing of alternate layers of felt and asphalt. On top of this was spread another course of concrete, and on the latter were set the foundations for the center columns and walls. A double row of terra-cotta ducts was placed against the walls, a hollow brick outer wall with the waterproofing being carried up in advance. Then the steel frames were erected, the jack arches turned, and the waterproofing spread over the roof, over which was laid a protecting layer of concrete. The waterproofing was thus protected from outside damage by the thin guard-walls of brick and the top layer of concrete. An admirable feature of the design was that it could be constructed in sections for either the full or part width, with the certainty that the several sections would fit together, the connections between the rigid members being made of plastic and easily molded concrete.

The sections of the tunnels, with the exception of the Murray-Hill tunnel, which was a three-center arch designed in order to lower the roof, were semicircular. The same section was used in certain deep cuttings in the two-track lines, where the space above the roof permitted an arch to be constructed. In these instances an arch was found more economical than steel frames.

STANDARD CONSTRUCTION

In the standard construction the center columns were made up of 4 bulb angles, 3 by 4 inches, by 10 pounds per foot, and one web plate 6 by $\frac{1}{4}$ inches. These were spaced 5 feet longitudinally of the subway and 12 feet 6 inches transversely, making the total width of the four-track tunnel 50 feet. The roof beams were 42, 60 and 70 pounds, according to the location. The Park avenue tunnels were 24 feet in width by 18 feet in center height, the tracks being 12

GEORGE S. RICE,
CHIEF ENGINEER RAPID TRANSIT COMMISSION.

feet center to center. The deep tunnels were 25 feet wide by 18 high. In its general features the steel viaduct was similar to other elevated railways, except that it was much stronger in order to provide for the weight of motor cars of 50 tons.

SEWERS

As the sewers in the city are commonly placed at a depth of about 13 feet, and as the excavation for the tunnel was to be over 18 feet at the minimum, it followed that a complete reconstruction of the system was necessary, involving the building of 7.21 miles of sewers along the route of the railway, and 5.13 miles of sewers in streets other than that followed by the route. Where sewers were encountered along the route, the method was to build two new sewers, one at each side of the railway and next to the abutting houses, and to diminish to the minimum all cross-connections either over or under the railway. Where they crossed the route they were gathered together and passed beneath the railway in iron pipes, and a new outfall sewer built from the lower end of the cross-connection on a new gradient to such a point as was rendered necessary by the topography of the street to make a new connection with the existing system. This did away with all siphons, with one exception, and left the sewers in a self-cleansing condition. As the sewer at Canal street was below tidewater, such a scheme was not possible. In that case a new route was selected for a new sewer, and the flow diverted to the East River instead of the Hudson, as formerly.

GAS AND WATER PIPES

Taking care of the pipes was a troublesome task. In general, the small ones, those of 12 inches in diameter and under, were placed on top of the roof, but the large mains were moved to the side of the subway wherever there was not sufficient space on top. At cross streets where the distance between the pavement and roof was insufficient to allow the longitudinal and lateral mains to cross each other, additional space was obtained by constructing a flat metal trough between adjacent roof beams and laying the lateral mains in it. When this space was not sufficient, the large mains were sub-divided into smaller pipes, equal in capacity to the large one. The bottom of the trough was made of 3-inch beams resting on the flanges of the roof beams, with concrete between. In extreme cases where every inch had to be saved a steel plate was set flush with the bottom flanges of the roof beams and supported by angles along the edges.

Almost all of the sewer and pipe work was preliminary to the building of the subway. The reconstruction was accomplished without interrupting the flow of any house connection, catch basin, or other sewer.

METHOD OF WORKING

Under Park row it had been planned to permit express trains to continue along a possible Broadway extension south, or to be switched back through a tail track. A station on the loop was located in City Hall Park, so as to be conveniently reached from all points, and thereby relieve the pressure at the Brooklyn Bridge station. The construction was carried forward by digging a trench on either side of the four surface tracks (electric conduit) down to grade. Cross drifts were then tunneled beneath the tracks connecting the trenches, and in these drifts timber supports were erected beneath the surface tracks. Then the intervening pillars of unexcavated sand were removed and the roof supported by timber props. The concrete floor and walls were then put in and the steel erected. This method was followed with but slight changes in all localities where similar material was encountered. As Elm street had not been officially opened for traffic, the sub-contractor availed himself of permission to take the whole width of the street and excavate for the entire structure.

OPEN CUT THROUGH ROCK

The section from Lafayette place to Thirty-third street presented considerable difficulty, owing to the presence of rock which in some places came directly beneath the yokes of the electric railway. At first the attempt was made to excavate half the street at a time, confining the traffic to the other half. It was found that this produced almost as much interference with traffic as the building of two railways. The sub-contractors were then permitted to excavate for the full width of the four tracks, supporting the surface tracks over the cut, concentrating the vehicular traffic on the same space and cutting off for the time being access to the abutting houses of each block. Arrangements were made to bridge the excavation at important buildings, and to truck merchandise by hand north or south to the nearest cross street. In order to support the surface railway the contractors placed on the outside of the track and immediately at the side of the excavation a pair of 24-inch rolled beams 40 feet long, and a similar pair in the trench between the surface railway tracks, this trench being afterward roofed over with planks. The ends of the beams were supported on wooden trestles. As the excavation progressed, heavy timber cross beams were inserted transversely beneath the surface tracks, and held by rods from the longitudinal beams. With this arrangement it was possible to remove all the earth beneath the railway and thus leave the whole space from the curb to a point beyond the center line of the street free for the constrution of the subway. The width thus secured was sufficient to put in place the

VIADUCT, MANHATTAN ST., N. Y. SUBWAY.

center row of columns. Water mains, gas pipes, and electric conduits in the excavation were supported by chains from cross timbers. To remove the excavated material, an overhead cableway on towers was erected longitudinally of the cut at each opening; or, where rock was found in quantities, a derrick was set up. Buckets on the cableway carried the soil forward to the end of the cut and there dropped it into carts. The appliances necessary for handling material took up no more room than the width of the excavation itself.

WORK AT UNION SQUARE

At Union Square, where the surface road was laid directly on the rock, it was decided to move the surface tracks to a new location near the easterly curb, in order to avoid the possibility of injuring them during blasting. Sufficient rock was blasted out for the south bound local and express tracks, and for the intermediate side track to be constructed at this point. The ducts of the street railway, which had to be kept in service in connection with the tracks themselves, contained not only the ordinary low tension feeders, but also high tension cables having a pressure of 6,500 volts each. Although in many cases the rock had to be blasted in direct contact with these ducts, in no instance were the cables broken or the service of the road interrupted.

Except for a short distance at its southern end, the length known as Section 4 was wholly in tunnel. It was impossible to build the four tracks of the subway in one tunnel, for the reason that if this had been tried the arched roof would have interfered with the old Harlem tunnel used by the Metropolitan Railway. Two double-track tunnels were built instead. These were separated a sufficient distance to leave a core of rock between them and directly under the old tunnel. In order that these tunnels might be kept as far away from the upper tunnel as possible, the roof section was designed as a three-center arch. The common shaft method of tunneling was here followed, but the same method of driving was not employed in the two headings. Where the rock was hard and compact enough to be self-supporting a top heading was advanced; in soft, disintegrated rock an upper heading and timbering were used.

FORTY-SECOND STREET

The section from Forty-first to Forty-seventh street presented some unusual features. In order that the travel on Forty-second street, at all times very heavy, might be interfered with as little as possible, the operations were first confined to the south side of the street. In a trench 15 feet wide the steel work for the south bound local track was erected. A drift was then opened north—across the street—for a distance of 20 feet and needle beams, consisting of 24-

inch 100-pound steel beams, were placed in it, one end resting on the completed roof and the other on the undisturbed rock. The street was supported on these beams by blocking. Beneath the beams the rock was excavated and the south-bound express track built.

ROCK WORK

The section from Forty-seventh street to Sixtieth street and Broadway was almost wholly in rock. The work was done with cableways similar to those used for Fourth avenue. The excavation was confined to the space between the curb and nearest rail of the surface railroad, subsequently drifting under the latter to a point just beyond the center of the street, in which space were erected the side, quarter, and center columns and the roof beams for one-half the subway structure. After the concrete arches had been put in, construction was extended under the remaining half of the street.

SUPPORTING COLUMBUS MONUMENT

At the junction of Broadway, Eighth avenue and Fifty-ninth street is a shaft monument to Christopher Columbus, having a height of 75 feet and a masonry base stepped out in the usual way. The westerly line of the subway excavation passed beneath this base just to the east of the center line of the shaft. It was decided to support the shaft and its base by underpinning. In order to do this the first step was the driving of a tunnel beneath the center of the shaft and to the west of the subway wall; this was filled with masonry. Under the eastern edge of the base was then placed a large girder supported on timber bents, north and south of the monument. The material beneath the base was then dug out, the subway structure built in place, and on top of the subway roof new foundations for the monument were carried up. When this work had been finished the girder was removed.

Broadway, from Sixtieth to One-hundred-and-fourth street, is 102 feet wide between the curbs, and midway throughout is a line of parkways 22 feet wide, on each side of which is a conduit electric railway. The work here was done through the parkways in open cut, under through trusses that had been set on the surface, one on each side of each track. These upheld the conduit while the work was carried on beneath.

The section to One-hundred-and-tenth street was almost entirely in deep tunnel. Work was prosecuted by means of shafts.

The methods of construction above mentioned cover the work of the entire route except the viaduct and Harlem River portions. The former, as has already been stated, differed very little from the ordinary elevated design, except that it

104TH STREET JUNCTION.

PARK AVE. AND 41ST ST.

N. Y. SUBWAY.

BROADWAY AND COLUMBIA UNIVERSITY.

was made heavier. This type was departed from at Manhattan street, where a two-hinged steel arch with a span of 180 feet was erected.

HARLEM RIVER TUNNEL

The Harlem River tunnel consists of two single-track tubes lined with cast-iron and separated by a vertical partition. The approaches were built in open cut. That portion of the tunnel under the river was constructed by an entirely new method, designed and successfully executed by D. D. McBean, member of the firm that contracted for this section. The Government required that the river be kept open for navigation, but permitted it to be temporarily narrowed. The western half of the tunnel was built in the following way:

NEW METHOD OF SUBMARINE TUNNELING

A channel was dredged across the river bottom to within a few feet of the full depth of the excavation required for the tunnel. In this channel foundation piles, and a row of specially prepared heavy timber sheeting were driven along each side and across the ends, and cut off to a true plane about 25 feet below the surface of the water. The roof of this chamber was formed of a platform of timber 40 inches in thickness and extending the full width and length of the tunnel section, which was sunk until it rested upon the top of the cut-off sheeting. Simultaneously with pumping the water from under the roof, compressed air was forced into the chamber under a pressure corresponding to the hydrostatic head, or depth of water above the roof. Inside this chamber the west half of the tunnel was built, and then the timber roof was removed.

Another simpler and cheaper method was pursued in constructing the easterly half of the tunnel. The sides of the pneumatic working chamber were prepared in the same way, but the sheeting was cut off about 12 feet lower down than in the first case, or exactly on the same level as the spring line of the arch of the tunnel. The top half of the tunnel proper was then built on pontoons which were floated over the tunnel site. The upper half of the tunnel was then lowered until flanges, which had been built upon its sides, rested upon the sheeting. This formed the roof of the working chamber. The foundation and bottom half of the tunnel were then constructed with the aid of compressed air.

CONTRACT NO. 2

The Brooklyn extension of the road, known as "Contract No. 2," extends from the Post Office south under Broadway to the Battery, thence under the East River to Joralemon and Fulton streets, and under the latter and Flatbush avenue to the junction of Atlantic and Flatbush avenues. At Bowling Green there is a spur to South Ferry and a loop. On the portion under Broadway it was at first intended to remove the street pavement, and put in a carefully

CONSTRUCTING TUBES.

JOINING ARCH AND TUBES.

HARLEM RIVER SECTION N. Y. SUBWAY.

planked roadway. Under this, excavation was to be made from two shafts, one in front of St. Paul's Church yard and the other in front of Trinity Church yard, where their location would not interfere with abutting buildings. It was not deemed wise to keep the gas mains under this roadway, since any leakage of gas, mixing with the confined air, might cause serious explosions. Arrangement was made with the gas company to lay two temporary mains on trestles over the sidewalks the length of the work. At the suggestion of the chief engineer, the contractor made the experiment of removing the soil beneath the pipes and pavement without disturbing the latter, supporting the pipes and pavement on a properly designed system of timbering, and thus use the existing pavement as a temporary cover in lieu of a plank roadway. This scheme worked so well that it was followed on the entire line south of St. Paul's shaft.

TUNNELING UNDER EAST RIVER

The width of the East River on the line of the crossing between bulkhead lines is 4,150 feet, with a depth at high water of 47 feet. The War Department required a depth of water above the top of the tunnel at low tide of at least 45 feet. This, taken in connection with the irregularities and varying materials of the bed of the river, together with the great volume of river traffic, forced the abandonment of the idea of building the tunnel in the open and floating it into place, and it was decided to do the work by means of shields and compressed air. Two double shafts were sunk, one within the Battery Park loop and the other in Joralemon street, near Henry, from which headings were started for the two tubes. The space between the outside of the shell and the rock was filled with broken stone and cement grout. This section is now nearing completion.

STATION DESIGN

From an operating point of view the stations have been designed in two general classes, local and express. This was accomplished by constructing four tracks from the Post Office to Ninety-sixth street, with two and three tracks in places above that point on both the east and west side lines. The express stations are the Brooklyn Bridge, Fourteenth street, Grand Central, Seventy-second and Ninety-sixth streets, at which stations all trains stop. These stations are located about 1½ miles apart. The other stops, at intervals of one-quarter mile, serve only the local trains. The platforms of all local stations south of Ninety-sixth street are 200 feet long; the platforms of the express stations are 350 feet long. Above Ninety-sixth street all stations have platforms of the longer length. Local stations usually have separate platforms, from which the passengers enter or leave the north or south-bound trains. These are located at the outside of the tracks, and in most cases with no provision for crossing from one platform to the other. At two stations, however, Astor place and Forty-second street and Broadway, underground passageways have been provided, and at five others, One-hundred-and-third, Columbia University, One-hundred-and-sixty-eighth, One-hundred-and-eighty-first and Mott avenue, there are bridges beneath the surface of the street but over the tracks.

TYPE OF STATIONS

In plan there are five types of local stations. The first includes those from Fiftieth street south. This type has two platforms, one on each side of the street, and made of as great a width as the width of the street permitted, extending from the side of the tracks to the area line of building, which is five feet from the building line. As far as possible these platforms are arranged symmetrically on either side of the cross street where the station is situated, a portion of the cross street being excavated to accommodate the waiting room, in which the ticket office, toilet rooms and service closets are located.

In order to provide the fullest possible facilities for reaching the platforms, each station is provided with eight stairways, four for each platform, located in pairs on the north and south sides of the cross streets. One of these stairways is an entrance and the other an exit. The entrance stairway descends from the sidewalk and reaches the rear of the waiting room where the ticket office is situated. The passenger descends the stairway, buys his ticket and goes forward to the platform, moving always in a straight line and without reversing the direction. The exit stairways lead from the back of the platform directly to the sidewalk. Passengers approach these exit stairways without passing the ticket office or meeting the incoming line of traffic. This stairway accommodation is much in excess of any similar accommodation provided in any station of the elevated railroad.

SECOND TYPE

The second type is represented in the local stations on Broadway north of Sixtieth street. In that part of the city Broadway is very wide and the platforms do not come beneath the sidewalks. As the congestion is not so much as in the commercial districts, the platforms are reached by one wide staircase. These, however, can readily be doubled as traffic develops.

Another type is on Lenox avenue from One-hundred-and-sixteenth to One-hundred-and-thirty-fifth street inclusive. Along this section the axis of the subway does not coincide with the center line of the street; so that the west platform is beneath the sidewalk while the other is under the roadway. As these stations are in the commercial districts of Harlem, more stairways have been provided than for the stations on upper Broadway, each platform being provided with two wide stairways.

DEEP TUNNEL STATIONS

The deep tunnel stations, at One-hundred-and-sixty-eighth street, One-hundred-and-eighty-first street and at Mott avenue, consist in each case of a wide arch spanning both tracks and the two platforms, access to the platforms being had by shafts, 98, 120, and 46 feet deep, respectively. Each shaft contains a stairway and two elevators, the latter having a capacity of 3,500 passengers per hour. The waiting room containing the ticket office is immediately beneath the sidewalk, and to this a short stairway leads. From the waiting room the elevators descend to a bridge crossing the tracks so that access can be had from this overhead passageway to either platform.

CITY HALL STATION

The City Hall station, being on a loop, contains but a single track which is curved. These two features made it possible to adopt a special design different in all respects from the others. The accompanying engravings, page 53, show some of the architectural features of the design. Another unique type is the station at Columbia University, which is reached through an ornamental house built in one of the parkways in the center of Broadway. The ticket office in this case is placed on the surface of the street. The stairway descends from this house to a bridge spanning the tracks and leading to both the up and the down platforms.

The principal features of the express stations are two large island platforms situated between the express and local tracks. At the Brooklyn Bridge, Fourteenth street and the Grand Central stations, access is had to these platforms by overhead bridges above the tracks but beneath the street surface. The island platforms of the Seventy-second street station are approached by stairways descending from an ornamental house in the center of Broadway. The platforms of the Ninety-sixth street station are reached by a passageway beneath the tracks. At these stations the island platforms serve either the local or express trains.

At the Bridge, Fourteenth, and Ninety-sixth streets, side platforms have been constructed in addition to the island ones; so that at these stations passengers going to or coming from the local trains will not be obliged to go to the island platforms and come in contact with those using the express trains. At the other two stations the width of the street would not permit the erection of such additional platforms.

The stations on the viaduct portion of the road are of the covered type.

That at Manhattan Valley has three tracks with two platforms. As these are 55 feet above the street a double moving stairway has been installed. This leads from a house in which are the ticket windows and waiting rooms, and thence to a platform directly beneath the tracks and connected by a short stairway with both platforms.

STATIONS NEAR THE SURFACE

All of the stations have been constructed as near the street surface as possible. This made two things possible; it permitted the stations to be supplied with natural light in the daytime, and reduced the length of the stairways to a minimum. Wherever the platforms are beneath sidewalks, the sidewalks are made of glass. Of the 37 subway stations, 20 are so well provided with natural light that very little artificial illumination is required during daylight hours. The length of stairways is not much more than one-half of the average length of stairways leading to elevated stations.

LIGHTING

In general the lights in the stations are incandescent lamps placed in recesses in the ceilings. Current for these is obtained from two sources, a regular lighting circuit and the track circuit. The latter is for use only in cases of emergency. All lights are controlled from a switchboard in the ticket booth.

The stations are made damp-proof by an inner and outer shell. The sidewalls and ceilings of the outer shell are built of steel columns and beams with concrete filled between them, and a layer of concrete forms the foundation of the floor. Water-proofing, protected by an outer lining of masonry, envelops the entire structure. This forms the constructive work of the stations, as distinguished from the finishing work of the inner shell which includes the sidewalls, ceilings and floors. The floors are all alike, and are made of concrete divided into plaques 3 feet square. The floors are graded so as to drain to catch basins which are connected with the sewer.

DESIGN OF STATIONS

The base of the walls at stations is built of a hard buff-colored brick, forming a double wainscot that extends around the whole platform 2½ feet high. This wall is set back from the face of the brick to allow for a finish of glass or of glazed tile. At the top of the tile a cornice of faïence or terra cotta is built into the wall, and at intervals of 15 feet, or opposite the platform columns, the cornice line is broken by an ornamental symbol designating the name of the station. At certain intervals a large tablet, consisting of a dark background of glazed mosaic, carries the name of the station in white mosaic, or gold letters or distinct figures. The finished floors and walls are joined with a sanitary cove base, so that corners where dust might lodge are avoided. The materials used in the wall treatment between the cornice and wainscot are glass, or glazed tile or ceramic-tile mosaic. The glass or glazed tile is 3 by 6 inches and covers most of the surface. The ceramic mosaic work is used for ornamentation. It is made up into narrow bands of single colors, ornamental friezes, pilasters and name tablets. Under each cornice plaque there is usually a pilaster design separating the wall into panels about 15 feet long. The panels are bordered with mosaic bands and friezes.

There are two kinds of ceilings; one is a flat suspended ceiling which covers all the steel and concrete in the roof; the other is arched and is also suspended, but only between the roof beams. Ornamental moldings are used to divide the ceiling into panels. Heat is furnished to all stations by electric heaters.

At appropriate stations suggestive designs have been worked into the walls. Thus there is the "Caravel" at Columbus Circle; the "Beaver" at Astor place, and the Arms of Columbia University at the Columbia University station.

COLUMBIA UNIVERSITY ENTRANCE—N. Y. SUBWAY.

CHAPTER XV.

EQUIPMENT OF THE SUBWAY.

COST OF EQUIPMENT

According to the conditions of the contract, the contractor was to supply the entire equipment. This comprised the power houses, conductors, train equipment, signalling apparatus, and the like. The outfit is part of the cost to be borne by the builder; and at the expiration of the fifty years, the period for which the contract runs, is to be turned over to the city as part of the subway plant. The equipment as it stands to-day represents an expenditure by the Interborough Company of between $15,000,000 and $20,000,000, thereby making its total investment about $60,000,000.

Before proceeding with its installation, a very thorough examination was made of all the prominent generating stations of this country and of Europe. This preliminary study resulted in the creation of not only the largest power house in the world—measured according to the horsepower capacity—but also the most complete one so far as each individual part is concerned.

It will be re-called that both Contract No. 1 and Contract No. 2 are controlled by the same interests. Therefore when the company received the second contract, in 1902, it immediately prepared plans for an electrical capacity sufficient to provide for the operation of the Brooklyn extension of the road.

POWER HOUSE

The power house occupies the site bounded by Fifty-eighth and Fifty-ninth streets and Eleventh and Twelfth avenues. The building is 200 feet wide on Eleventh avenue, and is divided into a boiler house 83 feet wide, and an engine room 117 feet wide, separated by a partition wall. Provision was made for six generating sections, with space remaining for a seventh. Each section has one chimney, together with the following equipment: 12 boilers, 2 engines direct-connected to a 5,000-kilowatt alternating generator, 2 condensing plants, 2 feed pumps, and all the appliances necessary to make each section complete in itself. All this required a structure 694 feet in length.

INTERIOR.

POWER HOUSE, N. Y. SUBWAY.

The advantages of this plan are thus summed up: *

ARRANGEMENT OF BUILDING

"The main engines, combined with their alternators, lie in a single row along the center of the operating room with the steam or operating end of each engine facing the boiler house and the opposite end toward the electrical switching and controlling apparatus arranged along the outside wall. Within the area between the boiler house and the operating room there is placed, for each engine, its respective complement of pumping apparatus, all controlled by and under the operating jurisdiction of the engineer for that engine. Each engineer has thus full control of the pumping machinery required for his unit. Symmetrically arranged with respect to the center line of each engine, are the six boilers in the boiler room, and the piping from these six boilers forms a short connection between the nozzles on the boilers and the throttles on the engines. The arrangement of piping is alike for each engine, which results in a piping system of maximum simplicity that can be controlled, in the event of difficulty, with a degree of certainty not possible with a more complicated system. The main parts of the steam-pipe system can be controlled from outside this area."

COAL-HANDLING PLANT

In the top of the building immediately over the boilers are seven coal bunkers, five of which are 77 feet and two 41 feet in length, all being 60 feet wide at the top. The total capacity is 18,000 tons. The six chimneys placed along the center of the boiler house separate the bunkers from each other. The chimneys are placed 108 feet apart, and are carried on plate-girder platforms in the fifth floor, the entire space below being thus left clear. The framing for both the chimney platforms and the bunkers is extended down to the foundation.

Both coal and ashes are handled by belt conveyors. Thirty-inch belts convey the coal along the dock where it is received, and by a tunnel to the southwest corner of the power house. From there it is raised 110 feet to the top of the boiler house, at the rate of 250 tons per hour, and distributed along the bunkers. The conveyors have automatic trippers which distribute the coal evenly in the bunkers. Another set of conveyors is placed under the bunkers for delivering different grades of coal from any particular bunker to the chutes in front of the boilers. All the conveyors are operated by electric motors.

---

* From the book on the "New York Subway" published by the Interborough Rapid Transit Company.

EXTERIOR AND INTERIOR, SUB-STATION, N. Y. SUBWAY.

The boiler room is intended to receive, ultimately, 72 boilers of the water-tube type, which will have a combined heating surface of 432,576 square feet. Fifty-two are now erected in batteries of two each, and between each pair is a 5-foot passageway. Thirty-six of the boilers are hand fired and have shaking grates. Twelve are furnished with automatic stokers.

Forced draft is provided in order to burn fine anthracite coal in sufficient quantity to obtain boiler rating with hand firing, and also to secure excess over the rating with other coal. The blowers deliver the air at a pressure of 2 inches of water.

STEAM PIPING

The steam piping from six boilers to one main engine is thus described: "A cross-over pipe is erected on each boiler, by means of which and a combination of valves and fittings the steam may be passed through the superheater. In the delivery from each boiler there is a quick-closing 9-inch valve, which can be closed from the boiler room floor by hand, or from a distant point individually or in groups of six. Risers with 9-inch wrought iron goose-necks connect each boiler to the steam main, where 9-inch angle valves are inserted in each boiler connection. These valves can be closed from the platform above the boilers, and are grouped three over one set of three boilers and three over the opposite set. The main from the six boilers is carried directly across the boiler house in a straight line to a point in the pipe area where it rises to connect to the two 14-inch steam downtakes to the engine throttles. At this point the steam can also be led downward to a manifold to which the compensating tie lines are connected. These compensating lines are run lengthwise through the power house for the purpose of joining the systems together as desired. The two downtakes to the engine throttles drop to the basement, where each, through a goose-neck, delivers into a receiver and separating tank and from the tank through a second goose-neck into the corresponding throttle."

ENGINES

There are nine main engines from 8,000 to 11,000 horsepower direct connected to 5,000-kilowatt generators, and three steam turbines direct connected to 1,875-kilowatt lighting generators, and two 400-horsepower engines direct connected to 250-kilowatt exciter generators. The main engines are of the compound type, having cylinders 42 and 86 inches and stroke of 60 inches, working under a steam pressure of 175 pounds.

The steam turbines are of the multiple expansion parallel flow type, consisting of two turbines arranged tandem compound. Each unit is of 1,700 electrical horsepower.

CONDENSERS AND PUMPS

Each engine has its own condenser outfit, and each has a circulating pump and vacuum pump which, for the sake of flexibility, are cross connected with each other so as to be used interchangeably. Each circulating pump has a capacity of 10,000,000 gallons of water per day, so that the combined capacity is 120,000,000 gallons per day. Two electrically driven compressors supply air throughout the power house for cleaning electric machinery and other purposes.

The operating room is supplied with one 60-ton and one 25-ton electric traveling crane; the area over the oil switches with one 10-ton hand crane, and the center aisle of the boiler room with one 10-ton hand crane. Both the electric cranes have a span of 74 1-3 feet and travel the entire length of the building.

The subway electric system comprises alternating generation and distribution with direct current car motors. The current is generated at a voltage of 11,000, and is delivered through three-conductor cables to transformers and converters in sub-stations, where it is transformed into direct current of 625 volts for delivery to the third rail. In the book above referred to we find the following:

ELECTRICAL POWER REQUIRED

"Calculations based upon contemplated schedules indicated that there would be needed for traction purposes and for heating and lighting the cars, a maximum delivery of about 45,000 kilowatts at the third rail. Allowing for losses in the distributing cables, in transformers and converters, this implies a total generating capacity of approximately 50,000 kilowatts; and having in view the possibility of future extensions of the system it was decided to design the power house building for the ultimate reception of eleven 5,000-kilowatt units for traction current in addition to the lighting sets. Each 5,000-kilowatt unit is capable of delivering during rush hours an output of 7,500 kilowatts or approximately 10,000 electrical horsepower, and, setting aside one unit as a reserve, the contemplated ultimate maximum output of the power plant is 75,000 kilowatts, or approximately 100,000 electrical horsepower." A generating unit of this size was adopted "because it is practically as large a unit of the direct-connected type as can be constructed by the engine builders unless more than two bearings be used—an alternative deemed inadvisable by the engineers of the company. The adoption of a smaller unit would be less economical of floor space and would tend to produce extreme complication in so large an installation, and, in view of the rapid changes in load which in urban

INTERIOR.

3011

COMPOSITE CAR N. Y. SUBWAY.

INTERIOR.

STEEL CAR N. Y. SUBWAY.

railway service of this character occur in the morning and again late in the afternoon, would be extremely difficult to operate." The company's engineers made a close study of steam turbines as prime movers for the alternators, and decided in favor of the reciprocating engine.

DYNAMOS

The alternators have a stationary armature exterior to the field; they are three-phase machines delivering current at a potential of 11,000 volts. The revolving part weighs 332,000 pounds, and the design is such as to eliminate the fly-wheel. The switches are electrically operated, and the circuits are made and broken under oil. "Provision is made for an ultimate total of twelve sub-stations, to each of which as many as eight feeders may be installed, if the development of the company's business should require that number. But eight sub-stations are required at present, and to some of these not more than three feeders are necessary. The aggegate number of feeders installed for the initial operation of the subway system is 34."

ELECTRIC CONDUCTORS

The conductors pass to the sub-stations through vitrified clay ducts built into the subway structure. The sub-stations are located at City Hall place, East Nineteenth street, West Fifty-third street, West Ninety-sixth street, West One-hundred-and-forty-third street, West One-hundred-and-thirty-second street, Hill-side avenue, and Fox street. In these stations the high potential alternating current is transformed into direct current at a potential of 625 volts; this current is conveyed to the contact rails by insulated cables.

The contact rails are carried upon block insulators resting upon malleable iron castings. The track rails are 33 feet long and weigh 100 pounds to the yard. One rail of each track is used for the operating current and the other for signal purposes. The third rail is guarded by a plank placed in a horizontal position directly above it.

After a thorough consideration of the question, the company decided to adopt a car with end platforms such as those generally used on American railways. The standard car is 51 feet long over all, 40 feet long in the clear inside, and 7 feet 10 inches wide in the clear, with a seating capacity of 52. The following is from the report of the Chief Engineer to the Commission, dated January 1, 1905:

COMPOSITE CARS

"In order to eliminate or reduce to the minimum all danger from fire, the result of which filling the subway with smoke would be disastrous, it was realized that the new cars should be made as nearly fireproof as possible. An all-metal car of reasonable weight was unknown, and at first did not seem practicable. A composite car was therefore designed having the sills of 6-inch steel channels for side sills, and 5-inch I-beams for center sills, and the superstructure of wood, but covered on the sides with copper so as to protect, for a while at least, the wood from taking fire by radiant heat. Great care was taken with the wiring details. All junctions and fusible plugs were located in asbestos-lined boxes, while the underside of the floor was covered with 'transiter,' a heavy asbestos board made for the purpose, and both fire and electric proof. Such a car, while not absolutely fireproof, is at least slow burning, and believed to be fireproof against any accident likely to occur in the subway. All details of construction were made more strong and heavy than is usual in cars for similar service, so that the weight of the car body is 27,650 pounds, as against 20,500 pounds for the car bodies on the Manhattan elevated.

ALL-METAL CARS

"While such cars as above described were being built, Mr. George Gibbs, consulting engineer to the company, and who was specially charged with equipment design, was studying a type of all-metal car, and finally evolved such a car of the same general dimensions as the composite car, the weight of the body being 28,500 pounds. In general the details of this car are center sills of I-beams, 17.25 pounds; side sills of angles 5 by 3 by $\frac{1}{2}$ inches, 12.8 pounds; with a plate of steel for the sides, which, with the side sills and a longitudinal angle (spiraled bulb angle) $4\frac{1}{2}$ to $2\frac{3}{4}$ inches, at the level of the window ledge, forms a plate girder to take the place of the ordinary iron body truss. The upper side and roof framing is of steel, while the interior lining of the car is aluminum. The floor is a cement compound. The only wood used is in the window sashes, doors and in the post furring, which is fire-proofed.

"On October 27, the date of the opening, there were delivered on the line 103 metal cars and 502 composite cars. At the end of the year 97 metal cars in addition had been furnished, and there were outstanding contracts for 100 metal cars. It is the intention to make the metal cars the motor cars, and the composite cars the trailers, until such time as the latter will be entirely superseded by the former.

TRAIN MAKE-UP

"As equipped electrically the motor cars have each two motors of a nominal capacity of 200 h. p. each, working on two axles of one truck. The total weight, on track, of a metal motor car completely equipped, but exclusive of passengers, is 76,925 pounds, and a composite trailer with ordinary trucks 51,300 pounds. The ordinary make-up of a local train is five cars, of which three are motors and two trailers, while an express train consists of eight cars, five motors and three trailers. The former therefore weighs empty 333,384 pounds, and has a total energy of 1,200 h. p., while the latter weighs 528,540 pounds with an energy of 2,000 h. p. In both cases the energy figures are a nominal rating and are capable of standing considerable overload, especially during the period of acceleration.

"For the regular train signals, automatic devices were adopted. The express lines were divided into blocks, the length of each being the distance in which a train traveling at full speed could be brought to rest with current cut off and emergency brakes applied. As this distance is obviously dependent upon the profile of the road, and as to whether the gradient is ascending or descending, the blocks are of varying length, from 450 feet to 1,000 feet. The ordinary arrangement of home and distant signals is established, but always with an overlap block; that is, each home signal guards not the next block, but the one after, so that there is always at least one whole block distance intervening between the home signal and the next train ahead.

SIGNALS

"At each signal box and connected with the home signal there is a mechanical trip set in the center of the track. When a home signal is at danger the trip is erect, so that if a motor-man for any cause overruns a home signal at danger the trip will cut off his power, set his brakes, and automatically bring the train to a stop before passing off the next block.

"On the local tracks home danger signals are located to guard all station approaches, curves, and any other point obstructing a free view of trains ahead."

LIGHTING

In order to maintain lights in the subway entirely independent of any temporary interruption of the power used for lighting the cars, a separate plant was installed in the power house. This is composed of three turbine-driven alternators, receiving steam from a special supply, and not from the supply for the large units. The primary current at 11,000 volts is led to transformers placed in fireproof compartments near the station platforms. The current is then delivered to two separate systems of wiring at 120 and 600 volts; the first provides the general lighting of the stations, while the second lights the subway between stations. In addition to this, and as a still further precaution, there are in each station a number of lamps connected to the contact rail circuit.

Lack of space will not permit an extended description of the many admirable features of the equipment of the subway provided by the Interborough Company. As it stands to-day it represents not only the best practice in electrical generation and distribution, but in many characteristics it is far in advance. The planning has been wisely and conservatively done and the construction has been thorough in all respects.

HARLEM TUNNEL—HALF SECTION.

N. Y. SUBWAY. TYPICAL UNDERGROUND CONSTRUCTION.

CHAPTER XVI.

WORK OF COMMISSION DURING CONSTRUCTION OF SUBWAY

The work of the Commission, while the construction of Contract No. 1 was going forward, was of the greatest importance to the future development of the "Greater City." The most essential part of the work was the provision for additional rapid transit facilities covering all the boroughs of Greater New York, and the consideration of franchises to foreign corporations desirous of gaining entrance to the city.

POWERS OF COMMISSION EXTENDED

The original Act of 1894 was passed before the consolidation, and provided for the construction of a rapid transit railroad only within the city of New York. It was, therefore, doubtful whether the Board had power to establish a route and general plan for the construction, at the expense of the city, of roads extending into boroughs other than Manhattan and the Bronx. In order to resolve this question, a bill was introduced in the Legislature to extend the powers of the Rapid Transit Commission into all parts of Greater New York. This became a law April 23, 1900.

Before the end of 1901 the Board had shown its intention to extend the rapid transit system to all the boroughs of the city as soon as the financial condition would allow; and in particular to Brooklyn, which was second only to Manhattan in population and importance.

The policy of the Board cannot be better expressed than in the following extract from its report for the year 1902:

POLICY OF BOARD

"Early in 1902 the Board was called upon to defend the essential proposition upon which it had been constituted. This was that the use of the underground and overhead portions of the streets of New York for railroad purposes should proceed according to a harmonious and far-seeing plan, possible only if all such uses, and every such use, of the streets were to be subject to the jurisdiction of the Rapid Transit Board, or of some other single authority of a similar kind, which should represent the interests of the entire city, and be so organized as to be able to carry out consistently and efficiently a plan requiring years, and perhaps many years, for completion. The establishment of this view followed the discussion over the so-called 'Pennsylvania Railroad Bill.'

"The vindication which was then accorded to the position of the Board, the creation, with an overwhelming approval of public sentiment, of the Pennsylvania Terminal franchise, the very advantageous terms of the Brooklyn-Manhattan contract, the authorization by the Board of additional tunnel connection with Jersey City, and, finally, the order of the Board that a plan be prepared for a great and systematic extension of rapid transit facilities in the Boroughs of Manhattan, Brooklyn, the Bronx and Queens, all these were normal fruit of the rapid transit agitation which brought this Board into being in 1894, and of the program to which the Board since that time, in season and out of season, and often under circumstances of extreme adversity, has at all times deemed itself committed. The Board had never lost faith that, if the citizens and the public authorities of the city would support it in its program, its practical results would be as large and comprehensively beneficial as those now well in sight.

RAPID TRANSIT SYSTEM FOR ENTIRE CITY

"The whole scheme of the Brooklyn extension, for which the contract was awarded in 1902, well illustrates the idea of a unified system of rapid transit for the whole city. But the Board does not for a moment assent to the proposition that the city, in order to secure such utility, is shut up to a contract with any one contractor. The opportunities for municipal rapid transit still remaining are such that in case lessees of the Manhattan-Bronx rapid transit railroad shall not find it to their interest, or for any reason shall fail, to propose to the city suitable terms for their undertaking such extensions, the city can still build other and through lines and award them to other lessees. The policy and intention of the Board are, to the very utmost that is practicable, to require every contractor for the construction and operation of a municipal railroad to stipulate to make fair operating arrangements upon the basis of a single fare for a single trip over any or all other municipally constructed railroads.

"The Board feels further bound to point out that, in the future, the terms of municipal rapid transit contracts can be had, and, therefore, ought to be, more favorable to the city than was the Manhattan-Bronx contract. That contract was made at a time when there was a widespread belief among railroad and financial people that it would be a business and financial failure, and when it was with the utmost difficulty and after very considerable delay that the city was able to obtain a contractor, and then only after the principal railroad proprietors in the city had refused to take up the enterprise. The remarkably favorable character of the bid for the Brooklyn-Manhattan extension (being for one-fourth or fifth part of its estimated cost) demonstrated beyond peradventure the very great value of the leases of its municipally constructed railroads which the city would be able to offer."

ACT CHANGED TO COVER FOREIGN ROADS

One of the most important achievements of the Commission during the year 1902 was a change effected in the Rapid Transit Act, Section 32. This amendment was made necessary by the application of the Pennsylvania Railroad, through a subsidiary company known as the Pennsylvania, New York & Long Island Railroad Company, for the right to construct a railroad beneath the Hudson River, Borough of Manhattan, the East River and a portion of the Borough of Queens, with a large terminal station to be located in the Borough of Manhattan. The original Act made no provision for the granting of franchises to existing railroads desirous of entering the city. As amended the Act empowered the Board to grant a franchise to "any railroad corporation owning or actually operating a railroad wholly or in part within the limits of the city in which the said Board has power to act; or of any railroad corporation now or hereafter incorporated, and for the purpose so declared in its articles of association, of constructing and operating a tunnel railroad or railroads in the said city to be connected with any railroad or railroads within the State of New York, or any adjoining State, and thereby forming a continuous line for the carriage of passengers and property between a point or points within and a point or points without the said city." *

Of still more importance than the granting of these franchises was the work done toward the general scheme, for the future of municipal and other rapid transit for the Boroughs of Manhattan, Brooklyn, the Bronx and Queens. The consideration of this question will be found in a following chapter.

ROUTE TO BROOKLYN

The routes and general plan of the Brooklyn-Manhattan extension were taken up in 1900 immediately after the contract had been awarded for the Manhattan-Bronx railroad. They were approved by the Board January 24, 1901; by the Board of Aldermen May 21, and by the Mayor on June 1 of the same year. As the consent of a sufficient number of abutting property owners could not be

* In the chapter on "Tunnels" will be found the terms of the grants to the Pennsylvania, New York & Long Island Railroad Company, New York & Jersey Railroad Company, and the Hudson & Manhattan Railroad Company.

secured, application for approval was made to the Supreme Court. The report of the commissioners appointed by the court was confirmed January 17, 1902.

NEEDS OF BROOKLYN

In preparing the form of the Brooklyn-Manhattan contract the Board was impressed with the idea that the public service required it to secure, if possible, not only transportation over the Brooklyn-Manhattan railroad for the fare paid, but also to provide, without additional fare, the most extensive systems of connections. In providing for transfers, it was necessary to consider the relative merits, on the one hand, of extensive connections in the Borough of Brooklyn, and, on the other hand, of an extensive system of connections in the Borough of Manhattan. It was clear that the convenience of the Brooklyn traveling public was first to be considered; since the extension would be used by residents of Brooklyn to a vastly greater extent than by residents of the Borough of Manhattan. Nevertheless, it might be open to doubt whether the convenience of Brooklyn would be better promoted by additional convenience of distribution of Brooklyn travelers over the Borough of Manhattan, or of additional convenience of access to the Brooklyn terminus of the road, with less convenience of distribution in the Borough of Manhattan. The committee of the Board, entrusted with the preparation of the draft of the contract, dealt with this question by making the extent of the connections one element of the bid.

A committee composed of Alexander E. Orr and Charles Stewart Smith was appointed to prepare a draft of the contract. In general the contract followed the form of the first one, but some of the provisions were more favorable to the city. The most important difference was the duration of the franchise, the time, before renewal, being reduced from fifty to thirty-five years. The renewal is to be for twenty-five years. Other conditions to be stipulated are as follows:

CONDITIONS OF CONTRACT NO. 2

The contractor must agree to construct the road, to provide the equipment and to operate it for thirty-five years. He must stipulate for connections with other rapid transit or surface lines in order to furnish continuous trips for a single fare not exceeding five cents. He must furnish $1,000,000 in cash, or securities such as savings banks are allowed to invest in, as security for the construction and equipment of the road. He must give a bond in a like amount to insure the payment of rental and the performance of every other obligation under the contract. All bonds given by sub-contractors must be deposited with the Board as additional security. After the construction of the road, the city is to hold, as further security for the payment of the rent, a first lien upon the equipment.

The city, on the other hand, is to guarantee to the contractor authority to construct and operate the road "free from all right, claim, or other interference, whether by injunction, suit for damages, or otherwise, on the part of any abutting owner or other person."

The contractor is exempted from taxation under the laws of New York "in respect to its interest in the railroad under the contract, and in respect to the rolling stock and all other equipment of the railroad, except that real estate for power houses, or otherwise forming part of the equipment, shall not be exempted, and that no property of the contractor not provided under and remaining subject to the contract by the city shall be exempted."

The contract contained the eight-hour provision with respect to laborers, workmen, and mechanics. The bid must include $1,000,000 for terminals, and for real estate otherwise required for the operation of the railroad.

The rental was to be the amount of interest the city must pay upon the bonds issued to provide the cost of construction, and a further sum of not less than one per cent. upon the bonds. The contractor must also pay rental upon the amount paid by the city to acquire rights of way, even when not acquired in fee.

STATION ADVERTISEMENTS

No advertisements to be displayed at the stations without special permission of the Board. The speed to be not less than 14 miles per hour, including stops.

The contractor may use the railroad for freight or express matter, provided such use does not interfere with right passenger service.

The report of the committee concludes as follows:

CONTRACTOR FAIRLY DEALT WITH

"The committee desires to remind the Board that although its success with the Manhattan-Bronx contract has made rapid transit prospects far better than they were, nevertheless it is the true interest of the city, not only to secure the lowest possible bid, but to establish the reputation of the city for wise and fair dealing upon the highest possible plane. The contractor should be treated with such scrupulous fairness that the city shall secure the very best and most loyal service, and that, whenever in the future the city has a contract to award for a municipal rapid transit railroad, it shall have a choice from the very best and most competent contractors. The committee has, in this view, followed the general provisions of the Manhattan-Bronx contract, according to the contractor, in precise and intelligible form, proper and efficient protection of his rights, as well as securing to the city full protection of municipal rights, and as far as reasonable protecting the contractor from caprice or uncertainty in the interpretation of his contract obligation. The committee is clear that, whatever may be the rule or the interest of the city with respect to other contracts, this is the only true theory with respect to a rapid transit contract."

The road is to extend from the junction of Park row and Broadway under Broadway, Bowling Green, Battery place, State street and Battery Park, with a loop under Battery Park and Whitehall street. From there it is to pass under the East River to Furman street, Brooklyn, and thence under Joralemon and Fulton streets and Flatbush avenue to the junction of Flatbush and Atlantic avenues. The entire line is to be underground. At the Battery the Brooklyn line passes under the Manhattan line so as to avoid a grade crossing. ROUTE

Three bids were received on July 21, 1902.

One was from the Brooklyn Rapid Transit Company, in the name of John L. Wells, an attorney of that company. This offered to do the work for $7,000,000 for construction and $1,000,000 for terminals. BIDS RECEIVED

The other two bids were by the Rapid Transit Subway Construction Company, one for $3,000,000 for construction and $1,000,000 for terminals, the other for $2,000,000 for construction and $1,000,000 for terminals. It will be recalled that this company was engaged, with John B. McDonald, in the construction of the Manhattan-Bronx line. Both these bids presented the following system of connecting service and transfer:

Connecting lines over which the contractor will assure to any passenger a continuous trip for a single fare not exceeding five cents without change of cars: The lines operated or to be operated by the Interborough Rapid Transit Company, in the Boroughs of Manhattan and the Bronx as now authorized, excepting in the case where the contractor shall have entered into an agreement with a connecting line to carry a passenger for less than five cents, the Interborough Company will not agree in such case to carry such passenger beyond Fifty-ninth street for the less fare. TRANSFERS

The two bids were identical in all respects except amount, and the larger was accompanied by a letter from Mr. McDonald stating that if the Board accepted that bid he would agree to construct an extension of the Manhattan-Bronx system from Forty-second street on Broadway south to Union Square for $100,000, provided the contract was awarded to him before July 1, 1903.

The Board accepted the lowest bid, and the contract was executed September 11, 1902. Construction was begun November 8, following.

ADVANTAGES OF BID ACCEPTED

The Board was of the opinion that two most important advantages would accrue to the city as the result of this contract. "The estimated cost of construction of the proposed road is from $8,000,000 to $10,000,000. By obtaining a responsible company, willing to use in large part its own money, so that it could build the road for only $2,000,000 of the city's funds, the city was saved the necessity of issuing $6,000,000 or more of bonds. Again, by awarding the contract to a company that could and did deliver, in accordance with the terms of its bid, a contract for connections and through service with the Manhattan-Bronx railroad, it was assured that these two roads would always be maintained and operated as parts of one great system. By that auxiliary contract the question of a single fare was solved as to both of the municipal railroads. One fare of five cents will carry a passenger to all parts of the Brooklyn-Manhattan and Manhattan-Bronx systems."

About the middle of 1903 the Interborough Rapid Transit Company informed the Board that it had made arrangements with the company operating the Fort Lee Ferry by which passengers could be carried over the rapid transit railroad and the ferry for a single fare of five cents, provided an elevated road could be built to connect the rapid transit viaduct with the ferry. The advantages of this proposition were so obvious that the Board readily agreed to the extension.

MOVING PLATFORMS

For several years the Board had under consideration the moving platform question. Early in 1903 the proposition came up for building one to run over the west end of the Williamsburg Bridge, along Grand, Center, and William streets to Wall, and then by some suitable connection to Hanover Square or Bowling Green. The device proposed was similar to that installed in Paris in 1900 and in Chicago in 1893. It consisted of moving platforms running parallel to each other but at different speeds, so that passengers could step from a stationary platform to a moving platform, and from that to another platform moving at a higher speed. A committee appointed by the Board was favorable to the plan in general, but it was thought best to consider several details in reference to the route in Manhattan so that it would not conflict with proposed or possible rapid transit railroads. In the year following, the matter was again brought to the attention of the Board, with reference to a crosstown line to be built along Thirty-fourth street. The Board expressed the opinion that the value of such a line, if the system was practicable upon a large scale, could hardly be a matter of doubt.

During the year the Board received application from the New York Connecting Railroad for a grant to connect its lines in Brooklyn with those of the New York, New Haven & Hartford Railroad in the Bronx, passing through the Borough of Queens and across Ward's Island and Randall's Island. This franchise was transmitted to the Board of Aldermen June 27, 1904, but was not approved by that body.

EQUIPMENT

Before the opening of the Subway (now known as Contract No. 1) the Board caused careful investigation to be made regarding the rolling stock and equipment that the Rapid Transit Company had contracted to furnish, with a view to determine whether the safety of passengers was properly provided for. Reports showed that the rolling stock represented the best state of the art of car construction; but it was thought that cars constructed entirely of metal were needed in order to eliminate dangers from fire. The experiments instituted by the Interborough Company in the construction of metal cars were successful, and many of these cars are now in use. The intention is to substitute metal cars as soon as they can be completed and put in service. The subway will then be equipped with a much better type of rolling stock than any other similar railway in the world.

Careful attention was also given to the system of signals and method of protecting the third rail. A more extended consideration of these features will be found in the chapter on "Equipment."

RENTAL TO BE PAID

The first contract provided for the division of the road into four sections, and that the payment of rental should begin, in respect to each, as soon as it was completed and ready for operation. These sections did not, however, agree with the portions of the road as they were successively put in operation. It therefore became necessary to adjust the questions of the method of computing rental in respect to the successive parts of the road as they were opened. On November 3, 1904, a supplemental agreement was made by the contractor and his sureties, which provided that the agreed percentage to be paid by the lessee should be calculated upon such proportion of the total cost of each section as the number of feet of single track in the part ready for operation should bear to the total number of feet of single track in the section.

In accordance with the contract, the contractor had deposited with the Comptroller $1,000,000 in cash as security for construction. When the time

CASH SECURITY RETURNED

approached for the opening of the road, he represented to the Board the hardship of retaining so large a sum to secure the completion of work which was very nearly finished. The Board returned the amount upon the condition that the securities upon the bonds for $5,000,000, including the Interborough Company, would agree that their responsibility extended to include any liability that would have been covered by the cash deposits if they had not been refunded.

The contract for the present subway contained the following clause:

"The contractor shall not permit advertisements in the stations or cars that shall interfere with easy identification of stations or otherwise with efficient operation."

In regard to this the Board said:

"This clause was inserted in the form of contract prepared by the Board because it was believed to be the part of wisdom to offer all possible inducements to bidders to undertake the novel and hazardous work of building the railway proposed. It was thought that although it was extremely desirable to prohibit the use of advertisements in the stations, yet this consideration must give way to the more important consideration of securing a contractor. Every previous effort of the city had failed, and it was known that the largest railroad interests in the city did not believe in the feasibility of the plans of the Board.

ADVERTISING SIGNS

"Shortly after the railway was put in operation large advertisements, in some cases coming down to the floor, were affixed to the walls of the stations by the firm of Ward & Gow, acting under an arrangement made between them and the Interborough Rapid Transit Company, the terms of which the latter have declined to communicate to the Board. These advertisements were of strong colors, and if brought in close contact with the name tablets in the stations, were thought to be likely to obscure them or confuse the eyes of the passengers."

In reporting upon this subject the chief engineer of the Board said:

"From a study of the operation of the road since its opening it is apparent that it is very much more difficult for passengers on the trains to locate the stations in the subway than it is on the elevated railroads, where passengers can recognize the locality from the surrounding buildings. Between the stations in the subway there is nothing to warn the eye of the passenger what point he is approaching. Except for some peculiarities in the shape or color of stations which are not very apparent to unobservant or preoccupied people, the names on the station walls are the only means of identification. It is therefore most essential for the easy identification of stations that their names should be clearly visible."

The counsel of the Board said that the full duty of the Board would be performed if it took pains to see that the advertisements did not in fact "interfere with easy identification of stations, or otherwise with efficient operation," leaving it to the lessee to defend itself in court against any attack that might be made.

ENTRANCES THROUGH PRIVATE PROPERTY

Arrangements were made by the Board for the acquisition of rights of way for station entrances at Astor place, Grand Central, and Forty-second street and Broadway. At the latter station, "Times Square," the owners of the property agreed to maintain an entrance through their building at all hours of the day and night, and to keep it suitably lighted. The Board therefore authorized the contractor to omit one of the kiosks planned for the corner of the street at that point. On this general subject the Board said:

"At certain other points entrances to private property have been under discussion, and it is the desire of the Board, so far as possible, to do away in present and future subways with entrances that occupy the public streets. On April 14, 1904, the Board adopted a resolution that it would consent that entrances to stations from private property should be given free of charge where, in the opinion of the Board, such an entrance would be for the benefit of the traveling public and would not be for other reasons objectionable, provided that in all cases the expense connected therewith should be borne by the applicants, and provided further that such permit should be revocable by the Board or other legal authority acting in its stead for the city of New York."

In the foregoing we have only briefly mentioned some of the most important acts of the Rapid Transit Commission from the date of the letting of the contract up to the present. After ten years of hard, incessant toil the Board was now to see the completion of the first portion of its task.

CHAPTER XVII.

OPENING THE SUBWAY.

OPENING CEREMONIES

The ceremonies incident to the opening of the Subway took place in the City Hall, October 27, 1904. Mayor Geo. B. McClellan, with Archbishop Farley, led the procession to reserved seats in the Aldermanic Chamber. Following them were President Fornes of the Board of Aldermen with Coadjutor Bishop Greer; President Orr with Father Lavelle of St. Patrick's Cathedral; John H. Starin with ex-Mayor VanWyck; Comptroller Edward M. Grout, and Deputy Comptrollers J. W. Stevenson and N. Taylor Phillips; Morris K. Jesup, Woodbury Langdon, John Claflin, Charles Stewart Smith, August Belmont, John B. McDonald, William Barclay Parsons, Edward M. Shepard, Albert B. Boardman, George L. Rives, George S. Rice and H. A. D. Hollmann. A large number of other citizens were present.

After a brief address by President Fornes and prayer by Bishop Greer the Mayor said:

MAYOR McCLELLAN

"Without rapid transit Greater New York would be little more than a geographical expression. It is no exaggeration to say that without interborough communication Greater New York would never have come into being.

"The present boundaries of our city included, ten years ago, a multitude of independent and heterogeneous communities, which would have continued, in all human probability, to work out their own destinies independently, had it not been that modern genius and modern enterprise afforded their population the possibility of movement.

"When the Brooklyn Bridge was opened Greater New York was born. Every addition to transit facilities has added to her growth, which can only reach its full development when a complete system of rapid transit shall be rapid in fact as well as in name. * * *

"We have met here to-day for the purpose of turning over a new page in the history of New York; for the purpose of marking the advent of a new epoch in her development. If this new underground railroad that we are about to open proves as popular and as successful as I confidently expect it to be, it will only be the first of many more that must ultimately result in giving us an almost perfect system of interborough communication. When that day arrives borough boundaries will be remembered only for administrative purposes, and New Yorkers, forgetting from what part of the city they come, and only conscious of the fact that they are the sons of the mightiest metropolis the world has ever seen, will be actuated by a common hope and united in a common destiny."

Chief Engineer Parsons, on being introduced by the Mayor, said:

"I have the honor and very great pleasure to report that the rapid transit railroad is completed for operation from the City Hall station to the station at One-hundred-and-forty-fifth street, on the west side."

President Orr said:

MR. ORR

"Mr. Chairman—On behalf of the Rapid Transit Commission, whom I have the honor to represent, I congratulate you, and through you the people of New York, upon the successful completion of a large part of the first division of the great work confided to our care a few years ago. I think it is unnecessary to occupy your time in speaking of the subway that you are about to open to the public, as it will soon speak for itself, and in a manner that I believe will carry conviction to every one who investigates it or enjoys its benefits, that it is in the line of an ideal system of local transportation for this city, and indeed I may add for all large cities where time, comfort, and safety are considered essentials. * * *

FRANCHISES

"It is unnecessary to argue, for I think it must now be apparent to every thoughtful mind, that among the most valuable assets a large city can possess are to be classed its franchise rights. This opinion has not always prevailed either here or in cities of the Old World, and as a consequence, many of New York's franchise rights have been disposed of without giving due consideration to future possibilities, which, if under her control to-day, would be of incalculable value. I use the word "incalculable" advisedly; for it is very safe to say that in things American it is impossible to forecast the future for a single generation, indeed I might say for a single decade. Will any one undertake to picture the New York of thirty years hence? In each of the civilized countries of later years there is only one great metropolitan city, largely the result of improved methods of national transportation, and all roads lead up to it in which are centered the culture, the refinements, and the wealth of the nation. Just as London is the metropolis of Great Britain and Paris of France, so is New York the metropolis of the United States. I know we have many large and growing cities, but if we are true to ourselves and do not overlook or recklessly cast aside our opportunities, this country of ours, great as it is, can only have one New York.

"With the growth of the city its franchise rights increase in value, and hence the need of their periodic readjustment so that the city may enjoy from time to time its fair proportion of the increase it helps to create. I do not wish it to be understood that I mean franchise rights should be denied to carefully considered enterprises at their fair value when applied for, for enterprise stimulates development; but enterprise should not object to pay at fixed periods of future readjustment its fair proportion of the increase predicated on the conditions as they will then exist, else the errors of the past, which in the light of to-day we now deplore, would fail of correction.

PENNSYLVANIA TUNNELS

"Who could have foretold, twenty-five years ago, that one of our most important railroad systems would make application to enter this city in tunnels under the streets, at a depth below their surface that would not interfere with any present or prospective street purpose, and agree to pay for the privilege an annual rent per mile of single track greater than the annual net earning power per mile of almost any steam railroad in the United States; and who will undertake now to estimate what will be the fair value of that franchise twenty-five years hence, which is secured to the city through the introduction into the agreement of a provision for readjustment at the end of that period? It is an imperative obligation, resting upon those endowed with the authority to grant franchise rights, to protect not only the present but also the prospective values of these most important assets.

SUBWAY CONSTRUCTION ONLY BEGUN

"And I am also led to believe that subway construction under municipal ownership is only in its first stage of development. Every city is divided into two great sections, the business and the residential, and the larger the city the further these sections will be apart, and passenger transportation is an important factor. Surface railroads are serviceable for short distances, and will always have their place, but they are not applicable to long distance street travel. At best they are an aggregation of grade crossings, subject to continual interruptions that cannot be obviated, nor can dependence be placed upon reaching a destination at a given time.

ELEVATED ROADS

"It cannot be denied that elevated railroads have proved of inestimable value in hastening the city's development, and also a great personal convenience as to time; but they are unsightly in appearance, interfere with light and ventilation in the congested streets, in many instances injure the value of abutting property, and at times are subject to serious delays through atmospheric changes. I question whether further elevated railroad-building will have many advocates in the future, except in sparsely inhabited outlying territory, or for bridge approaches, or that it would have been advocated, in the first instance, if the electric conditions of to-day had then obtained. In subway passenger service all these objectionable features are eliminated, and the promised 'Harlem in fifteen minutes,' and other places in proportion, *via* subway transportation, has passed beyond the realm of conjecture and become an established fact.

PIPE GALLERIES

"I also desire on behalf of the Commission to express the hope that in future subway construction the city will make provision for the installation of pipe galleries along the routes. It is true that these pipe galleries are not in any way a rapid transit requisite, and are, therefore, outside of the province of the Commission to construct, but they could be put in place at a minimum of cost during the process of tunnel excavation, would prevent the inconvenience of continual street disturbance in the future, and would, we believe, prove a profitable source of revenue to the city in proportion to their cost. It has always been a regret to the members of the Commission that permission could not have been obtained to install pipe galleries in New Elm street and lower Broadway during subway construction, by way of practically demonstrating the convenience and revenue to be derived from such a system.

CHAMBER OF COMMERCE

"When, in 1894, the Chamber of Commerce, that time honored guardian of the commercial interests of this city and State, realizing the need of enlarged local transit facilities as a means of retaining the prominence New York had already acquired and of insuring its continual growth, earnestly advocated the building of subways through which electric trains could be run at high rates of speed, they adopted the plan of municipal ownership that the late Abram S. Hewitt, when Mayor of this city in 1888, had urged without success. Happily Mr. Hewitt was one of the Chamber's most prominent members, and, guided by his intelligent supervision, and assisted by the late Judge Henry R. Beekman,

BLEECKER STREET.

SPRING STREET.

STATIONS, N. Y. SUBWAY.

GRAND CENTRAL EXPRESS.

the Chamber formulated the present Rapid Transit Act, under which, with a few subsequent amendments, the Rapid Transit Commission is now operating. It is unnecessary at this time to enumerate its provisions—they are pretty well known—but when this city is in the full enjoyment of its own system of rapid transit, a system not confined to one or two localities, but so comprehensive as to embrace the whole of Greater New York, which will transport its citizens from one station point to any other station point for a single fare (as I firmly believe will be the ultimate result), which will increase municipal revenues through the development of places that are now comparatively waste, which will help to safeguard to New York her well-earned position as the financial and commercial center of the United States, and all this at a mere bagatelle of cost to the treasury of the city, then, and not till then, will the genius of Mr. Hewitt and the enterprise and energy of the Chamber of Commerce be fully understood.

FUTURE BENEFITS

"Viewed from the standpoint of to-day, it is a singular fact that only a little more than four years ago subway construction under municipal ownership was regarded with suspicion and distrust by those largely identified with local and national passenger transportation, and, as far as I have been able to discover, with the single notable exception referred to above, by the prominent financiers of that period. If it had rested with the men controlling these great interests, I think I am justified in saying that municipal rapid transit would yet remain an unsolved problem.

MUNICIPAL OWNERSHIP

"It is, therefore, with a feeling somewhat akin to gratitude that the Commission makes record of the fact that on January 15, 1900, John B. McDonald, neither a railroad man nor a financier, but a contractor identified with large undertakings, after making a careful study of the situation, had the courage of his convictions and made an acceptable tender for the franchise contract and lease which the Commission were empowered to grant.

"Immediately after the contract was awarded, August Belmont became associated with Mr. McDonald and organized the Rapid Transit Subway Construction Company, by whom the subway has been built. That the work has been rapidly, admirably, and willingly performed is certified to by our engineer corps; and when public inspection is made evidences of refinement, comfort and safety will be observed that are not to be found anywhere in like structures. I am not in the confidence of Messrs. McDonald and Belmont as to the present or prospective financial outcome of their undertaking, but I am sure I express the

TYPICAL FOUR-TRACK CONSTRUCTION.

SPRING ST. STATION—FIVE TRACKS.

N. Y. SUBWAY.

hope of the members of the Commission, and of every New York citizen, that their courage and enterprise may reap a very generous reward."

Mr. Orr then paid a very warm tribute to Mr. Parsons, the chief engineer of the Commission, who had been elected to the position on the day the Board organized, as follows: "The Commission is responsible for the subway route. They were controlled in a measure by the amount of money at their disposition, and by the previous findings of the Appellate Division of the Supreme Court; but the merit of the plan of construction and its supervision from beginning to end is Mr. Parsons' alone. When we consider its twenty-four miles of length, running through some of the busiest and most congested sections of the city, the nature of the ground, largely of rock formation, the superstructures to be carried, consisting in most part of water and gas mains and surface railroads (the operating of which latter was not suspended for a single day), the difficult sewerage problems involved, and then the final result, it is not to be wondered at that Mr. Parsons' professional reputation has passed beyond the confines of his native city and received well merited national and international recognition. I never returned from any of my visits to the subway during the progress of the work without being more and more impressed with the magnitude of the engineering difficulties presented, and the magnificent manner in which they were being overcome. As long as the subway is made to render service to the people of New York, the Chamber of Commerce, Abram S. Hewitt, John B. McDonald, August Belmont and William Barclay Parsons should be held in remembrance as household words. * * * " MR. PARSONS

John H. Starin briefly reviewed the work of the Commission since its inception in 1894 and then said: MR. STARIN

"Since the execution of the contract between the city and Mr. McDonald, on the 21st of February, 1900, the work of construction has been carried on entirely under the supervision of this Commission. The Board has continued, with only a few changes in its membership, practically as at that time, and I may safely say that it has been as devoted to its work as if the railroad was being constructed with the money of its members. Winter and summer, in season and out of season, it has met both as a full Board, of which hundreds of sessions have been held, and in committees, of which the meetings are without number. And at all times its members have given a patient and expert care and attention to every question, no matter how trivial, that might in any way affect the quality and value and usefulness of the great railroad system that is to-day thrown open to the public. * * *

PUBLIC OPINION CHANGED

"Since the signing of the first contract in 1900, a great revolution in public opinion has taken place regarding city travel. My mind goes back to the time when the Commission of 1891 first came to the conclusion that underground rapid transit was the only cure for the ills that traveling New Yorkers were heirs to. In those days the number of persons who believed in an underground construction was most limited; indeed, it might have been comprised in a list made up of the Commissioners themselves, their engineers and assistants, and a few who had given the matter some study. Even among those who in the few subsequent years came to believe that such a plan was feasible and desirable, there were few sanguine enough to expect its construction; and to come down to 1900, even after the contract was signed, many could be found who said they did not expect to live to ride on such a road.

MANHATTAN-BROOKLYN EXTENSION

"No sooner had the first great work been well started than the Board confidently laid out a second one to bind together with Manhattan, by a subway and tunnel under the East River, the great sister borough of Brooklyn, which by consolidation, had become a part of the greater city, and over which the powers of the Board had been extended by legislative enactment. So thoroughly had the value of the underground idea been demonstrated, even at this time, in January, 1902, that a contract was secured by the Board for the city upon surprisingly favorable terms, and the Rapid Transit Subway Construction Company contracted to build the new line for $3,000,000, although its total cost will undoubtedly reach $10,000,000. * * *

"So the great work was commenced, and so it has gone on. That it has been successful beyond the fondest anticipation of its early advocates is cause for universal rejoicing. But, in the midst of that rejoicing, let us not forget the men who fought the battle and won the victory. Let us remember McDonald the contractor, and Belmont the capitalist, and William Barclay Parsons the engineer, and above all and beyond all let us remember Alexander E. Orr, the president of the Rapid Transit Commission."

MR. McDONALD

John B. McDonald spoke in part as follows:

* * * "The discussion and final building of the subway has been coincident with an evolution in public affairs in New York as marked as this great work. The city has grown from a population of 1,500,000 to 3,500,000, the

buildings from six to thirty stories, and commercially the City of New York now stands in the front rank in the world.

"When the final work of preparation had been concluded and the Rapid Transit Commission had formulated their specifications, prepared their plans, and advertised for proposals, my work began. It would be rank conceit to say that I did not approach this great undertaking with many misgivings as to my ability to accomplish the task; but I believed it practicable, necessary to the city, and, after careful study, determined to become a bidder for the work. After fair competition the contract was awarded to me.

"The work of organizing and giving a bond for the faithful performance of my contract finally resulted in bringing to my aid the distinguished financier, Mr. August Belmont, and his associates, and the organization of the Rapid Transit Subway Construction Company, whose generous support and co-operation I have had in carrying out this important work.

"In the sub-division of the work, there were brought to my aid as sub-contractors, men of means, ability, and experience not surpassed. What greater compliment can I pay them than to say: 'Behold their work'?" * * *

MR. BELMONT

August Belmont said that in an undertaking of this character there "is enough credit * * * to go round." After praising the courage, patience, industry and intelligence of those who had unitedly carried the plans to completion, he said:

"Attempts to install an underground system of railroads in the City of New York began many years ago. There had been some legislation and even some work prosecuted under such legislation, but the legislation and the work alike were inoperative. Until the present project was conceived, no real progress was made. Although much time and thought had been wasted upon these previous attempts, the resulting failures did not, as is frequently true of failure, furnish any suggestions for the guidance of those entering upon what, to all intents and purposes, was a wholly new undertaking.

DIFFICULTIES OF CONSTRUCTION

"Almost insurmountable difficulties stood in the path of the enterprise. The questionable right of the city to incur the obligations necessary to be assumed upon its part; the uncertainty as to the legal rights of abutting owners; the difficulties of carrying the subway through soil occupied by innumerable obstructions of pipes and wires; the fact that the work had to be prosecuted without interference with the operation of surface transportation lines and general surface traffic, which required the uninterrupted use of the thoroughfares under which the subway was to be constructed—all combined to give pause even to the most pronounced enthusiasm.

FINANCIAL

"Nor did the solicitude as to success end with the decision to proceed. At all points in the progress of the work great care was at all times requisite lest by unwise counsel and decisions, either in the physical or financial prosecution of the work, there might result a collapse which would defer indefinitely the completion of a work so essential to the municipal well-being of this metropolis, whose true development was hemmed in by the rivers at its very threshold.

"It was only by exhaustive preparation in almost infinite detail, both in the engineering and in the transportation and in the financial departments, that it has been possible for this enterprise to proceed to a successful termination without serious interruption or embarrassment and with credit to all identified with it.

NEW AND UNTRIED VENTURE

"If any especial credit is due to my associates and myself, it is that the financial end committed to our care required the exercise of a kind of courage not frequently demanded for an investment. It was a new and untried venture. No one had yet been willing to assume the risk in order to enjoy the possible resulting benefits and profits. The dangers attending its undertaking were clear and unmistakable; nor was the outcome guaranteed by any experience upon which it was possible to rely. It was essential before a decision to go forward could be reached, to eliminate, as far as possible, all apparent elements of probable failure.

"With all this I am entitled to add, I think, and I add it with no inconsiderable pride, the initiation and prosecution of the work have not involved any excessive capitalization. The capital represented by the par of the stock issued, together with the obligations issued by the city, represents substantially the cost of the investment for construction, equipment, and installation of the subway and the railway.

OBJECT LESSON

"It is my judgment, too, that the claim is not extravagant that the plan and the execution of this work have set an example which may fitly serve as an object lesson and a standard for similar quasi-municipal projects.

"In this case the City of New York was, by appropriate legislation, authorized to extend its credit by the issue of municipal securities, for the building of the subway, but that was the limit of its participation. Even this risk was reduced to a minimum, because municipal securities were to be issued and the proceeds devoted to the payment for the subway only as results, rigidly required by the contracts, were forthcoming from the contractor.

GUARANTEES BY CONTRACTOR

"The city had, before entering upon the undertaking, a substantial guarantee of performance by the contractor. Added to this protection there was demanded a much more substantial guarantee, not only that the interest upon these securities to be issued by the city would be met, but that, through the accumulation of a sinking fund to be provided by the private interests, the total municipal capital invested would be ultimately repaid. In the end, the subway, constructed at the expense of the city, will be delivered to it free from obligation.

"At a time when there are so many ill-digested and ill-considered plans under discussion, having for their object not only municipal ownership, but municipal operation of transportation lines, the State of New York has reached the true solution of this problem—that municipal participation is justified to the extent of furnishing credit for the construction of such a work, but should stop short of the operation of the property when constructed. To private interests should be committed the risks and the burden as well as the profit of constructing, equipping, and operating the road, the latter not being within the governmental functions or other legitimate province of municipalities.

"I think I am entitled to take you frankly into my confidence and say that nothing in my career has given me greater pause than the question as to whether I should permit my firm to assume financial leadership in this undertaking. It was not alone on account of the large sums of money it was necessary for me personally to risk in the new venture. Comparatively, that was not of first importance, for it was essential in a work as vast as this to secure extensive co-operation on the part of other financial interests, entitled to look to me in large degree for its success, which no preliminary investigation, however comprehensive and intricate, could assure with absolute certainty.

PRELIMINARY INVESTIGATION

"My associates and myself, however, had complete confidence in the exhaustive preliminary investigation, conducted at great length and with great care and having assured ourselves that the work could be completed within the estimates, we were willing without hesitation to assume the further risk, supposed by many at the time to be the main risk, that the growth of the City of New York would be sufficient to justify the providing of these new facilities for transportation.

"Now that the work has been completed and the subway, or, rather, this splendid arcade, is formally opened, although not a passenger for hire has yet been carried upon its tracks, being entirely assured of the success of this enterprise, we have in contemplation plans for still further adding to the rapid transit facilities of the system of elevated and subway lines now united.

"This great metropolis has now rid itself of the bonds that heretofore have limited and impeded its growth, and has included within itself, in all but legal description, a vast adjacent territory."

SUBWAY DECLARED OPEN

After benediction by Archbishop Farley the Mayor said: "Now I, as Mayor, in the name of the people, declare the subway open."

Mr. Belmont handed the Mayor a mahogany case, saying: "I give you this controller, Mr. Mayor, with the request that you put in operation this great road, and start it on his course of success, and, I hope, of safety."

The first train started from the City Hall station at 2:34 P. M.

18TH STREET STATION—N. Y. SUBWAY.

CHAPTER XVIII.

FUTURE RAPID TRANSIT IN NEW YORK.

During the past five years, or since the completion of the plans for the present subway, a large part of the time of the Commission has been taken up with the consideration of rapid transit schemes for the future. The work already accomplished was only looked upon as the beginning of a system of transportation that will ultimately embrace every portion of the city of Greater New York.

NEW ROUTES

The result has been the selection of new routes that extend to all parts of the city. The choice involved long and painstaking study. Natural advantages and the natural trend of population must be weighed. The relation of one section to another, and with Manhattan as a center, must be kept in mind. The lines must be so selected as to permit of expansion in the future without disturbing the efficiency and symmetry of the system as a whole.

In the spring of 1902 Mr. Orr, the president of the Board, requested the chief engineer to prepare a comprehensive plan of rapid transit for the whole city. In giving the instruction he said:

"The public has come to recognize fully the wisdom of development of the rapid transit facilities of Greater New York and of the use of its street property for rapid transit purposes upon a general and far-seeing plan. Rapid transit franchises, it is now believed, ought to be granted with reference to a systematic treatment of the subject under the guidance or initiatory control of a single body like this Board, with a tenure sufficiently long to assure not only the adoption of a comprehensive programme, but also, at least in part, its execution. This idea was embodied in the present rapid transit act, providing, as it did, not only for municipal construction of new rapid transit railroads, but also for the grant of rapid transit franchises to companies operating existing lines. * * *

COMPLETE SCHEME

"It is, therefore, clear that the public now has a right to expect from this Board the preparation of a general and far-reaching system of rapid transit covering the whole city of New York in all its five boroughs. It was in anticipation of that work that the Board in January last asked the Mayor and Comptroller for early information as to the extent to which the debt limit and other necessities of the city would permit rapid transit extension in addition to the Manhattan-Bronx and Brooklyn-Manhattan roads. When that information shall be received the Board will be better able to decide where the next rapid transit expenditure shall be placed.

RESULTS EXPECTED

"The far-reaching plan I have suggested could not, of course, be carried out at once, or, perhaps, completely carried out for many years. But if such a plan be now wisely prepared, and the streets of New York be dedicated to tunnel railroad purposes with a proper regard to the long and, no doubt, splendid future of the city, two things may be reasonably expected: First, that rapid transit construction will proceed upon the lines so laid down as rapidly as the means of the city and the amount of private capital ready for rapid transit investment will permit; and, second, that relatively unimportant franchises will not be granted in such way, or special routes be so devised, as to prevent or obstruct a permanent and sufficient programme.

"It is my conclusion from all this that, in laying out the East Side line you should study the whole rapid transit situation of all five boroughs, and that your report should aid the Board to prepare and submit to the local authorities the comprehensive plan for the entire city that I have suggested, the same to be carried out in sections or instalments, as financial conditions shall from time to time permit."

In February and March of the following year the chief engineer reported on comprehensive plans for rapid transit for the boroughs of Manhattan, the Bronx, Brooklyn and Queens. From these reports the following passages are taken:

INCREASE OF PASSENGER TRAVEL

"Tremendous increase in passenger travel on all lines during the past year clearly indicates that when the present subway system, now under construction from Brooklyn to the Bronx, is completed, it will almost be immediately congested, so that no great amount of permanent relief can be counted on. In order to meet the growing and imperative demands for increased facilities, arising from the natural growth of our city, it is evident that new lines should be laid down now and put under construction as soon as possible, and that steps should be taken to improve the existing facilities so as to permit them to carry the increased burden during the time when the new lines are being constructed."

ROUTES RECOMMENDED

The report recommended that the present subway be extended south from Forty-second street along the general line of Broadway, or parallel thereto on the west; and by extending it north from Forty-second street, at Park avenue, along Lexington avenue to One-hundred-and-forty-ninth street. It was also proposed that branches should be constructed from Broadway to the Pennsylvania Railroad station at Seventh avenue; along One-hundred-and-tenth street to Lenox avenue; from West Farms in the Bronx to Wakefield; and along the Southern Boulevard and One-hundred-and-eightieth street. A connection between the Bronx Park line and the Manhattan elevated was recommended from Brook avenue along Westchester avenue to Third avenue.

It was proposed to increase the number of tracks on the Second and Third avenue elevated roads; to extend the Sixth avenue road along Christopher street to Greenwich street; to add another track to the Ninth avenue road, and to connect the elevated system with a subway to be built along Tenth avenue to a connection with the present subway at Seventy-second street; and to arrange connection with the railroads terminating at the Grand Central Station.

It was suggested to provide an extension of the New York Central tracks south from Fifty-ninth street and Eleventh avenue by an elevated structure along their present right of way or possibly along West street to the Battery. To construct a branch of the Second avenue elevated along Sixty-fourth street and over the Blackwell's Island Bridge, with provision for future extension of the line.

BROOKLYN ROUTES

In Brooklyn it was proposed to build a subway under Nassau and Orange streets and the East River to Maiden Lane in Manhattan; thence along William, Center, and Grand streets to the end of the Williamsburg Bridge. This was intended to provide a loop for the elevated roads of Brooklyn by way of the Williamsburgh Bridge and this second tunnel.

The elevated trains were to be removed entirely from the Brooklyn Bridge, and the trolley cars transferred from the roadway to the original bridge tracks, thereby restoring the roadways to the exclusive use of vehicles. To connect the Second avenue elevated with the elevated structure of the Williamsburgh Bridge. To build an extension of the present subway from Flatbush and Atlantic avenues to Prospect Park and Plaza, and ultimately further. Also another extension from the same point along Fourth avenue to Fort Hamilton. A tunnel from Atlantic avenue to Whitehall street in Manhattan. Also extension of the Brooklyn elevated system in various directions.

The report of Mr. Parsons made no provision to connect the Borough of Richmond with Manhattan; the reason for this was that the great expense involved was entirely out of proportion to the population to be served.

The plans, as finally decided upon by the Rapid Transit Commission and transmitted for approval to the Board of Aldermen, until that Board was superseded by the Board of Estimate and Apportionment, were as follows:

THIRD AVENUE ROUTE.

This route begins in the Bronx near Lincoln avenue and the Southern Boulevard. A double track line running from there under the East River reaches Third avenue at One-hundred-and-twenty-eighth street. From that point it runs as a four-track road southerly under Third avenue and the Bowery to Chatham Square. At Chatham Square the narrowness of the streets compels a division of tracks. Two tracks will run southerly through the New Bowery and Pearl street to Broad street, and thence under South street to the Battery. Two tracks, diverging at Chatham square, will pass down Park Row, Nassau and Broad streets, joining the other tracks in Broad street near Pearl. Two single-track spurs are provided to connect the main line, through Thirty-fifth and Thirty-sixth streets, with the Seventh or Eighth avenue subway described below. These spurs, between Lexington and Fifth avenues, will be parallel to the other tracks forming a part of the Lexington avenue system; but they will be for the most part at different levels.

In the Bronx, two double-track lines will diverge from the point of beginning mentioned above. One of these lines will run northerly, terminating in a loop near One-hundred-and-forty-second street, and connecting with a proposed line to run under One-hundred-and-thirty-eighth street. The other line in the Bronx will run easterly under the Southern Boulevard to a terminus in the New York, New Haven & Hartford Railroad yards.

LEXINGTON AVENUE ROUTE.

This route begins near Forty-third street and Lexington avenue, with a short connection westerly to the existing subway in Park avenue. From Forty-third street, the line will run northerly under Lexington avenue as a four-track road to about One-hundred-and-twenty-ninth street, where it will divide and form two double-track extensions.

One of the extensions will pass under the Harlem River and along Third and Morris avenues in the Bronx to One-hundred-and-forty-ninth street, where it will connect with the existing subway near Cortlandt avenue. From about One-hundred-and-thirty-seventh to One-hundred-and-forty-second streets, this line will occupy the same streets as the Third avenue line above described; but these streets—Third and Morris avenues—are wide enough to contain four tracks in two separate tunnels.

The second extension in the Bronx will diverge with two tracks, as mentioned above, near One-hundred-and-twenty-ninth street and Lexington avenue, in Manhattan. It will cross from there under the Harlem River to Park avenue, and continue northerly under Park avenue to One-hundred-and-fifty-sixth street, from which point a further extension may be made northerly if required. At One-hundred-and-forty-ninth street and Park avenue another divergence is proposed, carrying two tracks under the New York Central yards, with a loop in the yards, and then parallel with the Harlem River along One-hundred-and-fifty-third street and under Cromwell Creek into Sedgwick avenue to about One-hundred-and-sixty-fourth street. This route has a triple branching in the Bronx.

From Forty-third street and Lexington avenue southerly, there will be four tracks as far as Thirty-sixth street. The two south-bound tracks will there turn west through Thirty-sixth street to Fifth avenue and then south. The two north-bound tracks will continue down Lexington avenue to Thirty-fifth street, and rejoin the other tracks in Fifth avenue. The four tracks will then continue southerly along Fifth avenue to Madison Square. There they will turn into Broadway and run south, passing under Union Square, to the City Hall Park. At that point a single-track loop will allow part of the trains to be turned back, while two tracks will continue down to Vesey street, and then through Vesey and Church streets to the Battery.

SEVENTH AND EIGHTH AVENUE ROUTE.

Beginning at the southerly end of this route, in the Battery Park, the line will run northerly under Greenwich street and West Broadway to Chambers street. From this point northerly, two alternate routes are planned. The most direct runs under Hudson street and Eighth avenue to about One-hundred-and-fifty-fourth street, where a northerly extension can be built hereafter. The other line continues northerly from Chambers street under West Broadway to Washington Square, where the line again diverges into two alternative routes. One of these runs under Washington Square, private property, and Greenwich avenue to Seventh avenue, and then northerly under Seventh avenue to a connection with the present subway under Times Square. The other alternative route runs under Washington Square and Fifth avenue to Twenty-third street, and then under Broadway to Twenty-fifth street, where it diverges again—two tracks running westerly under Twenty-fifth street to join the Seventh avenue subway, and so northerly to Times Square—and the main line running straight under Broadway to join the present subway near the same place.

A separate section of this proposed route is designed to run northerly from Seventh avenue and Forty-third street to Central Park, curving under the park so as to connect with the line under Eighth avenue at about Fifty-second street.

In regard to the above routes the Board said:

"The three routes referred to in this communication are all designed to be substantially of the same type as that which the present subway has made familiar. From end to end these lines will be below the surface. Not a foot of elevated structure is here included.

"It has been the effort of this Board to arrange the routes now submitted for the consideration of your honorable body, so that each of them should *first* be capable of separate operation; *second,* be capable of advantageous operation in connection with some existing means of passenger transportation within the city; *third,* be practicable to build at once, both from the engineering, transportation, and financial standpoints. In this way the largest measure of effective rapid transit will be secured, while at the same time an opportunity is afforded for active competition among strong rival bidders."

THIRTY-FOURTH STREET ROUTE.

This route runs through Thirty-fourth street, in Manhattan, from the East to the Hudson rivers, passing under the present subway in Fourth avenue and at a sufficient depth under the several north and south avenues to permit other subways to be constructed over it. It will have no track connections with any rapid transit lines in Manhattan, but it is expected that joint stations will be placed at the intersections of the principal avenues so as to facilitate transfers of passengers.

A separate section diverges from the main stem of this route between Second and Third avenues and runs on a descending grade to pass under the East River to Long Island City. The terminus in Queens will be in Jackson avenue near Borden avenue. At this point the various trolley lines converge, thus making transfers easy to and from the proposed subway. A physical connection can also be arranged, if found to be desirable, with the subway uniting the Williamsburgh Bridge with the Blackwell's Island Bridge.

This route is entirely in subway, the rails averaging about 40 feet below the surface.

The Board said in regard to this route:

"So far as this route is concerned, its advantages appear to be too obvious to call for argument. It will reach and serve such important points in Manhattan as the new Pennsylvania Railroad station, Herald Square with its neighboring shops and theatres, the Waldorf-Astoria Hotel, and the East Thirty-fourth street ferry. In Queens it will enable passengers by any of the steam or trolley lines now coming to the ferry to get quickly, and with only one change, to Manhattan; and it will carry them without change to points in Manhattan where they can transfer to any of the north and south railroads, and thus reach rapidly and conveniently any part of the city."

ROUTE TO VAN CORDTLANDT PARK.

This addition consists of an extension running along Broadway from its intersection with Two-hundred-and-thirtieth street to a point just north of Two-hundred-and-forty-second street, opposite Van Cortlandt Park. It will be an elevated structure throughout. The portion of Broadway in question is at present very little built upon, and the elevated road proposed would merely be a continuation of the one that already exists in the same street.

FIRST AVENUE ROUTE.

This route begins in the Bronx at the intersection of One-hundred-and-thirty-eighth street and Alexander avenue. At or near this point connections can readily be made with various rapid transit routes in the Bronx. From this point the line runs southerly along Alexander avenue, or just west of it, so as to avoid the Willis avenue bridge approaches; and then passing under the Harlem River it turns into First avenue near One-hundred-and-twenty-fourth street. From this point it runs southerly under First avenue to First street, then curves easterly and runs under Essex, Rutgers and Madison streets to the New Bowery. It then runs southerly under the New Bowery and Pearl street, by the side of the proposed Third avenue line, to a point near Dover street. From there it curves easterly under private property to Water street, and runs south under Water street to Pine street. It then passes under private property in the block bounded by Water, Pine, Wall and Pearl streets, and then runs under Beaver street, Bowling Green, and Battery place to Greenwich street.

From the northerly end of the line at One-hundred-and-thirty-eighth street a separate section is added which runs northerly under Alexander avenue, Melrose avenue, Webster avenue and Claremont Park, with a loop under the park. This line will afford a very direct connection between the more thickly settled parts of the Bronx and the lower east side of the city.

NINTH AVENUE ROUTE.

This route is, in effect, a continuation of the one just described. It begins at the southern terminus of that line in Battery place, and thence runs under Battery place and under West street to Gansevoort street, where it curves into Ninth avenue to Morningside Park, and thence under Manhattan avenue, St. Nicholas avenue, Kingsbridge road, Broadway and Sherman avenue to Amsterdam avenue at about Two-hundred-and-eleventh street.

Concerning the two last mentioned routes the Board said:

"Together with the Third avenue, Lexington avenue, and Seventh and Eighth avenue routes, they form the additional north and south lines in the Borough of Manhattan which this Board now contemplates, and which are all that it believes can wisely be planned for the present time. * * * It is only necessary to add that the routes herewith submitted are all in subway, and that, if they are approved, it is proposed to provide, in the contracts for construction, such modifications and improvements as the valuable experience already gained in such work may suggest."

JEROME AVENUE SUBWAY.

This route consists of a four-track subway running through Jerome avenue from about One-hundred-and-sixty-fourth street near its southerly end to the junction with Woodlawn Cemetery. From the southerly end of this line, two connections are provided with railways in Manhattan. The first is a three-track connection leading to the bridge over the Harlem belonging to the Putnam Division of the New York Central Railroad. The other is a two-track subway passing under the East River to a point in Eighth avenue near One-hundred-and-fifty-fourth street, so as to connect with a subway to be hereafter constructed under that avenue. A third spur is planned to connect with One-hundred-and-fifty-third street near Cromwell avenue, so as to afford a means of junction with the proposed Lexington avenue subway.

JEROME AVENUE ELEVATED ROAD.

This line consists of a three-track elevated structure running northerly from Jerome avenue near its intersection with Clarke place, to the junction of Jerome avenue with Woodlawn road. It is provided that connections may be made with the Jerome avenue subway and the Gerard avenue subway.

GERARD AVENUE SUBWAY.

This is a subway beginning at One-hundred-and-thirty-eighth street and Third avenue, at which point connections can be made with several other lines planned by the Board, and running thence west through One-hundred-and-thirty-eighth street and Gerard avenue to Jerome avenue near its intersection with Clarke place. At this point a connection can be made either with the Jerome avenue subway or the Jerome avenue elevated.

WHITE PLAINS ROAD ROUTE.

This route is practically an extension of the present rapid transit elevated viaduct. It is to begin at One-hundred-and-seventy-seventh street and West Farms road near Bronx Park, and thence a three-track elevated structure is planned to run along West Farms road, Morris Park avenue, and White Plains road, to the former village of Wakefield.

WESTCHESTER AVENUE ROUTE.

This route begins at Third avenue and One-hundred-and-thirty-eighth street, at which point connections may be made either with subways coming from Manhattan or with the Gerard avenue subway. From this point a subway is to run east under One-hundred-and-thirty-eighth street to the Southern Boulevard. At that point the road is planned to emerge from the ground and continue as a three-track elevated structure on the Southern Boulevard and Westchester avenue to the former village of Westchester.

The following remarks by the Board cover the five last mentioned routes:

"The three main lines which these routes cover are Jerome avenue, White Plains road, and Westchester avenue. These three divergent lines would not alone be practicable from an operating or financial point of view. They are of value chiefly as extensions of routes now or hereafter to be built in the Borough of Manhattan. With the exception of the White Plains road, these lines may form an extension of two or more systems, and it is believed that competition between bidders would exist as to these several lines.

"The Board recommends that elevated structures be authorized along part of Jerome avenue and along the White Plains road and Westchester avenue. It has done so with hesitation, but it is satisfied that its action in this regard is approved by a large majority of the residents of the Borough of the Bronx. The construction of subways in the Bronx, owing to the irregular and rocky character of the soil, would be extremely expensive—much more so, for example, than in the Borough of Brooklyn, where subway construction is comparatively cheap. It is thought, therefore, that while bids for elevated structures might be obtained, it would probably prove very difficult at the present time and probably for several years to come, to obtain bids for rapid transit subways. So far as the White Plains road is concerned, that would be merely an extension of an elevated structure already existing. And so far as the Westchester avenue road is concerned, it may be said that this road will be in appearance and effect simply an extension of the rapid transit viaduct already existing in other adjacent parts of both the Southern Boulevard and Westchester avenue."

BROOKLYN AND MANHATTAN LOOP LINES.

OOP LINES

The loop lines consist of a railroad beginning in East New York at the eastern extremity of Broadway, and running through Broadway across the Williamsburgh Bridge to Manhattan; and then running south in Manhattan to a series of tunnels between the Brooklyn Bridge and the Battery, which lead the line back to the Brooklyn Borough Hall Park; and from there easterly along Lafayette and Gates avenues back to Broadway. In addition, a line running north and south through Bedford avenue from the Williamsburgh Bridge plaza to the Eastern Parkway serves the purpose of an interior loop.

The route in Manhattan from the Williamsburgh Bridge passes underground in Delancey street near Norfolk; and then runs west under Delancey street to the Bowery, and under the proposed extension of Delancey street to the corner of Center and Grand streets. The line then continues southerly through Center and Williams streets.

THREE EAST RIVER TUNNELS

Provision is made for three tunnels, which may be described as the Old Slip tunnel, the Maiden Lane tunnel, and the Beekman street tunnel.

The route of the first is under William street, Exchange place, and Beaver street in Manhattan, and under Montague street in Brooklyn.

The second begins at the corner of William and Liberty streets, and then passes under Maiden Lane in Manhattan, and Pineapple street in Brooklyn.

The third passes under Beekman street in Manhattan, and Cranberry street in Brooklyn.

As stated, all three tunnels come together at City Hall Park, Brooklyn. From there a route runs under Willoughby street, the Flatbush avenue extension, Fulton street, and Lafayette avenue to its intersection with Bedford avenue. From this point one line continues by Lafayette to Stuyvesant avenue. Another line runs through Bedford avenue and Gates to Broadway.

There are several spurs forming a part of this route. The longest begins at Grand and Center streets in Manhattan and runs West under Grand and Desbrosses streets to the Desbrosses street ferry, and intersects all the north and south lines of travel in Manhattan. Another spur forms a connection, by means of a line under Canal street, with the Manhattan end of the Manhattan Bridge. A third connects with the City Hall loop of the present subway by means of a line under Beekman street. In Brooklyn, connections may be made with the subway now building in the neighborhood of Borough Hall Park and at the corner of Lafayette and Flatbush avenues.

This system will relieve the pressure upon the Brooklyn Bridge, as well as utilize the possibilities of the Williamsburgh Bridge. It will bring almost all parts of the Borough of Manhattan south of Houston street within easy reach of those parts of Brooklyn that may be described as East New York, Williamsburgh, the Lafayette avenue district, and the Bedford avenue district.

FOURTH AVENUE ROUTE.

This line extends from Fort Hamilton by Fourth avenue to Flatbush avenue, where connections may be made with the subway now constructing and with the Prospect Park extension. Connections are also provided for the Brooklyn and Manhattan loop lines above described, either directly by a line under Ashland place, or by a line curving from Fourth avenue and running under Atlantic avenue and Court street to the Borough Hall Park.

MANHATTAN BRIDGE ROUTE.

This route is designed to occupy chiefly the Manhattan Bridge and its approaches. Provision is made for a direct connection under the Flatbush avenue extension with the subway now being constructed, at the junction of Flatbush avenue and Fulton street. Provision is also made for a connection with the loop line running easterly under Fulton street and Lafayette avenue. As stated above, a spur in Manhattan will run from the proposed loop line under Center street to the Manhattan Bridge terminus in that borough.

By making the Manhattan Bridge an independent rapid transit route the Board, in negotiating a contract for its construction and operation, will be enabled to utilize it in connection either with the subway now under construction or with the Fourth avenue line, or with the Lafayette avenue line, or other lines, as may prove to be most desirable hereafter.

EASTERN PARKWAY ROUTE.

This line is planned to extend from the Prospect Park plaza under the Eastern Parkway to East New York avenue. Near that point a loop begins, running out from Howard avenue, Hunterfly road, Blake and Georgia avenues, and returning by Pitkin avenue. A spur is planned to run along Georgia avenue to the intersection of East New York avenue and Broadway, where the line running to the Williamsburgh Bridge will begin. An extension is also provided to run from the Prospect Park plaza along Flatbush avenue to Atlantic avenue, there connecting with the route to Court street and Borough Hall Park.

The Eastern Parkway route, in connection with the Broadway line, forms still another or exterior loop in Brooklyn, reaching a rapidly growing section of the city.

BROOKLYN, MANHATTAN AND LONG ISLAND CITY ROUTE.

This system consists essentially of two lines: One running from the Williamsburgh Bridge plaza to the Blackwell's Island Bridge through the Boroughs of Brooklyn and Queens; and the other running from Williamsburgh under the East River to Fourteenth street in the Borough of Manhattan.

The first of these two lines, beginning at the Williamsburgh Bridge plaza, runs through Driggs and Manhattan avenues, and under Newtown creek; and then under Jackson avenue in Long Island City.

The other line begins at the corner of Lafayette and Stuyvesant avenues, which is a point on the Lafayette avenue line above described. From there it runs through Stuyvesant, Bushwick, and Metropolitan avenues and North Seventh street in Greenpoint, and by a tunnel under the East River to the foot of Fourteenth street in Manhattan. Physical connection will be provided at the corner of Driggs avenue and North Seventh street, so that cars may be run from either Long Island City or the Williamsburgh Bridge plaza direct to Manhattan.

The route also includes two spurs; one running from the corner of Stuyvesant and Lafayette avenues under Lafayette avenue, Stanhope street, and Cypress avenue to Palmetto street. Another from the junction of Metropolitan avenue and North Seventh street along Union avenue to Broadway.

FOURTEENTH STREET, UNIVERSITY PLACE, GREENWICH STREET, ETC. (MANHATTAN).

This route is intended to be operated in connection with that just described. It crosses from Greenpoint to the foot of East Fourteenth street. The line now proposed runs along Fourteenth street as far as Ninth avenue. Two branches run southerly. One runs under Ninth avenue, Greenwich street, and Liberty street to connect with what has been called above the Maiden Lane tunnel. The other branch from Fourteenth street runs through University place, Wooster, and Canal streets to a connection at Canal and Center streets with the Brooklyn and Manhattan loop lines above described.

It will be seen that these two routes form still another loop (taken in connection with the Lafayette avenue line), by which cars could be run in either direction between the Boroughs of Brooklyn and Manhattan—not only reaching all points in Manhattan at least as far north as Fourteenth street, but also intersecting every north and south line of travel in that borough.

JAMAICA ROUTE.

This line is planned to start at the intersection of East New York avenue and Broadway—which is the beginning of the loop first mentioned above—and is to run out under Jamaica avenue to Grand street in the former village of Jamaica. When built it will, in connection with the Broadway and Delancey street line, afford a very direct means of communication between Jamaica and the lower part of the Borough of Manhattan, by means of either the Broadway or the Eastern Parkway lines in Brooklyn, and will also enable passengers to reach almost any part of Brooklyn.

Commenting upon these routes the Board said:

BROOKLYN REQUIRED DIFFERENT TREATMENT

"The geographical conditions of Brooklyn necessitate a different solution of the rapid transit problem from that which has been attempted in Manhattan. Instead of a series of independent straight lines running north and south, Brooklyn rapid transit railways must have as their most important feature a series of large loops. In several cases like the Fourth avenue line to Fort Hamilton, the Flatbush and Ocean avenue line, the Jamaica and East New York line, and the line connecting the Williamsburgh and Blackwell's Island bridges, railways radiating out into the more suburban neighborhoods are desirable; but the controlling and essential feature of any Brooklyn system must inevitably consist of loop lines embracing large areas in Brooklyn and comparatively small areas in Manhattan. In Manhattan these loops should be so far extended as to connect with as many as possible of the main north and south lines of travel.

BRIDGES TO BE USED

"The bridges across the East River should be utilized for rapid transit purposes. For this purpose the consent of the Department of Bridges is essential. The general plans now transmitted provide that all work of construction upon either the Williamsburgh Bridge or the Manhattan Bridge must be done in accordance with the requirements of the Commissioner of Bridges.

"In addition, the plans hereto annexed provide for four tunnels under the East River, with a total capacity of ten tracks. There are, besides these, the proposed Thirty-fourth street two-track tunnel, and the two-track tunnels already contracted for and in course of construction. If all these plans are carried out there will be fourteen rapid transit railway tracks in tunnel under the East River, and at least four such tracks over it on the bridges.

"It is believed that the plans now submitted for consideration will, when fully constructed, afford a complete and adequate solution of the difficult rapid transit problem in Brooklyn.

RAPID TRANSIT IN QUEENS

"The time has not yet come for dealing fully with rapid transit in the Borough of Queens. All that can be done at the present moment is to provide, as has been done in some of the routes transmitted this day to your honorable body, for lines connecting Queens with Manhattan and Brooklyn. Such connecting lines are three in number, namely: *First,* a tunnel under the East River running from East Thirty-fourth street to Long Island City; *second,* a subway running from the Williamsburgh Bridge plaza in Brooklyn to the end of the Blackwell's Island Bridge in Queens; and, *third,* a subway running from East New York to Jamaica.

"The extensive scheme of railroad construction contemplated by the various plans adopted by this Board, and now* submitted to the city authorities for approval, could not be constructed at once, even if it were desirable to do so. But a general and comprehensive scheme is almost essential in dealing with such a situation as exists in Brooklyn, so that every route, or part of a route, that may hereafter be built, shall fit into a symmetrical system to be ultimately developed.

"If the seven routes [this refers to the Brooklyn plans] submitted herewith shall be approved by the city authorities and by the property owners or the courts, this Board intends to make contracts for routes or parts of routes as rapidly as the means at the disposal of the city will permit, and as fast as satisfactory contractors can be found; and all such contracts in accordance with the law as it now stands, must be submitted to your honorable body for its approval and consent.

"The policy which this Board recommends is, in its essential features, the policy very successfully pursued by the city of Paris, where a series of loop lines have been planned, and are being built by the city in sections.

---

* This communication to the Board of Estimate and Apportionment was dated June 5, 1905.

DETAILED PLANS TO BE PROVIDED HEREAFTER

"Many details as to the mode of construction of the lines proposed, the location of stations and station entrances, the character of rolling stock, the method of operation, and other important matters, must be left to be settled hereafter in the contracts to be submitted for approval. It need only be said, at present, that it is the intention of the Board to avail itself fully of the valuable experience gained in the subways now constructed or constructing, and of the better knowledge that prospective bidders possess as to the possibilities of sub-surface passenger railways."

FULTON STREET ENTRANCE—N. Y. SUBWAY.

CHAPTER XIX.

FINANCIAL STATEMENT.

The following statements show the amounts expended by the Rapid Transit Railroad Commission from the time of its creation by the Act of 1894 to January 1, 1905: COST OF WORK DONE

The total amount expended for work done and materials furnished under the Manhattan-Bronx contract up to January 1, 1905 . . . . $33,614,000

The total amount expended for work done and materials furnished under the Brooklyn-Manhattan contract up to January 1, 1905 822,882

This latter item represents a construction cost of about $4,114,413, as the contract price was only about 20 per cent. of the actual cost of doing the work.

The total yearly expenditures for regular and extra work have been as follows: YEARLY EXPENDITURES

	1900	1901	1902	1903	1904	TOTAL
Regular work......	$1,685,000	$10,343,000	$11,436,000	$6,930,000	$3,220,000	$33,614,000
Extra work........	....	162,000	949,994	2,241,528	951,730	4,305,252
Total........	$1,685,000	$10,505,000	$12,385,994	$9,171,528	$4,171,730	$37,919,252

In the following table are presented the disbursements of the Commission during yearly periods from 1894 to January 1, 1905. It will be observed that the expenses of the administrative and general office were $299,278 and the legal expenses $290,714. The total expense of the engineering department, including all salaries, office rent and expenses, instruments and supplies, amounted to only $2,106,870, or the remarkably small proportion of 5 per cent. of the total expenditure of the Commission. In this expenditure is included work done in the preparation of plans not yet executed, in studies for the Brooklyn Bridge terminals, and for other objects not connected with either Contract No. 1 or No. 2, and which may justly be considered as outside work.

GENERAL FUND, 1894—1904.

DISBURSEMENTS.

Total amount of disbursements made under the direction of the Board of Rapid Transit Railroad Commissioners during the period from 1894 to 1904:

	Administrative and General Office.	Engineering.	Legal.	Total.
1894. Amount of disbursements	$2,929 10	$1,271 34	$28 30	$4,228 74
1895. " " "	6,048 49	26,250 29	25,688 13	57,986 91
1896. " " "	35,572 34	17,028 82	31,457 53	84,058 69
1897. " " "	5,230 06	21,395 86	38,925 73	65,551 65
1898. " " "	4,521 15	17,930 31	29,519 13	51,970 59
1899. " " "	2,826 94	3,698 00	20,551 30	27,076 24
1900. " " "	53,866 33	161,047 23	27,356 19	242,269 75
1901. " " "	39,023 86	348,258 30	31,861 62	419,143 78
1902. " " "	45,576 10	458,389 79	33,547 26	537,513 15
1903. " " "	45,719 42	520,664 27	24,332 55	590,716 24
1904. " " "	57,965 11	530,936 37	27,446 87	616,348 35
	$299,278 90	$2,106,870 58	$290,714 61	
Total amount of General Fund disbursements, from 1894 to 1904, inclusive				$2,696,864 09

CORPORATE STOCK, 1894-1904.

MANHATTAN-BRONX CONSTRUCTION FUND.

Total amount of proceeds credited of the Corporate Stock issued by The City of New York for the construction of the Manhattan-Bronx Rapid Transit Railroad during the period of:

			PROCEEDS.
1900.	Amount of Stock issued	$1,000,000 00	
	" " Premium	105,400 00	
			$1,105,400 00
1901.	Amount of Stock issued	$11,000,000 00	
	" " Premium	635,361 46	
			11,635,361 46
1902.	Amount of Stock issued	$12,500,000 00	
	" " Premium	803,663 70	
			13,303,663 70
1903.	Amount of Stock issued	$11,865,000 00	
	" " Premium	237,487 72	
			12,102,487 72
1904.	Amount of Stock issued	$5,885,000 00	
	" " Premium	82,938 37	
			5,967,938 37

Total amount of proceeds applicable to the construction of the Manhattan-Bronx Rapid Transit Railroad, from 1900 to 1904, inclusive............ $44,114,851 25

BROOKLYN-MANHATTAN CONSTRUCTION FUND.

Total amount of proceeds credited of the Corporate Stock issued by The City of New York for the construction of the Brooklyn-Manhattan Rapid Transit Railroad during the period of:

			PROCEEDS.
1903.	Amount of Stock issued	$301,000 00	
	" " Premium	715 29	
			$301,715 29
1904.	Amount of Stock issued	$1,065,000 00	
	" " Premium	15,359 13	
			1,080,359 13

Total amount of proceds applicable to the construction of the Brooklyn-Manhattan Rapid Transit Railroad from 1902 to 1904, inclusive......... $1,382,074 42

CONSTRUCTION FUNDS, 1894-1904

DISBURSEMENTS.

MANHATTAN-BRONX CONSTRUCTION FUND.

Total amount of disbursements made in the construction of the Manhattan-Bronx Rapid Transit Railroad during the period:

	Work and Materials.	Extra Work and Materials.	Terminals.	Real Estate.	Interest on Corporate Stock.	Total.
1900. Amount of disbursements..	$1,685,000 00	....	....	....	....	$1,685,000 00
1901. " "	10,343,000 00	$162,000 00	....	$9.515 45	$165,013 90	10,679.529 35
1902. " "	11,436,000 00	631,000 00	....	141,391 72	547,031 41	12.755,423 13
1903. " "	6,930,000 00	2.563,021 47	$1,048,251 72	512,004 90	947,481 56	12,000,759 65
1904. " "	3,220,000 00	991,729 86	701.748 28	863,195 62	1,305,865 78	7,082,539 54
	$33,614,000 00	$4.347.751 33	$1.750,000 00	$1,526,107 69	$2,965.392 65	

Total amount of Manhattan-Bronx Construction Fund disbursements from 1900 to 1904, inclusive... $44,203,251 67

BROOKLYN-MANHATTAN CONSTRUCTION FUND.

Total amount of disbursements made in the construction of the Brooklyn-Manhattan Rapid Transit Railroad during the period:

	Work and Materials.	Real Estate.	Interest on Corporate Stock.	Total.
1903. Amount of disbursements..............................	$202.457 06	$706 80	$5 87	$203.169 73
1904. " "	620.425 62	1.200 00	20,196 40	641,822 02
	$822,882 68	$1,906 80	$20.202 27	

Total amount of Brooklyn-Manhattan Construction Fund disbursements, from 1902 to 1904, inclusive.. $844,991 75

SUMMARY OF DISBURSEMENTS, 1894-1904.

Total amount of General Fund disbursements	$2,696,864 09
" " " Manhattan-Bronx Construction Fund disbursements	44,203,251 67
" " " Brooklyn-Manhattan Construction Fund disbursements	844,991 75
Total amount disbursed by the Board of Rapid Transit Railroad Commissioners from June 18, 1894, to December 31, 1904	$47,745,107 51

PASSENGER TRAVEL DURING FIRST YEAR.

The subway was opened for business October 27, 1904. During the first few days the road was crowded with curiosity travel, the total for five days being 1,294,000, or a daily average of 258,800. From that time the traffic fell to a minimum for a week day of 172,288 on November 10. From this minimum there was a steady and substantially even increase as the public became acquainted with the road, so that the daily average travel for November, including Sundays, was 205,030. The growth continued during December, on the last day of which 358,566 passengers were carried; the daily average for the month was 283,773. No railroad had ever before shown such a traffic at the end of two months after its opening. During the entire year the subway carried an average of about 300,000 passengers each day. The stations ranked in the following order in the amount of business done: Brooklyn Bridge, Grand Central, Fourteenth street, Fulton street, and Times Square.

The other transportation lines in the Borough of Manhattan, while losing somewhat as the result of the opening of the new line, did not lose anything like the total travel shown on the subway. It is evident that the new facilities created new travel. This new travel is largely due to the convenience of the combined local and express service. The local trains are used largely as collecting and distributing trains for the expresses, many local train passengers alighting at each express station, their places being taken by others coming from the express trains and who are to be discharged at the local stations.

As was to be expected, the Brooklyn Bridge station has done the largest business. This station absorbed all the travel south of the bridge during the first few months; but much of this was diverted after the opening of the stations on the Broadway extension to the Battery.

CHAPTER XX.

RAPID TRANSIT IN OTHER CITIES

LONDON.

LONDON A RAILROAD CITY

London is a city of railways. In the city and its suburbs there are 531 stations. With the opening of roads now under construction, this number will be increased to more than 600. The length of all the lines—trunk, local, and tubular—exceeds 630 miles. There are 22 stations that may be regarded as termini. Into these each day go 4,252 suburban trains, and 445 other trains. The main object of rapid transit enterprises has been to get people from scattered termini to their places of business. Works, now nearing completion, will give 52 new stations, and new connections with existing underground railways. Electrification of the local lines, and separation as far as possible from trunk line traffic, will greatly increase the number of trains and greatly promote public convenience.

Four-fifths of the half-million people brought into central London before half-past ten every day are conveyed by railways; the remainder by tramways. The interior underground and surface roads carry not less than 600,000,000 passengers per annum. Of this number the District, Metropolitan, North London, City and South London, and Central London, carried 258,000,000 passengers in 1904. The Great Northern and City carried 14,000,000. The Great Northern, Piccadilly and Brompton will carry 116,000,000; the Charing Cross and Hampstead, 95,000,000; the Baker Street and Waterloo, 116,000,000; and the electrified District and Metropolitan, 100,000,000.

ROADS UNDER PRIVATE CONTROL

These roads are all private enterprises. The city derives no benefit from the privileges granted; and, beyond the restrictions embodied in the acts as to methods of construction and operation, the companies are free to pursue their own policies.

THAMES TUNNEL

The first tunnel built for use in the transportation of passengers was that under the Thames, from Wapping to Rotherhithe. The structure was designed by Isambard Brunel, father of the designer and builder of the *Great Eastern*, and it was there that the shield method was introduced, but not in connection with compressed air. Sir John Rennie, speaking of this work before the Institution of Civil Engineers in January, 1846, said that it was noted "for magnitude, boldness in design, and ingenuity in the means of construction, as well as for the extraordinary difficulties by which the work was attended."

Operations were commenced, in 1825, by a private company. The work was soon suspended. In 1837, a Treasury loan having been granted, it was taken up again. The following description is from the address referred to:

DESCRIPTION

"The two arched openings are 1,200 feet long, with spans 14 feet long and 16 feet 4 inches high. The openings are separated by a pier 4 feet thick, having 64 lateral arches of 4 feet span between the openings. The whole is surrounded with massive walls. The external walls, including openings, are 38 feet wide and 22 feet high. The structure is approached at each end by a perpendicular shaft 50 feet in diameter and 80 feet deep. The tunnel was intended to be carried forward to the surface of adjoining streets at such inclination that carriages could easily pass through it from both sides of the river. The crown of the tunnel is 16 feet below the bed of the river.

METHOD OF BUILDING

"In order to carry into effect this very difficult work unusual means and precautions were necessary. The ordinary wooden center framing scarcely presented sufficient strength and connection for that purpose. Brunel, accordingly, invented a cast-iron frame (which he termed a shield) sufficiently large to embrace the whole width and height of the intended structure, and divided into 36 compartments, each sufficiently large for a man to work in, yet capable of being closed to prevent access of water when required. The whole was impelled forward, as the work progressed, by powerful screws bearing against the completed walls behind. This ingenious contrivance was perfectly successful. Although the work was twice stopped by the irruption of the Thames, the apertures were closed with bags of clay and other materials, and the structure was continued with extraordinary perseverance until finally completed and opened to the public in 1843. The whole was constructed with bricks set in Roman cement, and cased inside with the same material; and it gives every prospect of permanence and solidity."

One of the claims brought forward in favor of this scheme was that the entrance on the street would not occupy more space than an omnibus. The tunnel now forms part of the line of the East London Railway.

TOWER SUBWAY

The first underground system, in the strict meaning of that term, was the Tower Subway, which was started in February, 1869, and finished in the following December. It was designed by Peter Barlow, and finished by his son. It was intended to provide means of communication, by omnibus, under the Thames and other large rivers. It was advertised as "the only system capable of relieving the street traffic of the Metropolis."

The following information in relation to this tunnel is condensed from an address by Charles B. Vignoles, president of the Institution of Civil Engineers, in January, 1870:

The subway consists of two shafts, one on Tower Hill, and the other on the opposite side of the river, near Tooley street, in the Borough. Each shaft is 10 feet inside diameter and is sunk about 60 feet, penetrating well inside the London clay. They are connected by a circular tube 7 feet clear diameter and 1,350 feet in length. The grade at each end is 1 in 40. Passengers are conveyed up and down in lifts operated by steam. Transit through the tunnel is made by omnibus along a single line of railway, the hauling being done by wire ropes. The shield was forced forward by screws, as in the former case, the tunnel being lined with cast-iron plates as the work progressed. The shield overlapped the finished tube "like the covering to the object glass of a large telescope." The length under the Thames was finished in 15 weeks, the cost being $90,000. Mr. Vignoles says: "In this way between 3,000 and 4,000 persons can be conveyed between Tower Hill and Tooley street daily at a charge of one penny only."

Both of these schemes were strictly local in character, and were intended to provide convenient means for passing the river, and to relieve congestion in the immediate neighborhood of their termini. They were not meant to form an integral part of any comprehensive plan of rapid transit. That they were afterward so used was due solely to circumstances of location.

TWO TYPES OF UNDERGROUND ROADS

From a paper by Basil Mott and David Hay, read before the International Engineering Congress at St. Louis last year, we find that the existing underground railways of London are of two distinct types, namely, those constructed just below the surface, and approached by stairs from the street level, and the deep level, or tube railways, built in the London clay, at depths varying from 40 to 100 feet, and approached by elevators.

Fifty years ago an act of Parliament was obtained for the "North Metropolitan Railway, from Paddington to the Post Office, with extensions to Paddington and the Great Western Railway, to the General Post Office, to the

MANSION HOUSE STATION—LONDON UNDERGROUND.

ROADS OPENED London and North-Western Railway, and to the Great Northern Railway." Subsequently authority for further extensions was obtained, and the various parts of the road, which now constitute the inner circle of the underground system, were opened for traffic as follows:

Paddington to Farringdon street (Metropolitan Railway) . .	1863
Farringdon street to Moorgate street (Metropolitan Railway) .	1865
Paddington to South Kensington (Metropolitan Railway) . .	1868
South Kensington to Westminster (Metropolitan District) . .	1868
Westminster to Mansion House (Metropolitan District) . . .	1868
Mansion House to Aldgate (Joint Line)	1876
Aldgate to Moorhead street (Metropolitan)	1884

Other extensions, which are only partly underground, have been constructed as follows:

Hammersmith and Paddington, 1863.
Baker Street and Swiss Cottage, 1868.

East London Railway:

New Cross to Wapping, through Brunel's old Thames Tunnel,	1869
Wapping to Whitechapel, Great Eastern Railway	1876
Hammersmith and Ealing	1879
Connection with District Railway	1884
Earl's Court to Putney Bridge	1880
Putney Bridge to Wimbledon	1889
Whitechapel and Bow	1902
Ealing and South Harrow	1903

Messrs. Mott and Hay say:

CLAY-LEVEL TUNNELS "The enormous cost of constructing the shallow railways through the busy centers of London is, under existing circumstances, prohibitive; and, with the exception of the Whitechapel and Bow, no such railway has been carried out since the completion of the Circle from Aldgate to Moorhead street, in 1884. In order to avoid the heavy capital expenditure, the late J. H. Greathead proposed the alternative system of deep-level, iron-lined, tube railways constructed in the London clay, which is a strong impervious clay, and extends practically under the whole Metropolitan area."

At the present time the existing deep lines and those under construction or authorized are as follows:

DEEP LEVEL LINES

City and South London	Opened 1890
Waterloo and City	" 1898
Central London	" 1900
Great Northern and City	" 1904
Baker Street and Waterloo	Under construction
Great Northern, Piccadilly and Brompton . . .	"
Charing Cross, Euston and Hampstead	"
North West London	Authorized
District Deep-Level	"

All of the deep tunnels are iron-lined tubes, circular in section, constructed under the streets to avoid the purchase of property, and at a sufficient depth to prevent interference with pipes and sewers.

STATIONS

"The station tunnels, containing the platforms, are generally 21 feet 2½ inches internal diameter and from 300 to 400 feet in length, lined with concrete and tiled. The only property purchased is for the surface stations and the power station. Upon the station sites are sunk the shafts for lifts and stairs communicating with the platforms. The lifts are an essential feature of the deep-level tubes, and though adding to the cost of working the line, they enable the tunnels to be constructed in the clay, and have been generally adopted. These lifts are utilized during construction as working shafts from which all the tunnels are driven, and no openings are required in the streets. Consequently there is no disturbance of traffic."

Separate tunnels, having an average diameter of 11½ feet, are provided for the up and down lines. The advantages of separate tunnels are presented in the following:

DESCRIPTION OF TUNNELS

"In narrow streets, where double-line tunnels would be impossible without encroaching upon adjoining property, the two tubes can be placed one over the other without difficulty, and no property need be purchased.

"The ventilation is assisted materially by the trains moving always in the same direction in each tunnel.

"The gradients, approaching and departing from the stations, can be arranged to give a steep gradient with the load when departing. These gradients, where feasible in practice, are made 1 to 30, with a fall of 10 feet, which secures a very rapid acceleration, and reduces the power required approximately 25 per cent. The approaching gradients are usually from 1 in 60 to 1 in 100. With both lines in one tunnel the gradients, with and against the load, are necessarily the same.

"Where headway is important in passing under existing railways, or deep-level sewers, etc., two tunnels have an advantage.

"Two small single-line tunnels are cheaper than one large double-line one."

FIRST TUBE RAILWAY

The pioneer of all tube railways was the City and South London, opened for traffic in 1890. The following paragraph is from a report to the Board of Rapid Transit Railroad Commissioners of New York, by Wm. Barclay Parsons, chief engineer, in 1894:

DESCRIPTION OF TUBES

"This line is interesting for two reasons: First, it was built by a totally different method of construction from the other London railways; second, it uses electricity for its motive power. It consists of two cast-iron tubular tunnels. These tubes are at a distance of from 40 to 80 feet beneath the surface, following generally the lines of the streets, and nearly always on the same level and distant a few feet from each other. In one street, however, which was so narrow as to prevent the tubes from being driven side by side without encroaching upon private property, one tube was depressed and carried beneath the other. According to the company's report the road has cost £267,000 per mile.

"The road is operated from 6 A. M. to 11:30 P. M., with a headway in the busy portion of the day of about 4 minutes. The longest distance between any two stations is three-quarters of a mile, and the shortest slightly less than half a mile. The street level at the stations is generally about 50 feet above the platform level, communication being maintained by means of two staircases and two elevators. The elevators cost annually about £2,650 to operate; a cost per passenger of about 1-10 penny or over 5 per cent. of the gross receipts. The fare is 2 pence for any distance.

VENTILATION

"Ventilation is secured automatically by the piston action of the trains, which nearly fill the tunnel, so that each train propels in front of it a column of air which finds its way to the street through the stairways or elevator shafts, while the same train is sucking down through the previous station a similar amount of fresh air."

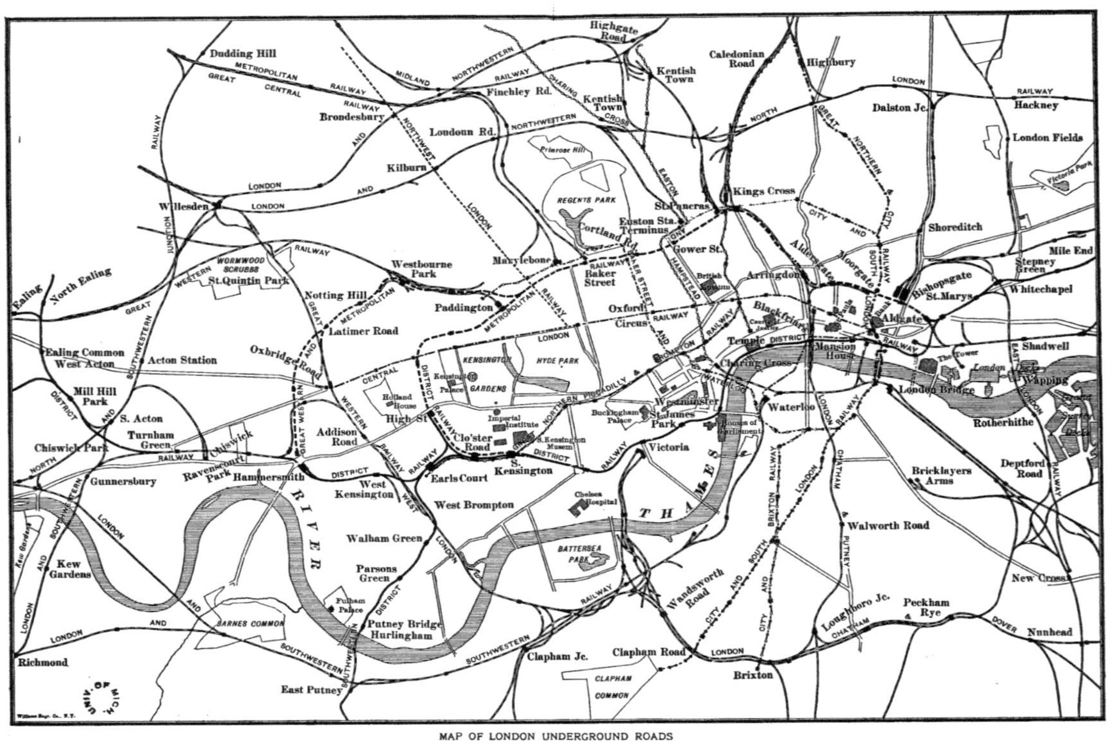

MAP OF LONDON UNDERGROUND ROADS

The following table is of value as showing the growth in the passenger traffic of this road: GROWTH

	June, 1891.	June, 1904.
Length of line	3 miles, 12 chains	6 miles, 9 chains
Train mileage	174,435	589,401
Receipts	£19,688	£80,204
Working expenses	£15,521 = 79 %	£36,569 = 45.58 %
Number of passengers carried	2,412,343	10,225,987
Dividend	Nil	2½ per annum
Number of carriages	30	142
Number of locomotives	14	52

The best known of the deep subways is the Central London. This is located under some of the most important sections of the city, as it extends from Shepherd's Bush to the Bank, a distance of about 6 miles. The first act authorizing the construction of this railway was passed in 1891; work was begun in 1894, and the line was opened in 1900. CENTRAL LONDON

At first the trains were drawn by electric locomotives, each train consisting of seven cars, giving a seating capacity of 48 passengers each, and drawn by a locomotive weighing 42 tons, the total weight of the train being 140 tons. It was found that the heavy locomotive caused vibrations in the tunnels, which were communicated to the surface and gave rise to complaints. It was, therefore, decided to adopt the system of multi-polar control, by which, from one point in the train, different cars could be actuated. The maximum service of a train every two minutes is maintained during the two busy morning and evening hours. The operation for the first six months of last year was: MOTIVE POWER

Passengers	22,921,651
Train miles	652,041
Car miles	4,654,423
Ton miles	76,637,950
Passengers per train mile	35.15

These figures show that the average number of passengers carried per train on each trip is 203. The seating capacity of each train is 330.

Particular attention has been paid to the ventilation of this tunnel. At the Shepherd's Bush end a large fan is operated which draws the air through the whole tube every night. This fan is sufficiently powerful to clear the air VENTILATION

BROAD STREET FREIGHT STATION, LONDON.

twice during the three hours while the traffic is stopped. Chemical examination of the air in the tube showed that it was by no means bad, while bacteriological observations gave results that were better than in the street.

The next important line to be opened was the Great Northern and City, in 1904. This runs from Finsbury Park to a station at the junction of Moorgate street, Princess street, and Lothbury. This tube connects with all the others by means of passageways. It is one of the most popular of all the tubes because of its extra diameter, its comfortable carriages, and its excellent ventilation.

BLACKWALL TUNNEL

Thirty years ago it was recognized that additional river crossings were needed below London Bridge, but it was not until 1887 that the Blackwall Tunnel Act was obtained. The first proposition was to build three tunnels, two for vehicular traffic and one for foot passengers. This plan was afterward changed, and it was decided to build one tunnel large enough to accommodate traffic of every description. During the latter part of 1891 the contract was let to S. Pearson & Son (who are now building the East River section of the Pennsylvania Railroad tunnels, New York,) for $4,215,640. Work was commenced the following year.

PLAN

The total length of this tunnel is 6,200 feet, of which 1,200 feet are below the river. The central section, for a distance of 3,112 feet, is lined with cast-iron. It is circular in section, with a clear diameter of 24 feet 3 inches, the roadway being 16 feet wide and the footpaths 3 feet 1½ inches. It has no connection with any of the underground roads.

In a lecture before the Society of Arts in January of the present year Robert P. Porter discussed the question, "Will the ever-increasing traffic of London at once absorb all this new accommodation?" He answers as follows:

EARNINGS

"The American metropolis, with a capacity for carrying 1,200,000,000 passengers per annum, is preparing to carry 2,000,000,000 passengers; but experts in that city believe that in less than ten years from the completion of the present facilities the requirements will be 3,000,000,000. In both cities what may be called the traveling habit increases with the increase of convenience in transit. The number of journeys, per head of population, has increased in a generation, in London, from 23 to 200 journeys, and, in New York, from 47 to over 400. Based on the earnings of the Central London on a passenger traffic of 55,000,000,

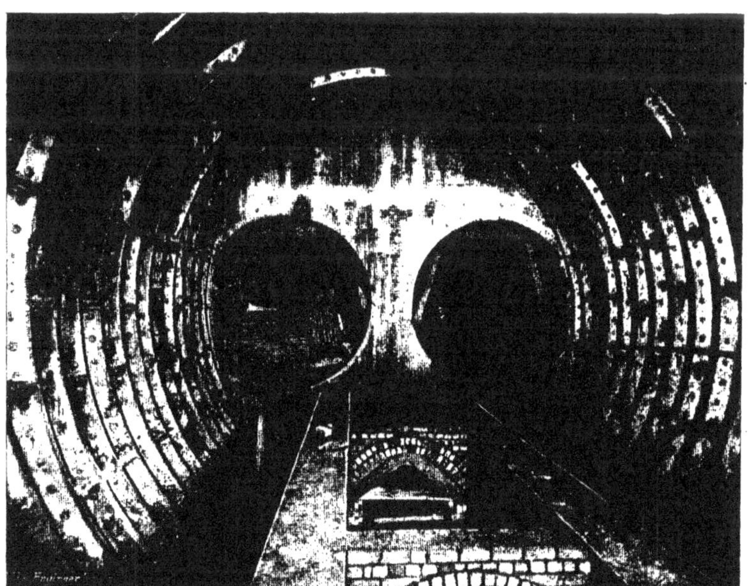

CROSS-OVER TUNNEL, LONDON.

the Baker Street and Waterloo should earn £230,000. The Great Northern, Piccadilly and Brompton, with a passenger traffic of 85,000,000, should earn £358,000, while the earnings of the Charing Cross, Euston and Hampstead line, with its 75,000,000 passengers per annum, should be in the neighborhood of £316,000. With a common power house the working expenses should be less than 50 per cent. of the earnings, the Central London being just over 49 per cent. With the growth of London the roads will undoubtedly become profitable investments."

BERLIN.

RINGBAHN

The Ringbahn, or Circle Railway, was opened in 1877. The route was laid out with little or no regard for public convenience, and, like other similar circular railways, it did not meet the needs of the people concerned. The Stadtbahn, an elevated road built wherever possible on masonry and earthwork, and employing iron for street and river crossings, was opened in 1882. It was constructed on a purchased right of way; and as the undertaking was found to be too expensive for private capital, the German Government completed the work, mainly as a military expedient to facilitate the movement of troops. The total length is 7½ miles. There are 5 miles of masonry arches, one mile of earth embankment, and one mile of iron structure. The route is through one of the best and most populous portions of Berlin. Much attention was given to architectural features. There are four tracks, two for local trains and two for trains from a distance. Of the 10 stations, those at the terminals and three others are for through trains, and at these baggage is received. The roofs of all the stations are made of iron and glass. The largest station is the Friedrich Strasse, having a length of 508 feet and a clear width of 125 feet. Statistics show that while the Ringbahn, with a much longer mileage, carried, in 1900, 37,000,000 passengers, the Stadtbahn carried 60,500,000.

STADTBAHN

ELECTRIC ROAD

Another line, called the Berlin Electric Elevated and Underground Railway, was commenced in 1897, and opened in 1902. It extends through the central part of the city from east to west. The underground part begins at the Zoölogical Garden, passes around Kaiser Wilhelm Gedächtniss-Kirche, and underneath the streets Tanuezien and Kleist to Nollendorf-Platz. Here the line rises to the surface. From this point it continues as an elevated structure through Oberaumstrasse, Skalitzecstrasse, Kottbuser Thor, and along Gitschinerstrasse, Hallesches Thor, and the Hallesches Ufer. It then crosses the Spree

Berlin and Spandau Canal
Gesundbrunnen
Schonhauser Allee
Humboldt Hain
Drilling Grounds
Prenzlauer Allee
Wedding
Goods Sta.
Weissensee
Putlitz Str.
Beussel Str.
Jungfernheide
RINGBAHN
(NORTH RING)
Drilling Grounds
Stettin
Landsberger Allee
Central Viehhof
Friedrichs Hain
RIVER
SPREE
Lehrte
Börse
Alex. Pl.
Westend
Charlottenburg
Thiergarten
Bellevue
Savigny Pl.
THIERGARTEN
Frankfurter Allee
Jannowitz Brücke
STADTBAHN
Schlesischer Bahnhof
Warschauer
CITY RAILWAY
Imperial Bank
Lietzen See
Zoological Garden
Potsdam Sta.
Eichkam
STADTBAHN
ELECTRIC
RAILWAY
Anhalt Sta.
ELECTRIC
RAILWAY
Stralau-Rummelsburg
Halensse
Halen See
Goods Sta.
Gorlitz
Treptow
Gross Görschen
Schöneberg
PUBLIC PARK
Military Sta.
DRILL GROUND OF THE BERLIN GARRISON
Schmargendorf
Wilmersdorf Friedenau
Ebers Str.
RINGBAHN
(SOUTH RING)
Pape Str.
Tempelhof
Hermann Str.
Rixdorf
RINGBAHN
(SOUTH RING)
Williams Engr. Co., N.Y.

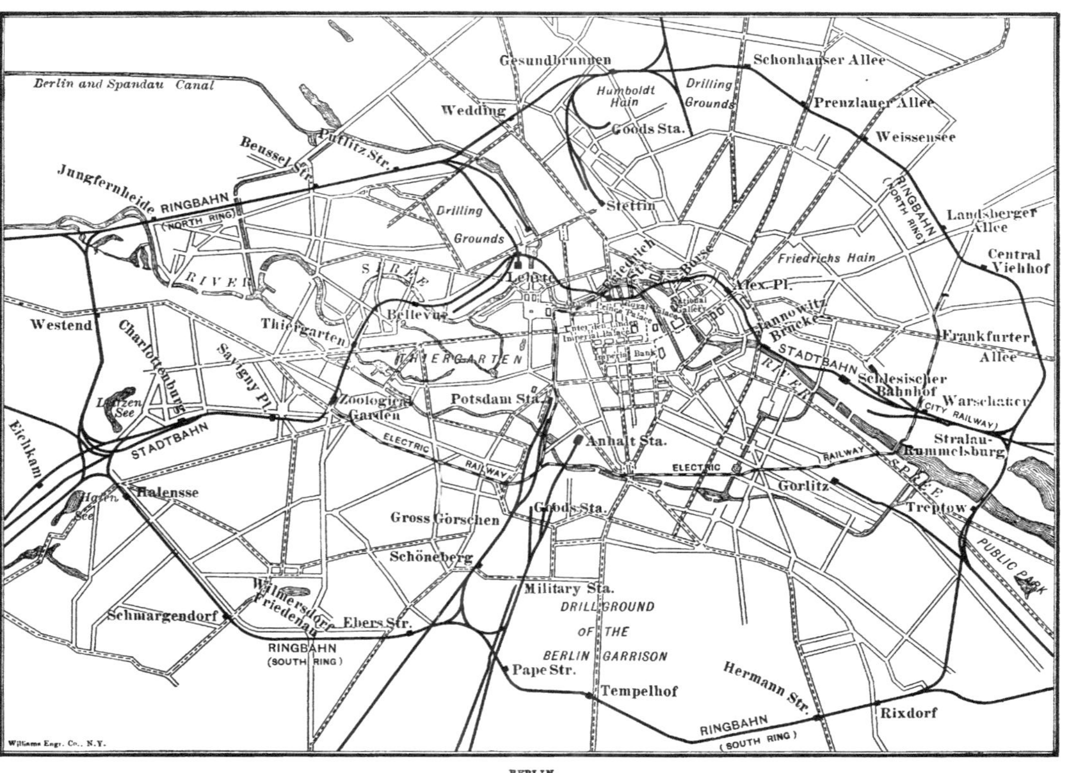

BERLIN.

BULOW STRASSE VIADUCT.

ELEVATED ROAD THROUGH BUILDING.

STATION AT SCHLESSISCHES THOR.

BRIDGE AND STATION AT STRAULAEUR THOR.

BERLIN.

INCLINE AT NOLLENDORF PLATZ—BERLIN.

River by the Oberbaum Brücke, and runs through Straulauer Thor and Warschauer Platz to Warschauer Brücke.

ROUTE

The total length of the underground and elevated lines is less than a dozen miles, the distance from the Warsaw Bridge to the Zoölogical Garden being about 7 miles. From the first station at Warschauer Bridge to Stralauer Gate is 351 yards, while from the latter to the next stop at Schlesisches Gate the distance is 495 yards. The next five overhead stations are at Oranien street, Kottbuser street, Prinzen street, Hallesches Gate and Möckern Bridge. These stops are from 606 to 1,120 yards apart, and the distance from Möckern Bridge to Buelow street is 1,665 yards. The stone arches of the overhead portion of the line comprise 1,026 yards, while the steel viaducts and bridges cover a distance of 7,960 yards. One of the conditions of the grant was that the overhead viaducts should have a clear headroom of 15 feet above the road level at all street crossings. The platforms are on the same level as the car floors. They are about 250 feet long, and are covered for more than half their length. There

BERLIN SUBWAY.

are no waiting rooms, the elevated portion of the station consisting merely of a hall, staircases, and ticket-distributing devices. The elevated structure has two tracks of standard gauge, placed 3 meters apart. The smallest curves have a radius of about 80 meters.

STRUCTURAL FEATURES

The tunnels were constructed under streets, the top of the arch being 2 feet below the surface. The distance between the transverse girders is 5 feet, the rise of the arches 8 inches, and the total width of the subway 21 feet 3 inches. Dryness is insured by the use of asphalt sheathing in the trenches, side walls, and roofs. The center of the span is supported by a row of steel columns. The tunnel has niches in the walls at every 75 feet, and is drained by a culvert in the center of each track, which leads to a sump from which the water is pumped into the sewers. The inclines from the tunnels to the viaducts have grades of 1.38. This portion of the system starts at the west of the city, north of Charlottenburg, near the Zoölogical Garden, and terminates at Nollendorf Place. The total length of tunnel is 1,856 yards, and the tunnel approaches are 622 yards long.

ELECTRICAL EQUIPMENT

The power house is near the center of the line, where the road meets the Ringbahn at the Potsdam station. The third rail system of distribution is used. The trains weigh 80 tons loaded, and consist of three cars, the first and last being motor cars. They are provided with motors upon each of the four axles. The motors are geared to obtain a train speed of 30 kilometers per hour. Each train is made up of two third-class and one first-class car. The train headway is from 3 to 5 minutes, according to the time of day, and the normal speed is from 18 to 25 miles an hour. Each train has a seating capacity of 125 people, with standing room for about 50 more.

COST

The total cost of constructing the tunnels, viaducts, stations, car sheds, and track equipment was $5,000,000, while the electrical equipment and rolling stock cost $1,000,000.

The line was built with private capital. The concession runs for a period of 30 years. The company paid a dividend of 3½ per cent. in 1903. The traffic in that year was 10 per cent. greater than in 1902.

THE BUDAPEST ELECTRIC SUBWAY.

Budapest, the beautiful capital of Hungary, has an electric underground railway about 2 miles in length, extending under Andrassy street—one of the finest residential streets in the world. Work was begun on this system in 1894,

VIEW SHOWING CONSTRUCTION—BUDAPEST.

KIOSK, BUDAPEST SUBWAY.

and completed about two years later. It is a double-track overhead trolley subway, a little smaller in cross section than the double-track Boston tunnel, which it closely resembles in design. The side walls are built of concrete masonry and support the steel channels which, with the arches sprung between them, form the roof. The street pavement is laid immediately upon these. Through the center of the tunnel is a row of steel columns supporting the roof.

PORTAL STADTWALDCHER—BUDAPEST.

The tunnel was constructed by the open-cut method, those portions of the street occupied by the work being closed to traffic.

The accompanying engravings convey a clear idea of the manner of prosecuting the work. The street is fenced off at each end of the excavation, and a fence is built down each side of the cut. The entrances are very ornamental in design, and in keeping with the neighborhood in which they are placed.

PARIS.*

The rapid transit problem of Paris has been solved in a manner widely different from that pursued in any other great city. This remark applies to the law providing for the construction, as well as to the methods used in prosecuting the work.

The law authorizing the Metropolitan Electric Railway System was adopted in March, 1898. Lines were to be built as follows:

LINES

From the Porte Vincennes to the Porte Dauphine.
A circular line following the old outside boulevards.
From the Porte Maillot to Ménilmontant.
From the Porte de Clignancourt to the Porte d'Orleans.
From the Boulevard de Strasbourg to the Austerlitz Bridge.
From the Cours de Vincennes to the Place d'Italie.
From the Palais Royal to the Place du Danube; and
From Auteuil to the Opéra through Grenelle.

FRANCHISE

The franchise was granted to the Campagnie Générale de Traction for a period of 35 years. This company was reorganized as a corporation whose only purpose should be the operation of the road, and by a State decree was called the "Compagnie du Chemin de fer Metropolitain de Paris."

The City of Paris took charge of all structural work; that is, of all tunneling, excavations, and viaducts, including the restoration of streets utilized to their former condition, and of the platforms in the stations, but not of the passageways giving access to them. All other expenses—such as those involved in the construction of tracks and electrical transmission lines, plants, and power stations, the purchasing of the necessary sites, the preparation of stairways and elevators for the stations and the cost of rolling stock, etc.—were to be met by the company.

The fares authorized between any two points on the railway are 15 centimes for a second-class and 25 centimes for a first-class ticket.

COMPENSATION PAID CITY

A part of the gross earnings is to belong to the City of Paris, at the ratio

* Much of the information contained in the following description of the Paris Subway is obtained from a valuable paper read by M. Biette, Chief Engineer of the Metropolitan, before the International Engineering Congress, held at St. Louis in October, 1904.

We are also indebted to M. Biette for the excellent photographs from which the accompanying half-tones were made.

LINES BUILT
CONTEMPLATED LINES
Porte de St.Quen
Porte de Clignancourt
Porte de la Villette
Porte d'Asnieres
Porte des Ternes
Av. de Villiers
Place du Danube
Porte Maillot
Pl.de l'Etoile
Gare de l'Est
Porte Dauphine
Opera
Place du Trocadero
Palais Royal
Place Gambetta
les Invalides
CHAMP DE MARS
Pte. de Montreuil
Pl.de la Bastille
Pl.de la Nation
Porte de Vincennes
Auteuil
SEINE
RIVER
Porte de St. Cloud
Porte de Versailles
Pl.d'Italie
Porte de Chatillon
Porte d'Orleans
Porte d'Italie
Williams Engraving Co., N.Y.

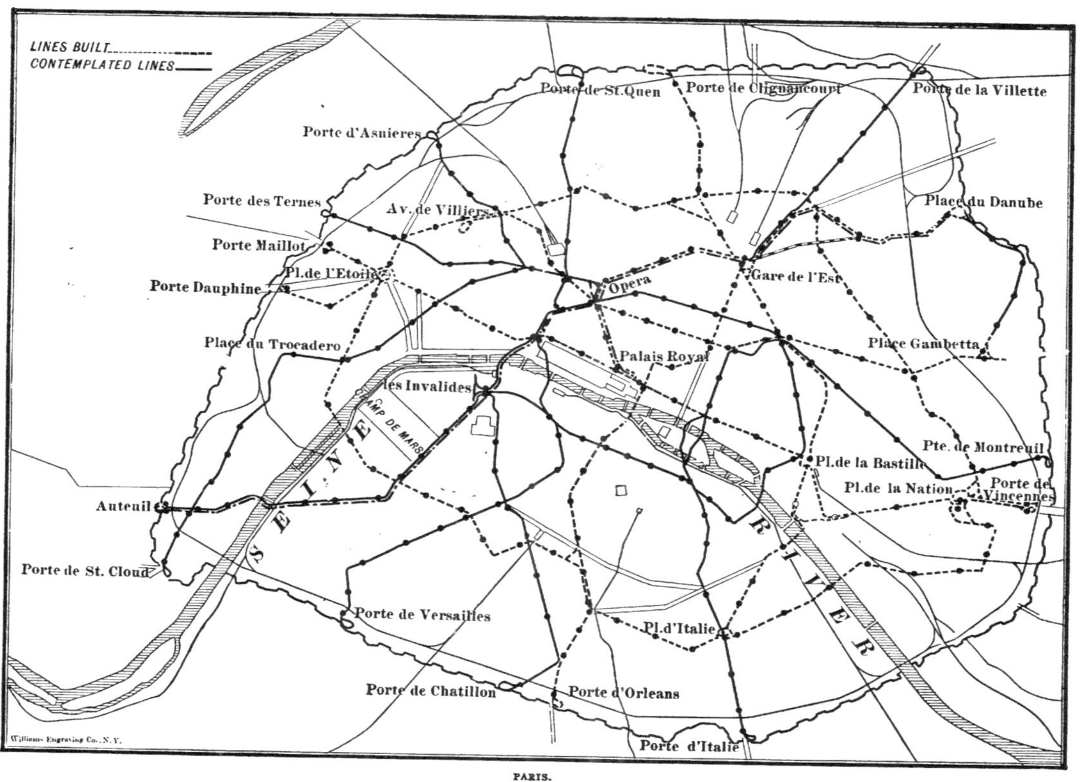

PARIS.

STATION, RUE D'ALLEMAGNE.

STATION, PLACE DE LA REPUBLIQUE.

PARIS.

VIADUCT—PARIS.

of .05 centimes for each second-class and .10 centimes for each first-class ticket. This is to be increased by .001 franc for each 10 million passengers till it reaches .055 and .105 franc, respectively, per ticket, as the number of passengers carried increases from 140 millions to 190 millions a year.

The lines form three distinct systems, and have a total length of 77 kilometers (about 45 miles), exclusive of the spurs connecting them. The first system must be finished by March, 1906, and the second and third ten years later. All the lines will be underground, except a part of the Circular Line, and the line from the Cours Vincennes to the Place d'Italie.

CITY PAYS PART OF COST

The city has been authorized to contract special loans amounting to 335 million francs for the purpose of defraying the expense of its part of the work. Of this amount 285 millions of francs will be needed to cover actual construction. The rest will be applied as follows: Borrowing expenses, 7 millions; cost of tearing up the streets at certain points, 28 millions, leaving a reserve of 15 millions, to be used later in the construction of branch lines and spurs. The total length of 77 kilometers is obtained by measuring the length of each line on its axis. If the side tracks, crossings, etc., are added, the total length will be 84.7 km., counting the single track for only half its actual length. The structural part of the railway will, therefore, cost the city an average of 3,400,000 francs per km. The cost to the company having the franchise is estimated at 1,500,000 francs per km., so that the cost per km. of double track is estimated at 4,900,000 francs.

APPRECIATION OF THE SYSTEM

The following paragraph illustrates the public appreciation of the subway system. M. Biette says: "According to the terms of the franchise annexed to the law of March 30th, 1898, the construction of the first three lines only was made compulsory, but the success following the opening of the first line was so great that it was decided to undertake the construction of the entire system. * * * The order in which the different lines are to be constructed was determined by the convention granting the franchise; but the City of Paris is allowed to construct more than one line at a time, provided the general order of construction is not changed. Advantage has been taken of this privilege. The new lines will increase the total length from 77 to 134 km."

IN OPERATION AND BUILDING

At the time M. Biette's paper was read the situation was as follows: Line No. 1, from the Porte de Vincennes to the Porte Maillot, the northern Circular Line; No. 2, from the Porte Dauphine to the Place de la Nation, along the boulevards on the right bank of the Seine, and the section of the southern Circular,

No. 2, between the Place de l'Etoile and the Seine, now in operation. The southern Circular Line, from the Seine to the Place d'Italie, along the boulevards, had been finished, so far as the tunnel was concerned, and it was necessary only to finish the great works at the two crossings of the Seine in order to connect it with the lines in operation. These works are now under way, and will be ready some time this year. Work has been commenced on Lines Nos. 4, 5 and 6, and the preliminary plans for the construction of Nos. 7 and 8 are under way.

The number of passengers carried in the first three years was as follows:

In 1901, 52,096,285.
In 1902, 63,021,068.
In 1903, 67,993,147.

DESIGN OF TUNNEL

From an engineering point of view the Paris tunnel cannot be described as a "tube," any more than the New York Subway. The London tubes, strictly so called, are circular in section, and formed of cast-iron plates. This form is admirably adapted to the soil of London, but was not considered suitable to conditions in Paris. The engineers adopted a plan having the following characteristics: There was to be no metallic tubing, except in crossing the Seine. A double-tracked masonry tunnel was to be built and was to run as near the surface as possible. This method was considered to have the following advantages: It would be economical to construct, facilities of operation would be greater, and the stations would be easier of access. It was thought also that the danger of disturbing adjacent buildings during construction would be less.

M. Biette remarks further:

"Objection to the surface plan adopted at Paris may be raised on the ground that it requires altering underground conduits, sewers, water and gas mains, electric cables, etc., which are very numerous in the subsoil of the metropolitan highways. This objection cannot be denied; but it has been possible to replace these conduits without serious trouble; and the expense incurred, although very heavy, is nothing compared to the increase in cost that the tube system would have caused to no purpose; such expenses, in any case, have no weight if the advantages of the plan adopted are considered."

STANDARD SECTION

The standard section of the double-tracked tunnel is formed by an elliptical arch, having a width of 7.10 m. and a rise of 2.07 m., supported by two side walls finished inside by circular arcs; the section is completed by an invert.

The width at the rail level is 6.60 m. Where it has not been possible to follow this design a metallic roof, supported by masonry walls, has been built. The parts of the tunnels connecting the different lines are single track, the arched roof being 4.30 m. wide. The stations are arched wherever the clearance allows; metal roofs are erected when this is not possible. A standard station, whether arched or metal-roofed, comprises two side platforms 75 m. long and 4.10 m. wide. They are reached by staircases opening on the streets, and leading into underground rooms where tickets are sold. Passengers reach the nearest platform by other staircases, and those more distant by similar staircases, after crossing the railway tracks by footbridges.

ELEVATED STRUCTURE

The elevated part of the system consists of a metal viaduct formed by a series of separate bents of variable lengths, composed of two side beams supporting the floor system on their lower flanges. These bents, as a rule, are carried on cast-iron columns; but when necessary to secure greater stability masonry pillars are used. In order that the viaduct may not interfere with street traffic, the length of the trusses conforms to local conditions. Spans of about 22 metres have been found most satisfactory, except where longer ones are needed for special reasons. Larger spans were resorted to in crossing important streets and railroad tracks; for instance, the crossing of the Northern and Eastern Railroads, on the right bank of the Seine, required three spans of 75.25 m. each. The lower chords of the girders are straight, and the upper ones parabolic.

The trackway ballast is supported by brick arches connecting the cross-beams. This system was adopted for the purpose of lessening the vibration from passing trains, and of reducing resulting noises and tremors to a minimum. When, however, the trusswork is longer than usual and this method would unduly increase the dead weight, the track is laid directly on a platform formed of cross-beams connected by stringers covered with metal plates. The minimum distance between the surface of the street and lower chords is 5.20 m., this clearance being sufficient to permit the passage of vehicles with high loads.

ELEVATED STATIONS

The elevated stations are constructed on the same plan as the viaducts, each having a total length of 75 m. Staircases lead from the street to intermediate platforms, where the ticket offices are placed, and from there to the station platforms.

As a rule, passengers have to change cars at junctions and points of transfer. This plan was introduced in order to avoid the danger of collisions in switching trains between lines, and loss of headway on given lines. Loss of time at terminals is avoided by the provision of loops, which permit trains to be moved directly from points of arrival to points of starting.

Two kinds of masonry are used in the underground work, sandstone and concrete; the first being employed for arches, and the second for side walls and floors. All visible facings inside the stations are covered with white tiles, or enameled brick; all other work with cement. All metal work, such as bridges, roofs, and stations, are made of soft rolled steel having an elongation of 23 per cent. under a breaking load of 43 kg. per square mm. of section.

The preliminary work, such as diverting sewers, water mains, and other conduits, is let out by public tender; this system being compulsory in France for public undertakings generally. The plan is described as follows:

METHOD OF BUILDING

"Each line is divided into sections, generally about 1,000 m. long, and never more than 1,500 m. long for underground work. For the elevated parts the length of the sections is limited to about 900 m. Each contractor has a time limit fixed for the completion of his work, and generally this limit is calculated by allowing one month for 100 m. underground, and three months extra for the preliminary organization of the plant. A large premium is given for each day gained on the limit fixed, and an equal fine imposed for each day of delay. By this arrangement the work is completed in a comparatively short time. Line No. 1, the first built, with a length of 10.5 km. (about 7 miles), was finished in 17 months of actual work, and Line No. 2, on the left bank of the Seine, with a length of 9.4 km., was finished in 18 months.

"On each section there is, generally speaking, only one point at which ground is broken; but other secondary points are sometimes authorized, as at stations or other works of special importance. At such points the contractor sinks vertical shafts in which electric elevators are installed for hoisting excavated material, and lowering materials of construction. In the ordinary construction of the tunnel the method followed is nearly always to construct the arch first, the side walls next, and then the floor.

"For stations, however, and arches of special works, where the span is more than 10 m., the side walls, or abutments, are first constructed in galleries, and then, as the case may be, the arch is constructed, or the metallic roof put in position; the core of the tunnel is then excavated, and finally the masonry for the floor is laid."

SHIELD NOT APPLICABLE

At first it was expected to construct Line No. 1 by means of a shield of the

VIEW SHOWING CONSTRUCTION—PARIS SUBWAY.

Brunel type. It was expected that the shield plan would do away with most of the breaking up of the streets. But better results were not obtained with it than with timbered headings. Where the design calls for a strong lining like cast-iron, and where progress is made through material of uniform consistency, the shield presents marked advantages; but in ground of a varying character, such as the sub-soil of Paris, the results are not so satisfactory. In that city excavations, bad fillings, foundations of old buildings, and the like, which prevent the regular advance of a mechanical device, are encountered. In ground of that kind it is often necessary to increase the strength of masonry, either by reducing the outside cross-section or by increasing the thickness. Such modifications are difficult to make when the shield is used.

ADVANCING HEADINGS

The heading was advanced by digging out the highest part of the tunnel and constructing the arch. In some localities good results were obtained by opening two headings simultaneously, one at the top and the other at the bottom, the last one being kept in advance of the first. The lower heading is used to carry out the earth, and the other to bring in the materials for the arch. The arch masonry is built in sections 3 m. in length. In solid ground the bench is nearly all taken out before the walls are begun; but in soft earth trenches of variable dimensions are cut before the bench is removed. When the arch and retaining walls have been completed, grout is forced behind the masonry so as to fill any spaces between the masonry and earth, these injections being made through holes left in the masonry during construction. The holes are provided over the whole surface of the arches and one-half meter down below the springings.

REMOVING EARTH

One of the most difficult problems to solve, in the construction of the Metropolitan Railway, was the removal of excavated material and the carrying in of materials of construction. If it is considered that when a bench is removed an average section produces from 800 to 1,000 cu. m. per 24 hours, it is easy to

BRIDGE ACROSS SEINE—PARIS.

understand how difficult it is to remove such amount of earth by means of ordinary carts in the center of the heavy traffic of Paris. Methods more modern, more rapid, and more economical were sought. For instance, in the central part of Line No. 1, running at a short distance from the Seine, the contractors did not hesitate to build special galleries, many hundreds of yards long, in order to connect the tunnel with the Seine, and thus allow the removal of the excavated material by boats. At other points the street car tracks connecting with the suburbs of Paris have been taken advantage of. Spurs have been constructed from these tracks to elevators in the working sites so as to allow the direct removal of excavated material without reloading. On Line No. 3 the earth coming from the central sections near the St. Lazare Station, the Opéra, and the Bourse has been carried beyond Paris by means of a temporary spur constructed specially to connect with the Ouest Railroad.

WORK AT THE SEINE

Lines 2 and 8 cross the Seine twice, and Lines 4 and 6 once. Lines 4 and 8 pass underneath the river through metal tubes. The Passy Viaduct is double-decked, one deck for carriage traffic and the other for trains. It occupies the site of a foot bridge connecting the Boroughs of Passy and Grenelle. It was necessary to do away with this bridge, but it was also essential not to cut the connection between the banks. The bridge was, therefore, moved back, parallel to itself, a sufficient distance to free the working sites of the viaduct. This bridge consists of two similar parts which correspond to the two arms that form the Seine at this place. The part above the wider arm had a length of 120 m., a width of 6.50 m., and a weight of 320 tons; the other had a length of 90 m., a width of 6.50 m., and a weight of 240 tons. Two methods were employed in moving the two spans. The wider arm was placed upon rolling timber platforms, supported on piles, and moved by means of windlasses, the distance being 30 m. The entire operation was performed, in four hours, without the slightest trouble, and without having interrupted in the least the traffic on the river. The other span was floated to its position on barges.

DIFFICULTIES ENCOUNTERED

The difficulties encountered by the engineers of these roads were of a type varying widely from those confronting the designers of underground roads in other large cities. The sewer, water, and gas pipes found in other works were here present, but a greater obstacle was the diversified character of the ground, which possessed different qualities in each section, and compelled the changing of the plans almost continually in order to overcome new troubles. One notable instance was as follows: Line No. 3 connects with the Circular Line, on the right bank of the Seine, at the Boulevard de Courcelles, between the Boulevard Malesherbes and the Avenue de Villiers. As originally planned this connection was to have been on the level, so that for a certain length the tunnel was made 18 m. wide, in order to accommodate four tracks and junctions between the two lines for handling the empty cars. But it was decided to provide for a possible extension of No. 3 toward the periphery, and as this could only be done by passing under No. 2, it became necessary to deepen the tunnel common to both lines, and to build at once the crossing of this line under the side wall of the great 18 m. arch. This task was done by alternating cross trenches, each 2 m. wide. The crossing under the other side wall of the arch, having a bad slanting direction, two galleries, joined together by a single track, have been substituted for the standard type of tunnel.

Another difficulty may be mentioned. This was caused by the formation of the sub-soil met in the construction of Line No. 3 at the Terminal Menilmontant, under the Avenue Gambetta and the Rue Belgrand. It is composed of gypsum marl that forms the bottom of a basin filled with clay or fine sand, both being impregnated with water. The water bearing sand forms a particularly troublesome element. The work was done as follows: The side walls were first undertaken in such a way as to obtain the drying of the thin sand. For this purpose a large number of wells were sunk from time to time through the layer of sand to the marl. These wells, sunk with all the care necessary, were provided with permanent means of drainage, and by their continued operation caused the semi-fluid ground to become firm enough to permit the construction of the tunnel.

Up to the present time the construction of the Metropolitan Lines has progressed rapidly; and a considerable advance, viewed from the length of actual construction, on the time allowance granted by the franchise, is noticeable.

The care taken to provide in Paris a rapid transit system that will serve the public needs admirably will be appreciated by those who carefully study the map of Paris given herewith, and the rapid transit lines laid down upon it.

It would be impossible, however for anyone to know how little the public were inconvenienced during the construction of the lines already completed, except by observation on the spot. A visitor to Paris, during the time of construction, might have gone about the city for days and have remained in ignorance of the fact that the work was going on.

GLASGOW SUBWAYS.

FIRST ROAD

In 1882 Parliament granted to the Glasgow City & District Railway a franchise to connect the two lines of the North British Railway, so that some of its trains could run through the city. This line is 3.12 miles long, and has four stations. It was opened in 1886. One mile was built by tunneling; 3,483 feet by cut and cover; 3,942 feet in open cut between retaining walls; 330 feet were under bridges, and 342 feet under the Queen street station, the main terminus of the railway. The road is double track. The tunnel is a brick arch, with a clear span of 26 feet in rock, and 27 feet in other material. On the urban portion of the line there are four stations, all of which are wholly or partly open at the top. The tunnel part of the road cost £334,000 per mile.

In 1888 the Caledonian Railway was authorized to construct the Glasgow Central Railway to connect its existing lines. This is a double-track road, 6.4 miles in length. In section the tunnel is a brick arch, supplemented with a concrete invert wherever the ground is soft. Where it was desirable to have the structure as near the surface as possible, a flat roof of plate girders was substituted for the arch. Most of the cut and cover work was done along Argyle street and the Trongate, the most crowded thoroughfares in the city. Before commencing the railway, it was necessary to rearrange all the street pipes and sewers for a distance of 2¼ miles.

BUILDING RESTRICTIONS

In the act granting permission to build the road, important clauses were introduced limiting interference with street traffic. Streets like Argyle were not to be torn up except between 12 P. M. Saturday and 5 A. M. Monday. Excavated material was removed through special openings, limited in area to 50 by 17 feet, and placed not nearer to each other than 200 yards. Streets of minor importance were torn up a portion at a time, but the surface had to be restored inside of three months.

Including those at the ends and the one at the terminus of the Maryhill Branch, there are 12 stations at average intervals of half a mile. Wherever possible the stations were made uncovered, only three being entirely roofed over. Five are partly underground, and four are entirely in the open. In general the stations are 600 feet in length and 47 feet in width, thus providing two platforms 13 feet wide.

CLAIMS FOR DAMAGES

Many claims for damages were made during the construction, but most of the suits were decided in favor of the company, the exceptions being cases where the time allowed for keeping the streets open was exceeded. Under the law in

England, no damages can be collected for commonplace or ordinary obstructions, the principle being that the right to make such obstructions is a part of the franchise, even though the company selects the site. A suit for damages was brought against the City & South London Railway because it had established its power station on property next to an orphan asylum, thereby rendering the latter uninhabitable. The decision was in favor of the defendant, on the ground that the company had statutory power to carry on the undertaking, and to do anything necessary to accomplish its object, even if it proved a nuisance, provided it exercised reasonable care and skill.

The total contract price for the work was £1,900,000, or about £300,000 per mile. The road itself, without equipment or station fittings, cost £1,020,000.

GLASGOW DISTRICT SUBWAY

In 1891 work was begun on the Glasgow District Subway, a line built for purely local traffic and having no connection with any other road. It is a two-track circular road, 6½ miles long, the route as far as possible following the street lines. The two tunnels are 11 feet in diameter, and are built of cast-iron plates. Each station, of which there are 15, is 150 feet long, with island platforms 10 feet wide and stairways 6 to 8 feet wide. Exclusive of land and equipment, the road cost £115,000 per mile.

GLASGOW HARBOR TUNNEL

The Glasgow Harbor Tunnel crosses the bed of the Clyde, and provides passageway for vehicles and pedestrians. It comprises three tubes, having a shaft at each end 80 feet in diameter and sunk 75 feet below the surface. Each tube is 16 feet in diameter in the clear and 720 feet long. Two of the tubes are paved for vehicles, the third being for foot passengers only. In each shaft are six elevators for handling vehicles and passengers.

BOSTON.

Boston was confronted with a peculiar transportation problem. Numerous radiating lines converged on a few streets at the center of the city. Some of the busiest thoroughfares were so occupied by electric cars that vehicular traffic was greatly interfered with. Many of the streets in the congested district were narrow and crooked, and were bordered by business establishments requiring the employment of many wagons. The problem was not so much one of providing rapid transit facilities as of relieving the streets within an area about one mile long and not much more than a quarter of a mile wide. The solution was reached by building a subway through the congested district, and placing all the trolley lines within it. The road has been finished, the congestion relieved, and the streets returned to the unrestricted use of pedestrians and ordinary vehicles. A comprehensive idea of the old and of the present state of affairs may be formed from an examination of the two engravings, given herewith, showing the conditions of Tremont street before and after the improvement.

BOSTON ELEVATED COMPANY

The Boston Elevated Railway Company was incorporated in 1894 with a capital of $10,000,000. This company was to build and operate certain lines of elevated railroad in Boston and vicinity. The company deposited, with the city Treasurer, bonds to the amount of $500,000 to indemnify the city for any damages. It is to be assessed, and to pay taxes the same as any street railway. On and after the first of January, 1907, the company is to pay a franchise tax of not less than 1 per cent., nor more than 5 per cent., of its gross earnings, as the Board of Approval may decide. This tax is to be paid into the treasury of the Commonwealth, and distributed to the different towns and cities affected, in proportion to the mileage operated in each.

This road must not be confused with the lines authorized by the Boston Transit Commission at a later period. It controls the elevated roads of the city, but has nothing to do with the subways, with the exception of a short section constructed solely for its own exclusive accommodation, as will be explained presently.

BOSTON TRANSIT COMMISSION

The Boston Transit Commission was created by an act approved July 2, 1894, and accepted at a special election held July 24, 1894. The commission is composed of five members, three of whom were named in the act, and two appointed by the Governor. The term of office was originally 5 years, but this was afterward extended to the first day of July, 1906. If the term of the commission should expire before the completion of the work, the duties are to be assumed by the mayor, city engineer, and treasurer. Any vacancy in the commission is to be filled by the mayor, subject to the approval of the board of aldermen. The act names the routes along which the commission may build subways, but the commission cannot extend these lines or construct new ones; it has no initiatory power. Provision is made for building a bridge over the Charles River. The commission may, on or before the completion of the subway, grant locations for tracks in it to any street railway company, and "shall order all surface tracks to be removed from Tremont street, between Boylston street and Scollay Square, and from Boylston street, between Park Square and Tremont street; and may order any other tracks that, in its opinion, have become unnecessary by the construction of said subway and tunnels, and which are

Back Bay Sta.
North Station
CHARLES RIVER
CHARLESTON BRIDGE
CAUSEWAY ST.
PUBLIC GARDEN
BOSTON COMMON
COLUMBUS
BEACON
BOWDOIN ST.
BOYLSTON ST.
PARK ST.
TREMONT ST.
COURT
CANAL ST.
WASHINGTON ST.
UNION ST.
HANOVER
COMMERCIAL ST.
COMMERCIAL AVE.
STATE ST.
ATLANTIC AVE.
EAST BOSTON TUNNEL
HARRISON AVE.
BEACH ST.
South Station
FORT POINT CHANNEL
PROPOSED TUNNEL IN WASHINGTON ST. SHOWN THUS
" CHANGES IN SUBWAY " "
" ELEVATED RAILWAY TO CAMBRIDGE " "
" CAMBRIDGE ST. SUBWAY " "
BOSTON SUBWAY AND EAST BOSTON TUNNEL " "
ELEVATED RAILWAY " "
ENTRANCES TO STATIONS WASHINGTON ST. TUNNEL "
Williams Engraving Co., N.Y.

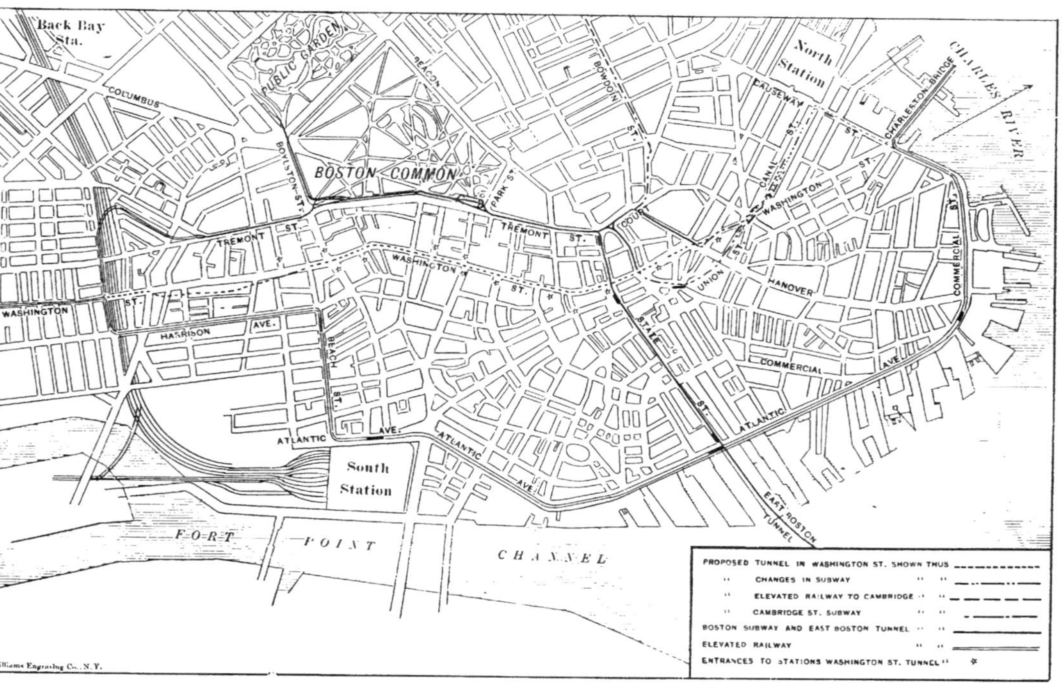

BOSTON.

above said subway and tunnels, or within a distance of 1,000 feet from any entrance to said tunnels, to be removed from the streets." Electric wires may be placed in the tunnel at such compensation as may be determined by the commission.

EXPENDITURE LIMITED

The work is to be paid for by bonds issued by the city treasurer, not to exceed $7,000,000, and such further amount for the Charlestown Bridge, in addition to the $750,000 appropriated by the city council, as may be necessary for its completion. A sinking fund is created into which are to be paid all premiums from the sale of bonds, and all proceeds from sale of lands or rights to use the subways.

On the completion of the subway the commission may contract for the use of the tracks to any street railway company for a period not exceeding 20 years, the compensation to be determined by the commission, subject to the approval of the railroad commissioners.

ADDITIONAL ROUTES

The act of 1902 provided for the construction of an additional subway from Broadway and Washington street to Court and State streets, and thence to Adams Square, Haymarket or Causeway street, together with connections with the East Boston Tunnel and the existing subway. This further subway was to contain two tracks exclusively for use by elevated trains, and two tracks for surface cars.

AGREEMENT WITH BOSTON ELEVATED

Within 90 days after the passage of the act, the commission executed with the company (Boston Elevated Railway Company, mentioned above) a contract for the exclusive use of this short section of the subway for a period of 25 years from the date of opening. The annual rental is to be 4½ per cent. of the cost of the tunnel. The cost of the tunnel includes all expenditures for construction and acquisition and interest at the rate of 3¼ per cent., per annum, on the debt incurred in construction prior to the beginning of the use. If the company execute the contract, it may, subject to the approval of the Board, construct certain additional lines of elevated railway. Upon the completion of the tunnel the company must remove its elevated trains from the existing subway. The commission had granted the use of the subway to this company as a matter of convenience for the public, and no permanent rights had been issued to the Elevated Company for such use. The arrangement was only of a temporary character, to be annulled upon the completion of the short section referred to.

AGREEMENT WITH WEST END COMPANY

In December of the same year a contract was made with the West End Street Railway Company, controlling the surface lines of the city, by which that company was granted the exclusive use of all the subways then constructed

PARK AND TREMONT STREETS—BOSTON. AS IT IS AND AS IT WAS.

FOUR-TRACK CONSTRUCTION—BOSTON SUBWAY.

and those to be constructed in the future. The term of the grant is 20 years. For this privilege the company pays the city the sum of $4\frac{7}{8}$ per cent. of $7,000,000, the compensation to begin when the company assumes control. The company also agrees to pay an additional sum of 5 cents for each passage made through the subway by a car not exceeding 25 feet in length, and a proportionately greater rate for each car of greater length. All equipment furnished by the company is to be the property of the company as long as it shall continue to operate the tunnel; this equipment is to be purchased by the commission, at a fair valuation, if the company ceases operations. The company is to make all repairs.

NO GRADE CROSSINGS

The routes built and building are shown on the accompanying map. The station at the corner of Boylston and Tremont streets is so designed that there is no grade crossing of tracks on which cars run in opposite directions, the separation being effected by means of a sub-subway for the south bound Tremont street cars. At Park street is a loop around which all cars pass that do not run beyond this point. There are four tracks under Tremont street along the line of the Common, these taking the place of the two surface tracks. Bids for the construction of Section I, which included all that portion of the subway on Boylston street to West street, with the exception of the station at the corner, were opened March 20, 1895. The first spadeful of earth was removed on March 28, 1895.

DESIGN OF TUNNEL

The incline is an open avenue descending from the surface of the ground opposite Church street to the subway portal. The length of the incline is 318 feet, and it descends about 17 feet in that distance. It has granite walls, underneath and back of which is concrete masonry, with all the deeper portions supported on a pile foundation. The two-track subway is 24 feet to 24 feet 8 inches in width inside, 16 feet 6 inches in height along the center, giving a clear height of 14 feet above the rails. The side walls are composed of 15-inch I-beams spaced 6 feet apart, standing on granite footing-stones. The space between the beams is walled with concrete, in which the beams are bedded. The roof is supported by 20-inch I-beams spaced 3 feet apart, the intervening space being bridged with brick and concrete masonry. The four-track sub-

PARK STREET STATION—BOSTON SUBWAY.

way is similar to the two-track, with the exception that its clear width is 48 feet, and that it has a row of columns along its center.

A provision of the act required that the commission "shall so conduct the work of construction that all streets and places under or near which a subway is constructed shall be open for traffic between 8 o'clock in the forenoon and 6 o'clock in the afternoon."

The method of building the subway will be understood from the following extract from the specifications:

METHOD OF BUILDING

"Trenches about 12 feet wide shall be excavated across the street, to as great a distance and depth as is necessary for the construction of the subway. The top of the excavation shall be bridged by strong beams and timbering, whose upper surface is flush with the surface of the street." [These beams usually consist of hard pine 10 inches by 8 to 12 inches, 20 feet long, placed side by side lengthwise of the street. Two or more 6-inch I-beams are used for supporting each rail of the street railway. The ties of the railway are usually under these beams and fastened to them with bolts. The surface of the beams is covered with plank, precisely flush with the paving of the street.] "These beams shall be used to support the railway track as well as the ordinary traffic. Portions of the bridging can be removed day and night. In each trench a small portion, or slice, of the subway shall be constructed. Each slice of the subway thus built is to be properly joined in due time to the contiguous slices. The contractor shall at all times have as many slice-trenches in process of excavation, in process of being filled with masonry, and in process of being backfilled with earth above the completed masonry, as is necessary for the even and steady progress of the work toward completion at the time named in the contract."

This method does not disturb the railway tracks at all, and leaves the whole surface of the street entirely free, in the day time, for normal use.

MASONRY TUNNEL

The masonry tunnel is built with concrete side-walls and brick arches that spring from one wall to the other. The arches have heavy concrete backing, and are further strengthened by vertical I-beams about 6 feet apart, imbedded in the walls, each pair of opposite beams being connected at their top by a tie-rod which passes just above the interior crown of the arch. The tunnel is 12.25 feet wide in straight sections, and considerably wider at the curves. The height from the invert to the crown is 16 feet. The side walls are 2 feet in thickness. The bell-mouth, where two tunnels join, is 30 feet wide and has a clear height of

21 feet. The side walls are 4 feet 10 inches thick and the brick arch 28 inches thick. The arch is strengthened by tie-rods 2 feet apart strained against washer plates. The bell-mouth grows smaller in cross-section until it unites with the normal wide arch of the subway, which has a span of 23 feet and a height of crown of 17¾ feet.

A roof-shield, similar to an ordinary shield, except that the lower half was omitted, was used successfully on a portion of the work. It was an arch-like structure, 12 feet long, with a rise of 8 feet 7¼ inches in its outer span of 29 feet 4 inches. It was built around two arched girders 3 feet 8 inches deep, placed 4 feet apart, leaving 4 feet of overhanging plates at front and back. The space between the girders was divided into 10 compartments, in each of which was placed a hydraulic jack. The track supporting the shield was placed on the side walls, cast-steel shoes being provided for the shield to rest and move upon. The greatest freedom and accuracy of manipulation were found possible with this arrangement, the control of the valves being effective in correcting slight changes in direction, overcoming uneven resistances, and in traveling around curves. As the shield moved forward the 1-inch space over the arch masonry, due to the thickness of the shield plates, was filled with cement grout (pumped through pipes left in the brickwork), so as to make a close connection with the earth above. The material passed through was compact clay and sand, and loose sand and gravel, with occasional boulders up to 4 feet in diameter. This is perhaps the first instance of the use of a shield in connection with a masonry tunnel. ROOF SHIELD

The walls of the stations are lined with enameled white brick. The steel columns are encased in concrete and painted white. The brickwork, and the exposed steelwork of the roof, are also painted white. The staircase walls are lined with white brick, and the roofs are made of metal and glass.

Prior to 1897, when all the Tremont street car traffic ran on the surface, the utmost limit of capacity of the surface tracks was found to be about 200 cars per hour each way. The rate of progress was often not more than two miles per hour. In October, 1898, one month after the complete transfer of the surface traffic to the subway, the number of cars passing freely each way at the same point within the subway, during the hours of greatest travel, was 282, the rate of speed, including stops, being between 7 and 8 miles per hour. This meant that the cars between the Public-Garden entrance and the Park street DAILY TRAFFIC

BELL MOUTHS UNDER TREMONT STREET—BOSTON SUBWAY.

station, moved on a fixed schedule time of 4 minutes in the subway, instead of an uncertain time on the surface varying from 10 to 20 minutes.

When the Park street station was opened the commission was confronted with a problem apparently without a counterpart in steam or street railway practice. Between the hours of 4:30 and 6 in the afternoon the outgoing platform of this station was served by about 180 cars per hour. These belonged to more than 20 different routes, and came to the platform without any fixed order. The passengers did not know what cars were coming nor where they would stop. Dire confusion was the result. The trouble was obviated by the introduction of a large indicator upon which just before the arrival of a car, the name of the car and the location of its stop were shown.

EAST BOSTON TUNNEL

The East Boston tunnel extends from Maverick Square, East Boston, under the harbor to the city proper. It carries two electric railway tracks. The East Boston approach consists of an open incline 139 feet long, and a wide-arch subway 680 feet long. The tunnel portion has a total length of 4,430 feet. Under the harbor the tunnel is $20\frac{1}{2}$ feet inside height by 23 feet wide. The tunnel was excavated by means of a roof-shield, as previously described, compressed air being employed to prevent entrance of water. In building the tunnel the invert was put in and the side walls carried up to within 16 inches of the springing line of the arch. The walls were terminated at this height in order to serve as foundations for the tracks upon which the roof-shield was to run.

METHODS

Side drifts, 8 feet square, were dug in advance of the shield, and then the core was taken out and the invert and side walls put in. Curved steel ribs made of 10-inch channels, spaced 30 inches apart, were used as centering for each ring of arch. After lagging had been placed on the ribs, the concrete was put in. The final keying up of each ring of the arch was done through two holes, about 13 inches in diameter, in the rear girder, at the top of the shield. Curved sheet-iron troughs were extended from these holes to the top of the arch. Concrete thrown into the troughs was pushed into the unfilled space at the crown of the arch. As soon as one ring of arch had been finished, the shield was pushed forward 30 inches and another ring put in. The space left vacant over the completed ring by the advancing tail-piece of the shield was filled with grout forced through a vertical pipe placed at the crown of each ring. This was probably the first successful example of fresh concrete work in connection with the shield method.

The following is a summary of the cost of the several works up to June 30, 1904:

COST

Original subway	$4,158,988.26
Alterations	243,438.77
Charlestown bridge	1,570,197.98
East Boston Tunnel	2,744,088.01
Boston Tunnel and Subway	156,310.23
Grand Total	$8,873,023.25

BOSTON ELEVATED ROADS.

The elevated railroads of Boston, controlled by the Boston Elevated Railway Company, extend in a north and south direction through the business portions of the city. When the present extensions shall have been completed it will extend from Forest Hills on the south, through the city to Charlestown and East Boston on the north and east. The present system, which is elevated throughout, passes along the docks through Atlantic avenue.

As we have already explained, the Transit Commission is building a tunnel under Washington street for the exclusive use of the elevated road; this and the East Boston tunnel under the harbor have been leased to the elevated company.

CHICAGO.

Chicago has inaugurated, and is now rapidly extending, a system of tunnels that bids fair to have a marked influence upon the rapid transit problem in that and other cities. The plan is original in its design; comprehensive, in that it covers the congested district, and, as far as may be judged at the present time, effective, in that it provides the desired relief. The fundamental idea has been to place the transportation of merchandize, mail, and express matter, and all supplies and refuse, in tunnels, and in that way reserve the streets for the exclusive use of the people. It is evident that such a scheme, in order to be thoroughly successful, must cover the district perfectly; it would fail if any portion, however insignificant, were omitted. Every building, the occupants of which require material of any description from without that particular territory, must be reached by the system.

W. 19TH ST.
W. 18TH ST.
W. 14TH ST.
W. 12TH ST.
W. TAYLOR ST.
W. HARRISON ST.
W. VAN BUREN ST.
JACKSON BOUL.
W. ADAMS ST.
W. MUNROE ST.
W. MADISON ST.
W. WASHINGTON ST.
W. RANDOLPH ST.
W. LAKE ST.
WATER ST.
KINGSBURY ST.
ORLEANS ST.
N. FRANKLIN ST.
N. W'n Sta.
WELLS ST.
LA SALLE AVE
N. CLARK ST.
DEARBORN AVE.
N. STATE ST.
CASS ST.
RUSH ST.
PINE ST.
MICHIGAN ST.
ILLINOIS ST.
Union Sta.
S. CANAL ST.
S. CLARK ST.
S. STATE ST.
WABASH AVE.
MICHIGAN AVE.
Gt. Cen. Sta.
FIFTH AVE.
LaSalle St. Sta.
Polk St. Sta.
Cen. Sta.
Suburban Sta.
LAKE ST.
S. WATER ST.
HARRISON ST.
CONGRESS ST.
VAN BUREN ST.
JACKSON BOUL.
ADAMS ST.
MUNROE ST.
MADISON ST.
WASHINGTON ST.
RANDOLPH ST.
12TH ST.
13TH ST.
14TH ST.
16TH ST.
18TH ST.
South
Branch
of
Chicago
River
North
LAKE MICHIGAN

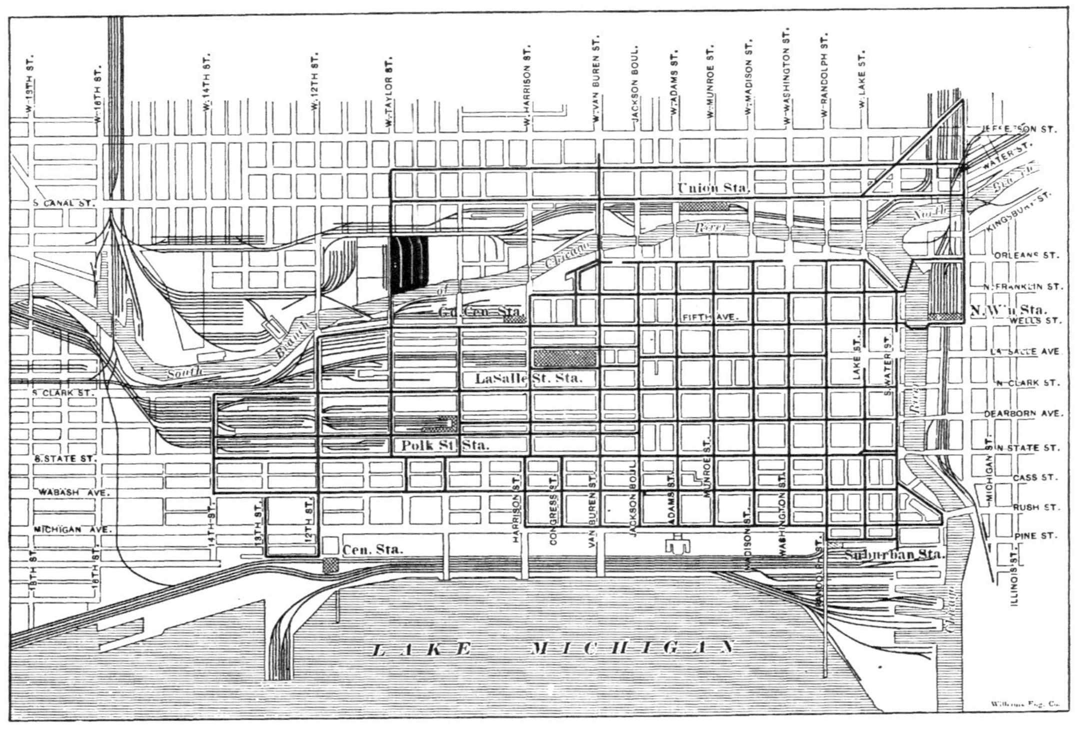

CHICAGO.

CONGESTED DISTRICT

The business center of Chicago occupies an area of about one and a half square miles. Within this space are the great department stores, the office buildings, the newspaper offices, some large factories, and terminals, including six freight depots for 25 trunk lines entering the city. In addition to all this, the district is enclosed in a loop formed by four converging elevated roads. Some conception of the condition may be formed from the fact that the teaming, necessary to the transfer of goods in this district, has grown to greater proportions probably than in any other city of the world, regard being had to the space occupied. On thirty-two miles of streets, the daily movement of merchandise averages about 112,000 tons. During the busy hours as many as 1,000 teams have been counted passing a street corner in an hour. Fortunately for those advocating the freight tunnel plan, the streets, as shown upon the accompanying map, are straight and laid out at right angles.

The following item from a Chicago paper clearly, although facetiously, outlines the project:

CHICAGO SUBWAY DEFINED

"What the subway means to Chicago: Clean streets, pure air, sunlight for the people, underground subway for freight traffic; just the reverse of New York and London, where the people are put underground, and teaming and trucking given the preference. Coal, ashes, dirt, excavations from building sites, offal, etc., taken off the streets and hauled underground. All the dirt and annoyance are abolished. Every building in the business district is equipped with tunnel connections, and thus brought into direct communication with every railroad and steamship line in the world. Freight, merchandise, and fuel are hauled in; ashes, dirt, and refuse hauled out. Uninterrupted free traffic on the surface for the people who walk, drive, or ride in surface and elevated cars. The streets for the people; the tunnels for merchandise, coal and freight."

The inception of this project was probably due to a strong public feeling that the charges for telephone service in the city were too high. Taking advantage of this feeling, the Illinois Telephone & Telegraph Company was incorporated, and granted permission to build tunnels and conduits under the streets for telephone wires. This was in 1899. In 1903 the terms of the charter were broadened so as to include apparatus for the transmission of newspapers, mail matter, parcels, merchandise, coal, etc.

ORDINANCE

The ordinance of 1903 provides that at the expiration of the charter in 1929 "all tunnels and conduits heretofore constructed, and all tunnels hereafter constructed, under said ordinances, shall, without the payment of any consideration, become and be the absolute property of the city of Chicago, free from liens and incumbrances."

The ordinances contain the following provisions: The trunk or main line tunnels must not be more than 12 feet 9 inches in width and 14 feet in height; the small tunnels not more than 6 feet in width and 7½ feet in height. The crown of the tunnels must not be less than 19 feet below the city datum. The company must lower or remove its tunnels if the city decides to build water tunnels or subways with which they would interfere. Space must be reserved, in each of the tunnels, for the use of city telegraph, electric light, and telephone wires. The company has the right to connect up any of its tunnels with the lots of private owners abutting on such streets, and also with the branch offices or delivery stations of said company, by proper passageways or connecting tunnels. The company may lease its works to another duly authorized company, but it shall not maintain or operate cars or vehicles of any kind for the conveyance or transportation of passengers, nor shall it have the right or authority to lease space in its tunnels to any person, firm, or corporation to carry passengers in any manner.

The city reserves the right to regulate all charges and rates for the services rendered.

DURATION OF FRANCHISE

At the end of 20 years from the granting of the franchise, the city may purchase the entire property and equipment, with the exception of the wires, necessary to the carrying on of the telephone business; but the telephone company must pay a reasonable rental for the use of the tunnels. The city is to pay in cash the value of the property as determined by three appraisers in the usual way. The appraisers, in determining the fair cash value of the property, "shall not take into consideration its earning power or the value of any franchise or license, but shall allow for the property the then cost of duplication, less depreciation."

CITY TO PURCHASE

If, at the expiration of the grant, the city should not desire to purchase nor to operate the tunnels, the privilege is to be granted to the corporation making the most advantageous proposal. If the proposal of the Illinois Telephone & Telegraph Company is not as advantageous as that of some other corporation, such other corporation may purchase the property at an appraised valuation.

For the privileges granted, the company must pay to the city in January of

TRAIN AT STREET INTERSECTION—CHICAGO.

each year the following percentages of its gross receipts for the preceding year: "For the first ten years of the grant, 5 per cent.; for the second ten years of the grant, 8 per cent; and for the balance of the grant, 12 per cent. On all gross receipts the company derives from the rental of space in its tunnels and conduits it shall pay into the city treasury 20 per cent. annually."

PENALTIES

If the company fails to complete the work authorized by the franchise within 5 years, it shall pay to the city $200,000 within 60 days after the expiration of the 5 years. In case of failure to pay this amount within the time specified, the company forfeits "all rights acquired under this ordinance, together with its plant and equipment."

If the company fails to construct and operate 50 miles of tunnels, within 10 years from the passage of the ordinance, it forfeits its plant and equipment. Within 5 years it must also have a telephone equipment adequate for the service of 20,000 subscribers, or forfeit its plant.

ILLINOIS TUNNEL COMPANY

The original company has been succeeded by the Illinois Tunnel Company, which now acts as both constructing and operating company. Twenty-eight miles of subway have been finished, and, when fully equipped, 60,000 tons of freight can be handled daily. The longest line is about 1 mile. It lies under Wabash avenue, one block west of the lake front. There are eight principal passages, one under each street parallel with Wabash avenue and west thereof, making nine north and south tunnels in all, with four secondary tunnels running in the same direction. At right angles with these are 15 tunnels under the cross streets. The accompanying engravings show the form of the tunnel, and the switches and connections at the intersections.

METHOD OF BUILDING

The work was done by what is known as the pneumatic system, in which the air-lock of the ordinary pattern is placed in the completed section, and air at from 5 to 7 pounds pressure carried in the heading. This method was not absolutely necessary, as the soil was of such a nature that it would stand without caving or swelling.

Following closely all excavation work, channel-iron ribs were placed in position, with lagging behind them. Concrete was then rammed in between the lagging and earth, and in this way every void was completely filled. The lateral conduits were built with a 13-inch invert and 10-inch walls. The trunk system was constructed with 21-inch invert and 18-inch walls.

In order to prosecute the work smoothly and rapidly, the excavated material had to be disposed of without delay. This was accomplished by the use of tramcars on a track of 14-inch gauge. A line of double tracks was laid, and the cars were hoisted by elevators up the shafts to a headhouse built on the curb line. The material was dumped into wagons standing on the street. Most of the hauling away was done at night to avoid interference with street traffic. The first 12 miles of tunnel were built without causing a complaint from any source, and without accident of any kind. Over 12 miles of tunnel were completed in ten and one-half months of actual work.

FREIGHT TRAIN AT STREET INTERSECTION—CHICAGO.

Connections with buildings for telephone service are made by drifts, 3 feet in diameter, from the tunnel to points within the curb line, and by driving 2, 3, 4, or 5-inch pipes to meet the drifts. In this way the necessary cables are taken into the buildings of subscribers.

THIRD RAIL TRACTION SYSTEM

The four-way intersections have curves of 20-foot radius, the sharpest curves on the main line being 16-foot radius. The track is 2-foot gauge laid

TYPICAL STREET INTERSECTION—CHICAGO.

with 56-pound rails. The Morgan third-rail traction system is used. This consists of a perforated steel plate, ½ inch thick by 4 inches wide, forming a rack, which is bolted between two lines of timber stringers, as shown in the engraving. These both protect and support the rack. Engaging with the teeth formed in the rack is a gear driven by the motor of the locomotive. By means of this construction the rack serves both for traction and as a third rail conductor. The current is taken up by the teeth of the driving gears and led to motors

TYPICAL DISTRIBUTING STATION—CHICAGO.

geared to the axles. The track rails are used for the return current. A speed of between 15 and 20 miles per hour is attained.

CARS The cars are of steel construction throughout, and are 12 feet in length over all. They are of the double-truck, eight-wheel type. The design is such that a car can be used either as a flat car or gondola, and the contents can be dumped without removing either the sides or ends. The box car is 48 inches wide, 10 feet 6 inches long, stands 63 inches above the rails, and has a capacity of 30,000 pounds.

The district consumes 4,000,000 tons of coal annually. Contracts have been made for hauling the supply for many of the large buildings, and for the removal of the ashes, the contracts being in force for periods of a year. The Post Office Department has a contract with the company for the handling of mails between the general post office, the sub-stations, and the railway stations, to run for a period of 5 years, the consideration being approximately $175,000 per annum.

The company has an authorized capital stock of $30,000,000, and a bond issue of like amount. Of the $30,000,000 in bonds, $15,000,000 has been issued, the remainder being held in reserve for future extensions of the plant.

Chicago is now considering the advisability of building a passenger subway system, having the following as it main features:

PASSENGER SUBWAY

An underground subway system making it practicable and serviceable to put in operation a one-fare system without the issue of transfers; no grade crossings; cars to be run from the different divisions of the city to other divisions as may be convenient for the people; foot walks ten feet wide along all lines; a system that will take care of new sewers, a high pressure water system, and a storm-water system.

It will be seen that the subway work already done in Chicago, and the suggestions for further developments, present features radically different from anything so far attempted in other cities in our land and abroad. The practical merits of the plans—those already accomplished and those proposed—are so evident that one cannot but believe that they will be followed elsewhere in greater or less measure. It cannot be supposed for a moment that trains for the transportation of passengers will be run on the surface, because of the danger to other traffic. It can hardly be supposed that the people of great cities will be content with elevated systems involving noise and the disfigurement of streets. It would seem that underground ways must come into common use, not only for passengers and for freight, but also for sewers, for water pipes, and for conduits of different kinds. In this way, and in this way only, can the surface of streets be reserved for ordinary traffic, and the incessant breaking up of pavements avoided. For not only are the streets of our great cities, and those of European cities, greatly overcrowded by traffic, but here and there serious breaking up of pavements is going on all the while. The cases, indeed, are not infrequent when different gangs of men are employed on the same street—the one replacing pavement, the other opening the ground for some different purpose.

CHICAGO ELEVATED ROADS.

ROUTES

As we have just mentioned, the congested section of Chicago is embraced in a small area on the lake front near the center of the city. The elevated railroad systems cover the outlying districts to the north, west and south; all of the roads meeting in a loop encircling the business portion. This provides for the quick handling of all traffic from three cardinal points, and for the unlimited extension of the residential districts in like directions. These features, in combination with a flat country in each direction, vastly simplified the elevated problem. The absence of heavy grades and sharp curves is unique in elevated railroad practice.

The elevated roads started with the incorporation of the Chicago & Oak Park Elevated Railroad, in August, 1892. This was formerly known as the Lake Street Elevated Railroad. The franchise carried the right to build a double-track elevated structure from Wabash avenue and Lake street west to Wisconsin avenue and South Boulevard. Since then the following elevated roads have been constructed:

The South Side Elevated line, with two routes extending directly south. This road is being extended by east and west lines at Thirty-ninth and Sixty-first streets.

The Metropolitan West Side line, with roads to the west and northwest.

The Northwestern Elevated, with a line due north. This road is extending its system further to the north.

The loop where all the roads meet in the city is controlled by the Union Loop Company, which leases the use of the loop to the other four roads.

PHILADELPHIA.

Philadelphia is now engaged in the construction of a comprehensive system of rapid transit. The conditions there are more favorable than those in any of the other cities we have mentioned. The city was originally laid out regularly. The streets running north and south are parallel, and those running east and west are at right angles to the others. Two of the streets, Market and Broad, divide the city east and west and north and south, and are of unusual width. These features permit of rapid transit lines that are straight, and provide convenient points for diverging lines.

The legal foundation of all the corporations created for the purpose of constructing and operating elevated systems of municipal railways in Pennsylvania is the Act of Assembly of June 7, 1901. Section 1 provides that any number of persons, not less than five, three of whom are citizens of the commonwealth, may form a company for the purpose of constructing and operating passenger railways, either elevated or underground, or partly elevated and underground, and for the collection and distribution of mails of the United States; permission to erect or construct to be obtained from the local authorities of the city in which the road is to be operated. ACT OF ASSEMBLY

Section 2 provides that the charter shall be subscribed to by at least three of the corporators, who shall certify, in writing, to the Governor, the name of the company, number of years it is to be continued, and other details in regard to the road, amount of capital stock, etc. This section prescribes also the powers and privileges of the corporation. These are the usual privileges of such a body; but, in addition, power is granted to sell or lease any road or franchise, or any parts thereof, to other companies, or to acquire other roads and franchises.

Section 8 gives such corporations rights of eminent domain.

Section 12 provides that construction shall be begun, in good faith, within two years, and be completed within five years thereafter.

A supplement to this act enlarges the power of such corporations, so that they are authorized to build either an elevated or underground, or both an elevated and underground railway, over the route described in their charter, after having obtained the consent of the local authorities. ELEVATED OR UNDERGROUND

Corporations, incorporated under the original act, were given power to construct branches and extensions. The amendment of March 25, 1903, gave them power, with the consent of the local authorities, to abandon any portion of the road, or to merge with other companies, and when two or more roads shall be so merged, the commencement of the work, in good faith, upon any part of the route, on any of such merged roads, shall be a commencement upon all the merged roads, within the meaning of the act; provided that the work shall be completed within five years upon all the merged roads, unless the time for such completion shall be extended by the proper local authorities. This was an important addition, for the charters of a number of the following mentioned elevated and subway lines would have been forfeited if it had not been for this provision, as work, even yet, has not been begun on them.

MARKET STREET COMPANY

The Market Street Elevated Passenger Railway Company was authorized to build and operate an underground road from Delaware avenue on Market street, around the Public Buildings under any and all streets bounding the same, and continuing on Market street to the county line, with the right to come out upon the surface of Market street west of Twenty-second street, or through private property acquired by the company, and to connect with the tracks of any other passenger railway company. The road must be operated electrically, or by any other power excepting steam. The company is to construct tubes or conduits for carrying city telegraph, telephone and fire alarm wires. Subsequently the company was further authorized to construct a loop, branch, or road beginning at the intersection of Broad and Market streets, on the south side of the City Hall, there connecting with its tracks, and thence extending south on Broad street to Walnut street to Fifth, thence to Arch, to Broad, to Filbert, and there connecting with its main tracks at Fifteenth and Market. This provided for two tracks on Market street east of Broad, and four tracks west of Broad in addition to the tracks already authorized. The alternate privilege was also granted of using Chestnut street instead of Walnut. The company is also privileged to bridge the Schuylkill so as to connect the subway tracks with the elevated tracks to be built to the west.

ROUTES OF DIFFERENT COMPANIES

Similar ordinances were passed for the Ridge Avenue Elevated Passenger Railway Company to build a double-track elevated railway from Passyunk avenue along Ninth street to Vine, to Ridge avenue, to Main street, Manayunk.

The Frankford Elevated Passenger Railway Company is privileged to build a double-track road from South street along Delaware avenue to Vine, to Front, to Callowhill, to New Market, to Laurel, to Frankford avenue.

The Passyunk Avenue Elevated Passenger Railway is to extend from Delaware avenue along South street to Front, to Bainbridge, to Passyunk avenue, to Juniper, to Snyder avenue, to Schuylkill River.

The Germantown Avenue Elevated Passenger Railway is to extend from Front street along Germantown avenue to Germantown & Perkiomen turnpike, to the county line.

The Broad Street Subway Passenger Railway Company is authorized to construct an underground road from Government avenue under Broad street, around the Public Buildings, and continuing under Broad street to the county line.

PHILADELPHIA RAPID TRANSIT COMPANY

On none of these lines was the requirement as to the beginning and completion of the work complied with; and the rights and privileges granted by the several ordinances would, therefore, have been forfeited, had it not been for the act above referred to providing for the extension of time of completion. All of the franchises have been acquired by the Philadelphia Rapid Transit Company, which operates all the surface lines in Philadelphia.

DESCRIPTION OF WORK

The plan proposed for the Market street line, now building, was an adaptation of the Boston method, and provided for both elevated and surface cars. The franchise for the line gave the right to build both an elevated road and a subway. There is a double-track elevated structure on Market street from the county line to the Schuylkill River, the surface tracks being underneath. A four-track bridge over the river carries both elevated and surface lines to the entrance of the subway at Twenty-third street. From this point to the Public Buildings is a four-track tunnel, the outside tracks for the surface cars, and the inside tracks for the elevated trains. The elevated tracks will continue around the City Hall and thence down Market street to the river front, where they will join an elevated structure on Delaware avenue from Arch to South streets. The surface car track will leave the other at the City Hall and pass south on Broad street in a single-track subway to Walnut street, to Fifth, to Arch, to Broad, to the City Hall, where it will unite with the westbound elevated track to the county line.

The tunnel is built with a concrete floor, steel-concrete side walls, and roof of I-beams with arches between, and rows of columns between the tracks. A considerable portion of this line has been finished. The bridge over the Schuylkill is practically complete.

Work is now progressing on the elevated portion of the road west of the Schuylkill.

An ordinance, passed in 1903, provided that each system of the railway must be finished before the streets are torn up for another system. The several sections must be completed in the following order:

From Sixty-third and Market streets to Delaware avenue and South street, the system just mentioned, in three years from the passage of the ordinance.

Subway loop on Broad street and Walnut or Chestnut street, Fifth and Arch streets, one year additional.

Subway on Broad street, from Cayuga to Walnut or Chestnut, in two years additional.

Branches in West Philadelphia in two years additional, and the remainder within two years additional.

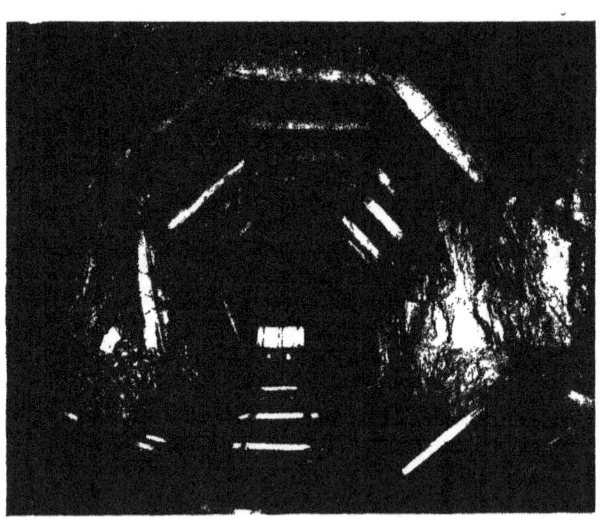

EAST RIVER TUNNEL DURING CONSTRUCTION—N. Y. SUBWAY.

CHAPTER XXI.

PRESENT RAPID TRANSIT LAWS.

The failure of the two earlier Commissions, and the inadequate quality of the legislation under which they had acted, resulted in a study of the legislation needed by this Chamber. A bill was prepared by a committee appointed for the purpose which became a law in 1894. This law was amended in 1895, 1896, 1900, 1901, 1902, 1904 and 1905.

COMMISSION

The first section of the Rapid Transit Law as it now stands provides for the appointment of a Board of Rapid Transit Commissioners in each city having over 1,000,000 inhabitants according to the last preceding national or State census. Such board shall be made up of the Mayor, the Comptroller or other chief financial officer of the city, the president of the Chamber of Commerce of the State of New York, by virtue of his office, and the following named persons: William Steinway, Seth Low, John Claflin, Alexander E. Orr and John H. Starin. Vacancies shall be filled by a majority vote of the remaining members of the Board. Four members of the Board constitute a quorum for the transaction of business. Each of the commissioners, other than the Mayor and Comptroller, shall take an oath faithfully to perform the duties of his office.

ESTABLISH ROUTES AND FORM PLANS

From time to time the Board is to consider and determine whether it is for the interest of the city to build a rapid transit railway or railways for the conveyance of persons and property. Upon the request of the local authorities the Board shall consider and determine such questions forthwith. If the Board considers such a railway necessary, it shall establish the route thereof and the general plan of construction. Such plan shall show the general mode of operation, and contain such details as to the manner of construction as may be necessary to indicate the extent to which any street, avenue or other public place is to be encroached upon and the property abutting thereon affected, and the concurrent votes of at least six members of the Board shall be necessary to determine such route. The route may be located over, under, upon, through, or across any streets, avenues, bridges, viaducts, and lands within the city, and partly through blocks between streets or avenues; provided that the consent of the owners of

CONSENT OF PROPERTY OWNERS

one-half in value of the property bounded by such streets, and also the consent of the local authorities having control of such streets and avenues have been procured. In case the consent of such property owners cannot be obtained, the General Term of the Supreme Court in the district of the proposed construction shall appoint three commissioners, who shall give due hearing to all parties interested, and determine whether such railway ought to be built. The finding of the commissioners, confirmed by the court, shall be taken in lieu of the consent of the property owners. It is made lawful for the commissioners to locate the route of a railway by tunnel under any public parks, lands, or waters, and across any of the streets or avenues now occupied by an elevated railroad in the city of New York. An elevated railway must not be built on Broadway south of Thirty-third street, nor on Madison avenue.

PLANS TO BE SENT TO BOARD OF ESTIMATE AND APPORTIONMENT

Section 5 provides that after any determination by the Board of any routes and general plan a copy of such conclusions shall be sent to the Board of Estimate and Apportionment. It shall be the duty of that board, upon receiving such plans, to appoint a day not less than one week nor more than ten days after the receipt thereof for their consideration. Such consideration is to be continued from time to time until a final vote shall be taken. Within sixty days of the receipt of the plans a final vote must be taken, the vote to be upon a resolution to approve the plans. Upon the adoption of such a vote by a majority of all the members of the Board of Estimate and Apportionment, and the approval of the Mayor, the plans shall be deemed to be approved by the city authorities. Having obtained the approval of the city authorities, the Rapid Transit Commission shall obtain, if possible, the consents of property owners along the line of the road. The value of the abutting property shall be obtained from the assessment roll of the city. If such consents cannot be obtained, the Board may, in its own name, make application to the Appellate Division of the Supreme Court in the judicial district in which the railroad is to be constructed, for the appointment of three commissioners to determine and report, after due hearing, whether such railroad ought to be constructed and operated. Two weeks' notice of such application shall be made by publication in papers to be designated by the court. The three commissioners shall determine, after public hearing of all parties interested, whether such railroad ought to be constructed and operated, and report the evidence taken to the court, together with their determination. If the decision of the commissioners should be in favor of construction, and this should be confirmed by the court, such decision is to be taken in lieu of the consent of the property owners. Such report shall be made within sixty days after appointment of the commissioners, unless the court shall extend the time.

Having obtained the consents, the Rapid Transit Commission shall at once proceed to prepare the plans and specifications "including all devices and appurtenances deemed by it necessary to secure the greatest efficiency, public convenience and safety, including the number, location and description of stations" and plans for turnouts, switches, sidings, buildings, platforms, stairways, elevators, telegraph and signal devices, and other appliances which the board may approve as "the best and most efficient system of rapid transit in view of the public needs and requirements." The plans may also include subways or tunnels for sewer, gas, or water pipes, electric wires and other conductors proper to be placed underground.

Stations and station approaches may be under or over streets of the route, or cross streets.

SEWERS, WATER PIPES, CONDUITS, ETC.

The Board may from time to time alter such plans and specifications, but always so that the same shall accord with the general plan of construction; but whenever a contract shall have been made for the construction of the railway, no alteration shall be made without the consent of the contractor and his sureties. When the line disturbs any sewer, water pipe, or other duly authorized subsurface structure, the work of construction at such points shall be conducted in accordance with the reasonable requirements of the Commissioner of Public Works. All expense attached to the work shall be borne by the contracting company. Where galleries or subways shall be constructed for sewer, water pipes, or other underground structures, they shall be in the care of the Board and be maintained by the city. Any revenue derived from them shall be paid to the treasury of the city, except that where bonds shall have been issued to pay for the construction of such railroads, such amounts shall be paid into the sinking fund to be established out of the annual rentals of the road. Any corporation which, at the time of construction of such subways, shall own pipes or conduits in a street traversed by the road, shall be entitled to the use of such galleries and no rent shall be charged for such use except a reasonable charge to defray the actual cost of maintenance; but if the new galleries are of greater capacity than the old ones, the rent shall be charged only for such increased capacity.

MAY SELL FRANCHISE

If, after having secured the necessary consents and prepared the plans and specifications, it shall not have been determined by vote of the people "as provided by sections* twelve and thirteen of chapter seven-hundred-and-fifty-two of the laws of eighteen-hundred-and-ninety-four," that such railway shall be constructed for and at the expense of the city, as afterward provided, then the Board shall sell at public auction the franchise to build, maintain and operate the road.

TERMS OF SALE

The terms of sale shall provide for the construction of the railway under the supervision of the Board, and for the approval of an engineer to be appointed by the Board, the salary of the engineer to be paid by the company owning the franchise. The successful bidder must deposit with the chief fiscal officer of the city cash or securities in such amount as may be determined by the Board to constitute a guarantee of full compliance with the terms of sale. The road is to be begun and finished at times specified by the Board. Should the company fail to begin or finish the road in the times named, then the Board shall have power to re-sell the franchise and so much of the road as may have been constructed. The proceeds of such re-sale shall be applied first to the payment of the expenses of the re-sale, and then to the discharge of any liens that may have been created upon the property, and the balance to be paid over to the company. The terms of sale must specify the amount of capital of the corporation, and number of shares of capital stock it shall be authorized to issue, the percentage to be paid in cash by the subscribers, the maximum amount of bonded indebtedness which such corporation may incur, and the rates of fares and freights which such corporation may charge for the carriage of persons and property. But the rate of fare from any point on the road northward or southward within the city of New York shall not exceed five cents. The Board may reject all bids and re-advertise the franchise for sale as often as it may deem necessary in the interest of the city, and shall finally accept that bid, which, under all circumstances, is most advantageous to the public and the city; and no bid shall be accepted without the concurrent vote of six members of the Board. The sale may be adjourned from time to time at the discretion of the Board. All such sales must be made for a definite term of years.

Within one year, and not less than six months, prior to the expiration of the period for which the franchise shall have been sold, the Board shall proceed to re-sell the right to maintain and operate the road. Such sale is to be made in the manner prescribed for the original sale. Any corporation thereto-

*These sections are quoted in full later.

fore organized under the provisions of the act may be a purchaser on such re-sale; but if no such corporation be the purchaser, a new corporation shall be formed to maintain and operate the road. Such sale is to be made in the manner prescribed for the original sale.

POWERS OF BOARD

The Board may rent such offices and employ such engineers, attorneys and other persons as it may deem necessary to the proper performance of its duties. It may sue in the name and on behalf of the city. It may bring actions to recover damages for any violation of contract. Every action or proceeding brought by the Board shall have preference above all causes not criminal on the calendar of every court, and may be brought on for trial or argument upon notice of eight days for any day of any term on which the court shall be in session.

PAYMENT OF EXPENSES OF BOARD

The Board of Estimate and Apportionment, or other board on which is imposed the duty and in which is vested the power of making appropriations of public moneys for the purposes of the city government, shall, on requisition duly made by the Board of Rapid Transit Commissioners, appropriate such sum or sums of money as may be requisite to properly enable it to perform its duties. Such appropriation shall be made forthwith upon presentation of a requisition from the Board, which shall state the purposes for which such moneys are required. It shall be the duty of the Auditor and Comptroller, after such appropriations have been made, to audit and pay the proper expenditures and compensation of the commissioners, upon vouchers furnished by the commissioners.

BONDS

For the purpose of providing funds with which to pay these sums, the Comptroller or other chief financial officer of the city is authorized to issue and sell revenue bonds of the city in anticipation of receipt of taxes, and out of the proceeds of such bonds to make the required payments. The amount necessary to pay the principal and interest of the bonds shall be included in the estimate of moneys necessary to be raised by taxation to carry on the business of the city. All expenses of the Rapid Transit Commission, including the compensation of the Commissioners, shall be repaid, with interest, by the successful bidder for the franchise. The compensation to be paid the Commissioners shall be determined by the general term of the Supreme Court in the department in which the city shall be located.

The articles of association of the corporation building and operating the road shall be signed by not less than twenty-five persons. The articles must state that they are made and filed for the purpose of taking and exercising the

SUBSCRIPTION TO CAPITAL STOCK OF CORPORATION

rights purchased. The articles must be approved by a vote of six members of the Board. Immediately after the articles of association shall have been approved and filed, the Board of Rapid Transit Commissioners shall open books of subscription to the capital stock of the corporation, and shall give public notice of such opening. When the full amount of such capital stock shall have been subscribed by not less than fifty persons, and such percentage of the amount subscribed as may have been fixed by the Board in the terms of sale shall have been paid in, in cash, the Board shall call a meeting of the subscribers for the purpose of organizing the corporation. At such meeting of the subscribers thirteen directors shall be elected, each of whom shall be a holder in his own right of at least one hundred shares of stock.

BY-LAWS

The by-laws to be adopted must provide the term of office of the directors, which shall not exceed one year; the manner of filling vacancies; the time and place of the annual meeting of the directors; manner of calling and holding special meetings; the number of stockholders who shall attend in person or by proxy any stockholders' meeting in order to constitute a quorum; the officers of the corporation, the manner of their election by the directors, and their powers and duties; the manner of amending the by-laws.

If in their judgment the public interest requires it, the Board may, at any time after the full organization of the corporation, by the concurrent vote of six members, alter or add to the detailed plans and specifications, provided these plans do not change the route of the railway and are not inconsistent with the general plan of construction. Such change must be approved by a vote of two-thirds of the directors.

ROAD FREE FROM TAX UNTIL OPERATION

Every corporation organized under this act shall have its principal office and be taxed on its property in the city where the railway is situated. But no taxes of any kind shall be imposed upon any portion of the railway not in actual operation for the transportation of passengers or freight.

The capital stock of the corporation may be increased or reduced upon the approval of the Commissioners, and the approval of two-thirds in amount of all the stockholders.

POWERS OF CORPORATION

The corporation shall have the right to acquire such real estate as may be necessary for stations, depots, engine houses, machine shops, etc. In case the corporation cannot agree with the owner of such property upon the terms, it shall have the right to acquire title in the manner prescribed by the condemnation law.

The corporation shall have the right to cross, intersect, join, and unite its railway with any other railway at any point on its route and upon the grounds of such other railway company, with the necessary turnouts, sidings, switches and other conveniences in furtherance of the objects of its connections. And every corporation whose railway shall be intersected by the new railway, shall unite with the new railway in forming such intersections and connections; if the two corporations cannot agree upon the amount of compensation to be made therefor, the same shall be determined by commissioners to be appointed by the court, in the manner provided in the act in respect to acquiring title to real estate. If the two corporations cannot agree upon the manner of such crossings and connections, then the commissioners shall determine the same.

The corporation shall convey persons and property on its railway by the power or force of steam, or by any motor other than animal power. It may enter upon and under streets and avenues and public places. No road must cross a steam railroad at grade.

MAILS TO BE CARRIED

The corporation shall, when applied to by the Postmaster-General, convey the mails of the United States on its road; and in case the parties cannot agree as to the rate of transportation therefor, and as to the time, rate of speed, manner and conditions of carrying the same, the Governor of the State shall appoint three commissioners who shall determine the prices, terms and conditions. This price must not be less than the corporation would receive as freight on a like weight of merchandise transported in their merchandise trains, and a fair compensation for the post-office car. If the Postmaster-General shall require the mail to be carried at other hours, or at a higher speed than the passenger trains are run, the corporation shall furnish an extra train for the mail and be allowed an extra compensation for the service.

FRANCHISE TO ROADS ALREADY BUILT

The Board may also from time to time grant a franchise, upon application of any railroad corporation owning or actually operating a railroad wholly or in part within the limits of the city, or of any railroad corporation now or hereafter incorporated, for the purpose of constructing and operating a tunnel railroad in the city, to be connected with any railroad or railroads within the State of New York, or within any adjoining State, and thereby forming a continuous line for the carriage of passengers and property between a point or points within and a point or points without the city. The Board may, by a vote of six of its members, determine the route or routes by which such railroad corporation may connect with other railroads, or the stations thereof, or

PRIVILEGES OF EXISTING ROADS

with ferries, or may establish or extend its lines within the city, and may authorize such corporation to lay additional tracks on, above, under or contiguous to a portion or the whole of the route of its railway within the city, or to acquire terminal or other facilities necessary for the accommodation of the traveling public on any street or place except Battery Park.

BOARD TO DETERMINE ROUTES AND PLANS The Board shall fix the location and plans of construction of such railroad or railroads, the times within which they shall be constructed, the compensation to be made to the city, and such other terms and requirements as the Board may consider just and proper. But every such determination, authorization and license shall be made upon the condition that the railroad corporation to which the grant shall be made, shall, from the time of the commencement of the operation of such railway annually pay to the city a sum or rental, and that the amount of such rental, for a period of not more than twenty-five years, shall be prescribed by the Board.

RENTAL TO BE PAID BY CORPORATION

READJUSTMENT OF SERVICE Such authorization shall provide for re-adjustment of the amount of rental at the expiration of the period for which the same shall be prescribed, and for re-adjustment from time to time in the future of the amount of such annual payment at intervals each of not more than twenty-five years.

PROPERTY OWNERS' CONSENT But such construction and operation of any such railroad shall only be upon the condition that the consent of the owners of one-half in value of the property bounded on, and the consent also of the local authorities having control of that portion of the street upon, above, or under which it is proposed to construct the road, be first obtained. In case the consent of such property owners cannot be obtained, the Appellate Division of the Supreme Court in the department in which such railroad is to be built, may, upon application, appoint three commissioners who shall determine, after a hearing of all the parties interested, whether the road ought to be constructed or operated, and their determination, confirmed by the court, may be taken in lieu of the consent of the property owners.

DISPOSITION OF SEWERS, WATER PIPES, ETC. Wherever the route selected by the Board intersects, crosses, or coincides with any tracks occupying the surface of any street, or the construction interferes with any pipes, sewers, subways, or underground conduits, any corporation organized under the act, or any contractor constructing any railway under a contract made with the Board, is authorized to remove the tracks or pipes, etc., in such manner as to interfere as little as possible with the operation of the railroad tracks, or the usefulness of the pipes and sewers. All these must be replaced as soon as possible. All such removals and restorations shall be made at the cost of the corporation or contractor building the road. For the purpose of facilitating construction, the contractor may, with the approval of the Board, lay upon or over the surface of any street, temporary tramways to be used only for the removal of excavated material or the transportation of material for use in the construction.

Section 34 is quoted in full, since it is that under which the present subway is being constructed:

PEOPLE VOTE FOR ROAD

"In case the people shall determine by vote, as provided in sections twelve and thirteen of chapter seven hundred and fifty-two of the laws of eighteen-hundred-and-ninety-four, that any such railway or railways shall be constructed for and at the expense of the city, then and in that event it shall be the duty of said Board to consider the routes, plans and specifications, if any, previously laid out and adopted by them or their predecessors, and for which the consents have been obtained referred to in section five of this act; and either to proceed with the construction of such railway or railways, and provide for the operation of the same, as hereinafter provided, or to change and modify the said routes, plans, or specifications in such particulars as to said Board may seem to be desirable; or, from time to time, and with or without reference to former routes or plans, to adopt other or different or additional routes, plans and specifications for such railway or railways, provided always that in all cases in which any such change or modification shall be of such character as to require the consents thereto referred to in section five of this act; and in all cases where other or different routes or general plans may have been so adopted the said Board shall proceed to secure the consents required to be obtained by section five of this act as therein set forth.

CITIES FORMED BY CONSOLIDATION

"If any city has been or shall have been formed by the union of or consolidation of one or more cities and other territory, and if in or for one of such cities so consolidated or united there shall have been a Board of Rapid Transit Railroad Commissioners as provided in this act, the board of rapid transit railroad commissioners for the said city formed by such union or consolidation shall have for and within such city so formed all the powers, and be subject to all the duties and responsibilities, which at the time of such union or consolidation belonged to the Board of Rapid Transit Railroad Commissioners of the former city so as aforesaid possessing such board for or in or with respect to such former city. If in such former city the vote of the qualified electors thereof shall have been for municipal construction of rapid transit road as prescribed in sections twelve and thirteen of chapter seven-hundred-and-fifty-two of the laws of eighteen-hundred-and-ninety-four, then the system of municipal construction of rapid transit railways provided for in this act and all the provisions with respect thereto in this act contained shall be applicable to, and in full force within, all the districts or boroughs and throughout the entire area of the said city formed by such union or consolidation.

NEW ROUTES AND GENERAL PLANS

"The Board of Rapid Transit Railroad Commissioners for any city shall, prior to the time of the final grant of any franchise under the provisions of this act, or the making of a contract for construction and operation of any railroad under the provisions of this act, have power to rescind and revoke any resolution or resolutions of such board adopting any routes or general plan for a rapid transit railroad adopted by such Board, and, in the discretion of such Board and in lieu thereof, to adopt new routes and general plan. Every such rescindment or revocation which shall have been heretofore made shall be deemed to have been lawful and authorized by this act as the same was prior to the present amendment hereof.

CONTRACT FOR BUILDING ROAD

"As soon as such consents, where necessary, shall have been obtained for any rapid transit railroad or railroads, and the detailed plans and specifications have been prepared as provided in section six of this act, the said Board, for and in behalf of the said city, shall enter into a contract with any person, firm, or corporation, which in the opinion of said Board shall be best qualified to fulfill and carry out said contract, for the construction of such road or roads, including such galleries, ways, subways, and tunnels for sub-surface structures as said Board may include in the plans for such road or roads under the authority of section six of this act, such road or roads, galleries, ways, subways or tunnels to be constructed upon the routes and in accordance with the plans and specifications so adopted, for such sum or sums of money, to be raised and paid out of the treasury of said city, as hereinafter provided, and on such terms and conditions, not inconsistent with the aforesaid plans and specifications, as said Board shall determine to be best for the public interests. The sum or sums of money to be paid for the construction of such road or roads shall be separately stated in the contract from the sum or sums to be paid for any galleries, ways, subways, or tunnels for sub-surface structures, the construction of which is provided for in such contract. And said Board may in any case contract for the construction of the whole road, or all the roads provided for by the aforesaid plans in a single contract, or may by separate contracts, executed from time to time, provide for the construction of parts of said road or roads, or for the construction at first of two or more tracks over a part or parts of such road or roads and afterwards of one or more additional tracks over a part or parts of such road or roads as the necessities of said city and the increase of its population may in the judgment of said Board require.

WORK DIVIDED

"The Board may also, in a contract for a part of any such rapid transit railroad, insert a provision that, at a future time, upon the requirement of the Board, the contractor shall construct the remainder or any part of the remainder of said road, as the growth of population or the interests of the city may, in the judgment of the Board, require, and may, in such contract, insert a provision of a method for fixing and ascertaining at such future time the amount to be paid to the contractor for such additional construction, and to the end of such ascertainment, may provide for arbitration or for the determination by a court of the amount of such compensation, or of any other details of construction which shall not be prescribed in the contract, but which shall be deemed necessary or convenient by the Board.

AMOUNT TO BE PAID FOR FUTURE CONSTRUCTION

"Any such contract may provide, if the public interest shall, in the opinion of the Board, justify the provision, that the construction of any section or portion of the railroad included in such contract may, with the consent of the Board, be suspended during the term of operation of the railroad as hereinafter mentioned, or any part of such term; provided, that during such term or part of term the lessee or contractor shall use, in lieu of such portion of the road, a railroad owned or leased by the lessee or contractor or a portion or section thereof, which shall, with the railroad or portion of railroad constructed by it under its contract with the Board, form a continuous and convenient route.

WORK MAY BE SUSPENDED

"Every such contract shall also provide that the persons, firm, or corporation so contracting to construct said road, or roads, shall, at his, or its own cost and expense, equip, maintain and operate said road or roads for a term of years to be specified in said contract, not more than fifty years, and upon such terms and conditions as to the rates or fare to be charged and the character of service to be furnished and otherwise, as said Board shall deem to be best suited to the public interests, and subject to such public supervision and to such conditions, regulations and requirements as may be determined upon by said Board; provided, that the right to use or operate any galleries, ways, subways or tun-

ALL LEASES TO EXPIRE AT SAME TIME

nels for sub-surface structures, which are required to be constructed under said contract, shall not pass under the operating provisions of said contract; and further provided that in case the contract shall provide for construction at different times or at intervals of time of different parts of a road, or if the contract shall provide for the use by the contractor of an existing railroad as part of continuous route as aforesaid, then and in any such case the Board of Rapid Transit Railroad Commissioners may, in its discretion, prescribe periods for the operation of the different parts of said road so that at one period of time in the future the Board may be enabled to make a single operating contract or lease of the entire road.

PROTECTION BY CITY

"Every such contract shall further provide by proper stipulations and covenants on the part of the said city, that the said city shall secure and assure to the contractor, so long as the contractor shall perform the stipulations of the contract, the right to construct and to operate the road as prescribed in the contract, free of all right, claim or other interference, whether by injunction, suit for damages or otherwise, on the part of the owner, abutting owner, or other person.

PAYMENT REQUIRED OF CORPORATION

"Every such contract shall further provide that the person, firm or corporation so contracting to construct, maintain and operate said road shall annually pay into the treasury of said city, as rental for the use of said road, a sum which shall not, except as hereinafter provided, be less than the annual interest upon the bonds to be issued by said city for the construction of said road as hereinafter provided for, and in addition to said interest, a further sum which shall be equal to a percentage of not less than one per centum upon the whole amount of said bonds; provided, that in estimating such annual interest and additional percentage there shall be deducted from the amount of said bonds the amount thereof issued to pay for rights, terms, easements, privileges or property other than lands acquired in fee, and also the amount thereof issued to pay for the construction of galleries, ways, subways and tunnels for sub-surface structures.

TIMES OF PAYMENT

"And provided, further, that the said contract may, in the discretion of the said Board, provide that the payment of the said further sum of not less than one per centum upon the amount of said bonds as aforesaid, shall begin at a date not more than five years after the date at which the payment of rental shall begin, and that the said annual rate, instead of one per centum, may be a rate not less than one-half per centum for a further period not exceeding five years; but in case the contractor shall, during any year in which the said payment of one per centum shall be suspended or reduced as aforesaid, earn a greater profit upon his, its, or their net capital invested in the enterprise than five per centum, then the surplus of his, its, or their earnings for such year up to the extent of at least one per centum shall be paid as rental as aforesaid.

"Such rental and the term for the operation of the railroad included in any such contract shall begin, as to said road, or any section thereof, when the same shall be declared by the Board of Rapid Transit Railroad Commissioners to be completed and ready for operation.

METHOD OF ESTIMATING PAYMENT

"For the purpose of estimating such one per centum per annum upon the ascertainment of the amount of such rental, there shall be included such portion of the said bonds as shall have been issued to pay interest on bonds theretofore issued under the provisions of this act, except bonds issued to pay for rights, terms, easements, privileges, or property other than lands acquired in fee. The aforesaid annual rental shall be paid at such times during each year as said Board shall require, and shall be applied first to the payment of the interest on said bonds, as the same shall accrue and fall due, and the remainder of said rental not required for the payment of said interest shall be paid into the sinking fund, for the payment of the city debt, if there shall be such sinking fund in said city, or, if there be none such, then said balance of said rental shall be securely invested, and, with the annual accretions of interest thereon, shall constitute a sinking fund for the payment and redemption at maturity of the bonds issued, as hereinafter provided.

RENTAL TO PAY INTEREST ON BONDS AND SINKING FUND

RENEWAL OF LEASE

"Any such contract may also provide for a renewal or renewals of the lease of said road upon the expiration of the original term and of any renewals of the same, upon such terms and conditions as to said Board may seem just and proper, and may also contain provisions for the valuation of the whole or a part of the property of said contracting person, firm or corporation, employed in and about the equipment, maintenance and operation of said road, and for the purchase of the same by the city, at such valuation, or a percentage of the same, should said lease not be renewed at any time.

"Any such contract may provide for the construction of said road in sections, and, except as herein otherwise provided, every such contract shall specify when the construction of the railroad included therein or of the several sections of the same shall be commenced, and, in each case, the date of completion. It shall also state the date on which the operation of the road, or any section thereof, shall commence.

BOND OF CORPORATION

"The person, firm or corporation so contracting for the construction, equipment, maintenance and operation of the railroad or railroads included in any such contract shall give a bond to the city, in such amount as said Board of Rapid Transit Railroad Commissioners shall require, and with sureties to be approved by said Board, who shall justify each in double the amount of his liability upon said bond. Said bond shall be a continuing security, and shall provide for the prompt payment by said contracting person, firm or corporation, of the amount of annual rental specified in the aforesaid contract, and also for the faithful performance by said contracting person or corporation of all the conditions, covenants and requirements specified and provided for in said contract. In lieu of said continuing bond such contracting person, firm or corporation may, upon the approval of the said Board, deposit with the comptroller or other chief financial officer of such city cash equal in amount to the entire amount of the said bond or securities which are lawful for the investment of the funds of savings banks within this state and are worth not less than the entire amount of such bond. If such bond shall have been given after the deposit of cash and securities in lieu thereof as aforesaid, and the approval thereof by the said Board, the said bond shall be surrendered by the said city to the said contracting person, firm or corporation duly cancelled by the Comptroller or other chief financial officer of the said city. In the event of the deposit of cash or securities as aforesaid, the contract may provide for the payment to the contractor of the income of such securities or of interest upon such moneys at a rate not higher than the highest rate received by the city upon the deposit of its funds with banks, and may also provide for withdrawal of securities so deposited upon deposit of cash or securities of the same value, provided that all such securities shall be such as are lawful for the investment of the funds of savings banks.

SECURITY REQUIRED OF CORPORATION

"The said contracting person, firm or corporation shall also simultaneously with the execution and delivery of every such contract, deposit with the Comptroller or other chief financial officer of such city the sum of one million dollars in cash or in securities of a value not less than one million dollars, which securities shall be of the character of those in which the savings banks of this state are authorized by law to invest moneys, and shall be approved by the Board of Rapid Transit Railroad Commissioners, which cash or securities shall, under such terms and conditions as shall be provided in the said contract, be further security for the faithful performance by such contracting person, firm or corporation of all the covenants, conditions and requirements specified and provided for in said contract relating to the construction and equipment of said road. If in any case the cost of construction embraced in a contract is estimated by the said Board of Rapid Transit Railroad Commissioners at the sum of ten million dollars or less, the contract may in the discretion of the said Board fix the amount of such deposit at such a sum less than one million dollars as the said board may determine, but in no case shall such deposit be less than ten per cent. of the contract price of such construction. The city in and for which said road shall be constructed shall also have a first lien upon the rolling stock and other property of said contracting person, firm or corporation, constituting the equipment of said road and used or intended for use in the maintenance and operation of the same, as further security for the faithful performance by such contracting person, firm or corporation of the covenant, conditions and agreements of said contract, on his, their or its part to be fulfilled and performed, and in case of the breach of any such covenant, condition and agreement said lien shall be subject to foreclosure by action, at the suit of such city, in the same manner, as far as may be, as is then provided by law in the case of foreclosure by action of mortgages on real estate. The said Board of Rapid Transit Railroad Commissioners may, however, from time to time, by a concurrent vote of six of the members of said Board, relieve from such lien, any property to which the same may attach, upon receiving additional security, which may be deemed by said board so voting to be the equivalent of that which it is proposed to release and otherwise upon such terms as to such Board so voting shall seem just. The said Board may in or by any such contract and in its discretion, require, and this act, as the same was prior to the present amendment thereof, shall be deemed to have authorized the said Board to have heretofore required any other security upon any such contract.

CITY TO HAVE FIRST LIEN UPON PROPERTY

"Upon the completion of the construction and equipment of the railroad or railroads provided in any such contract to the satisfaction of the said Board, and when the operation of the same shall have commenced pursuant to said contract, it shall be the duty of the Comptroller or other chief financial officer to pay to the said contracting person, firm or corporation said sum in cash or the said securities so to be deposited as above provided as security for construction and equipment, and the said contracting person, firm or corporation shall also be then entitled to be credited upon the rental which he, they or it shall have contracted to pay to said city for the use of said road a sum which shall be equal, as the case may be, either to the interest on the sum so to be deposited for the

DEPOSIT TO BE RETURNED UPON COMPLETION OF ROAD

time of such deposit at the rate of interest provided for in the bonds which shall have been issued and sold by the city to provide for the construction of said road, or the interest, dividends or other income which said city shall have received from the said securities.

IN CASE OF DEFAULT BOARD MAY TAKE POSSESSION AND OPERATE ROAD

"The said contract shall further provide that in case of default in paying the annual sum or rental therein provided for, or in case of failure or neglect on the part of said contracting person, firm or corporation, faithfully to observe, keep and fulfill the conditions, obligations and requirements of said contract, the said city, by its Board of Rapid Transit Railroad Commissioners, may take possession of said road and the equipment thereof, and as the agent of said contracting person, firm or corporation, either maintain and operate said road, or enter into a contract with some other person, firm or corporation for the maintenance and operation thereof, retaining out of the proceeds of such operation, after the payment of the necessary expenses of operation and maintenance, the annual rental hereinbefore referred to, and paying over the balance, if any, to the person, firm or corporation with whom the first contract above mentioned was made, and if such proceeds of the operation of said road, after the payment of the necessary expenses of maintenance and operation, including the keeping in repairs of the rolling stock and other equipment, shall in any year be less than the annual rental hereinbefore referred to and provided in the first contract, then, and in that case, the said contracting person, firm or corporation, and his or its bondsmen, shall be and continue (but in the case of any bond hereafter executed each bondsman only to the extent of the liability expressly assumed by him upon the bond) jointly and severally liable to the aforesaid city for the amount of such deficiency, until the end of the full term for which the said first contract was originally made.

BOARD MAY ASSIGN PRIVILEGE

"No contract entered into under authority of this act shall be assigned without the written consent of the said Board of Rapid Transit Railroad Commissioners, concurred in by six members of said Board. The said contracting person, firm or corporation, with such written consent and upon such terms and conditions as the said Board shall prescribe, may either assign the whole of such contract or separately the right or obligation to maintain and operate the said road or roads for the remainder of the term of years specified in such contract and all rights with respect to such maintenance and operation, or included in the leasing provisions of such contract, but subject to all the terms and conditions therein stated; provided, however, that the assignee or assignees shall, in and by such assignment, assume all of the obligations of the original contractor, under or with respect to such leasing provisions and all obligations which relate in any way to such operation and maintenance, and provided, further, said Board before giving its consent shall be satisfied that the pecuniary responsibility of the assignee or assignees shall be no less than that of such original contractor; and provided, further, that all of the security or securities which the city shall have received for the performance by the original contractor of such leasing provisions and of all provisions of the contract with respect to such operation and maintenance shall continue in full force as provided in such contract, or any modification thereof, as security for the performance by such assignee of all obligations of the contractor under or with respect to such leasing provisions and such maintenance or operation.

PROVISIONS OF LEASE

"It shall be deemed to be part of every such contract that, in case the Board of Rapid Transit Railroad Commissioners shall cease to exist, the legislature may provide what public officer or officers of the city shall exercise the powers and duties belonging to the Board of Rapid Transit Railroad Commissioners under or by virtue of any such contract, and that in default of such provision, such powers and duties shall be deemed to be vested in the Mayor of the city.

SUCCESSORS OF BOARD

"Every such contract shall provide that if the contracting person, firm or corporation shall fail to construct or operate the railway according to the terms of the contract, and shall, after due notice of its default, omit for more than a reasonable time to comply with the provisions of such contract, the Board of Rapid Transit Railroad Commissioners may bring an action in the name and in behalf of the city to forfeit and vacate all the rights of such contracting person, firm or corporation under such contract, and for damages and otherwise as may be necessary for the sufficient and just protection of the rights of the city; or may, upon such terms as to the Board of Rapid Transit Railroad Commissioners seem just, and with such person or corporation as to the said board may seem proper, make another operating contract and lease of the said road for the residue of the term of the contractor in default; and may bring action in the name and on behalf of the city to recover from the contractor the amount due from the contractor, less the amount which shall have been received by the city, under or by virtue of such new contract, and for all other damages sustained by the city by reason of such default.

DUTIES OF BOARD IN CASE OF DEFAULT

"The said Board may by any such contract determine when and how the work of construction of the rapid transit railroad or railroads included therein shall proceed.

PRIVILEGE OF ROADS WHOLLY OR PARTLY WITHIN CITY LIMITS

"Any existing railway corporation owning or actually operating a railway wholly or in part within the limits of the city in and for which said Board has power to act, and approved by the said Board of Rapid Transit Railroad Commissioners, shall be competent and is hereby authorized to enter into any contract for the construction and operation of any railway pursuant to the provisions of this chapter; or, after such a contract shall have been made, shall be competent and is hereby authorized, with the approval of said Board, to contract with the original contractor or his assignee or assignees for the maintenance and operation (including the equipment thereof) of any railway constructed or in process of construction pursuant to the provisions of this chapter, and shall have all the powers necessary to the due performance of such contract.

RIGHTS OF CORPORATION ORGANIZED UNDER RAILROAD LAW

"A corporation may be organized under the railroad law of this state, for the purpose of undertaking the construction and operation of a railway pursuant to the provisions of this act, or for the purpose of maintaining and operating a railway (including the equipment thereof) already constructed or in process of construction pursuant to the provisions of this chapter, or for both such purposes; and any corporation so organized, upon the approval in writing of the said Board of Rapid Transit Railroad Commissioners, shall, in addition to the powers conferred by the general act under which such company is organized, be empowered, and is hereby authorized to enter into any contract permitted by law for the construction and operation, or for the maintenance and operation when constructed (including the equipment thereof if desired), as the case may be, of any such railway constructed or to be constructed at the expense of the city as in this act provided. The certificate of such approval shall be filed in the office of the Secretary of State and a copy thereof certified to be a true copy by the Secretary of State or his deputy shall be evidence of the fact therein stated.

"A corporation so organized shall not be required to procure the consent of the Board of Railroad Commissioners of the State as provided for in section fifty-nine of the railroad law. Where in this section the consents referred to in section five of this act are mentioned, they shall be construed to include any consent given by the commissioners appointed by the General Term or Appellate Division of the Supreme Court, and confirmed by the said General Term or

Appellate Division in lieu of the consent of property owners as hereinbefore provided."

The equipment to be supplied by the corporation shall include all rolling stock, boilers, engines, wires, conduits, machinery, tools, and appliances of every nature used for the generation or transmission of power, and including all power-houses, and all apparatus for signaling and ventilation. EQUIPMENT

Before awarding any contract the Board shall advertise for proposals for three successive weeks, and shall publicly open all proposals.

For the purpose of providing the necessary means for such construction, at the public expense, "and of meeting the interest on the bonds, in this section hereinafter provided for, accruing thereon prior to the completion and readiness for operation of the portion of such road or roads for the construction of which such bonds shall have been respectively issued, the Board of Estimate and Apportionment, or other local authority in said city, in which such road or roads are to be constructed, having power to make appropriations of moneys to be raised by taxation therein, from time to time, and as the same shall be necessary, and upon the requisition of said Board of Rapid Transit Railroad Commissioners, shall direct the Comptroller, or other chief financial officer of said city, and it shall become his duty to issue the bonds of said city at such a rate of interest, not exceeding three and one-half per centum per annum, as said Board of Estimate and Apportionment, or other local authority directing the issue of such bonds, may prescribe. BONDS TO BE ISSUED BY THE CITY

"Said bonds shall provide for the payment of the principal and interest in gold coin of the United States of America. They shall not be sold for less than the par value thereof; and the proceeds of the same shall be paid out and expended for the purpose for which the same are issued, upon vouchers certified by said Board of Rapid Transit Railroad Commissioners.

"Said bonds shall be free from all taxation for city and county purposes, and shall be payable at maturity out of the sinking fund for the payment of the city debt, if there be such a sinking fund of said city; but if there be no such sinking fund, then out of a sinking fund to be established and created out of the annual rentals of said road as hereinbefore provided. But this provision that the said bonds shall be payable out of such a sinking fund shall not diminish or affect the obligation of said city as a debtor upon said bonds, or any other right or remedy of any holder or owner of any such bonds, to collect the prin- BONDS cipal or interest thereof. The amount of bonds authorized to be issued and sold by this section shall not exceed the limit of amount which shall be prescribed by the Board of Estimate and Apportionment or such other local authority having power to make appropriations of moneys to be raised by taxation; and no contract for the construction of such road or roads shall be made unless and until such Board of Estimate and Apportionment or such other local authority shall have consented thereto and prescribed a limit to the amount of bonds available for the purposes of this section which shall be sufficient to meet the requirements of such contract in addition to all obligations theretofore incurred and to be satisfied from such bonds."

Changes may be made in the contract, or the plans, with the consent of six members of the Board; but in no case shall the annual rental to be paid to the city be reduced below the minimum rate provided.

BRIDGES

The board of directors of any company incorporated for the purpose of building a bridge, or bridges, connecting a city of more than one million inhabitants with any other city in the State, and to construct an approach thereto extending generally in an easterly and westerly direction, may in lieu of constructing such approach, build and operate an elevated railway, the route of which shall be coincident with the approach or approaches. "The entire route of any elevated railway, constructed under the provisions of this section, shall not exceed three miles in length, nor shall any part of said railway, except at the termini thereof, be less than sixteen feet above any street, avenue or public place, or less than fourteen feet above any existing elevated railway which may be crossed, intervened, or intersected thereby."

The Board may acquire any necessary real estate by condemnation or other legal proceedings.

When the contractor shall require any property for the construction and operation of the road, such property shall be deemed to be required for a public purpose; and, with the approval of the Board, may be acquired by the contractor in all respects as such property may be acquired by the Board. Such property acquired by the Board, when no longer necessary for rapid transit purposes, shall be sold, with the approval of the Commissioners of the Sinking Fund.

Sections 40 to 62, both inclusive, contain provisions for the acquisition of real estate.

In case it shall be determined by vote of the people to construct the road at the city's expense, then the road shall be the absolute property of the city, and shall be deemed to be part of the public streets and highways, to be used and enjoyed by the public upon the payment of such fares and tolls, and subject to such reasonable rules and regulations, as may be imposed and provided by the Board of Rapid Transit Railroad Commissioners. ROAD PART OF STREETS AND HIGHWAYS

The act prohibits the construction or operation of any railroad upon the surface of any street, avenue, or highway in the city of New York; but this prohibition does not extend to bridges, or viaducts, or approaches connecting bridges with the surface; nor does it prevent the construction, or operation upon the surface, of any street, or avenue, or bridge-approach in the city of New York, for such a distance as may be reasonably necessary in order to connect underground lines with bridges, viaducts, or surface lines. NO ROAD TO BE UPON A STREET SURFACE

NOTE.—The following sections of the Act of 1894, Chapter 752, do not, *in terms,* amend any portion of the Rapid Transit Act of 1891, although the whole Act of 1894 is, in fact, an amendment of the earlier statute. These sections are accordingly numbered with respect to their position in the Act of 1894, and without reference to the numbering of the sections in the original act.

"Section 11. The Commissioners of Rapid Transit heretofore appointed under the act hereby amended, or who became such commissioners by its terms, upon the organization of the Board which shall succeed them pursuant to said act as hereby amended, shall cease to be such commissioners and shall transfer and deliver to the Board of Rapid Transit Railroad Commissioners, provided for by the act hereby amended, as so amended, all furniture, books, maps, records, plans, and other papers and property of what kind soever appertaining or belonging to or in the custody of the Board of which they were commissioners, or in their possession, or under their control as such commissioners, or held by them, or for which they are responsible in their official capacity. The expenses incurred by said commissioners for which an appropriation or appropriations shall have been made pursuant to section ten of the act hereby amended, shall be paid upon vouchers to be furnished by said Commissioners and otherwise, as provided in said section. Said Commissioners shall also be entitled to receive a reasonable compensation for the services which have been rendered by them, which may have been, or which shall be, determined on their application in the manner provided for in said section. The Comptroller, or other chief financial officer of said city, is hereby authorized and directed to issue and sell revenue bonds of such city in anticipation of the receipt of taxes and out of the proceeds of such bonds to pay said compensation so ascertained and determined, and the amount necessary to pay the principal and interest of said bonds shall be included in the tax levy of said city for the year next following the issue and sale of the same.

METHOD OF VOTING

"Section 12. The said Board of Rapid Transit Railway Commissioners shall cause the question, whether such railway or railways shall be constructed by the city and at the public expense, to be submitted to the qualified electors of the city within which such railway or railways is or are to be constructed, and to that end it shall be the duty of said Board, after completion of the detailed plans and specifications, as required by the act hereby amended, at least thirty days prior to the next general election, to file with the public officer or officers within the county in which such city is located, who may be charged with the duty of printing the ballots to be used at such election, a request that separate ballots be printed and supplied to such electors, one-half in number of which shall read, 'For municipal construction of rapid transit road,' and the other half in number of said ballots shall read, 'Against municipal construction of rapid transit road.' Upon such request being so filed, such ballots shall be printed and supplied to such electors at such general election, and separate ballot boxes shall be provided for the reception of the same in each election district within such city, and the provisions of chapter six-hundred-and-eighty of the laws of eighteen-hundred-and-ninety-two, entitled 'An act in relation to the elections constituting chapter six of the general laws,' and any act or acts amendatory thereof, or supplemental thereto, shall apply thereto as far as the nature of the case may allow. No ballot which may be provided under this section shall be deemed invalid by reason of any error in dimensions, style of printing, or other formal defect, or through having been deposited in the wrong ballot box, but all such ballots shall be canvassed and returned as if such formal defect had not existed, or as if they had been deposited in the box provided for the purpose. Upon the canvass of such votes by the Board of County Canvassers of the county in which such city is located, it shall be the duty of said Board to file with the county clerk of said county a statement which shall declare the total number of votes cast in said city 'for municipal construction of rapid transit road,' and the total number so cast therein 'against municipal construction of rapid transit road.'

And the said railway or railways shall be constructed by the said city and at the public expense, if it shall be found from such statements so filed that there is a majority of the votes so cast in favor of such municipal construction.

"Section 13. In case the majority of votes cast at such election shall be in favor of such municipal construction of said railway or railways, it shall be the duty of said Board of Rapid Transit Railway Commissioners, within thirty days after the official declaration of the said vote, to proceed to construct the said railway or railways, and to make and let all contracts required for the performance of the work necessary to be done and performed in and about the construction thereof. All such contracts must, before execution, be approved as to form by the counsel to the corporation, or chief legal adviser for said city."

EAST RIVER TUNNEL--N. Y. SUBWAY.

CHAPTER XXII.

APPRECIATION OF THE CHAMBER.

The proceedings of the Chamber in appreciation of the services of its members on the Board of Rapid Transit Commissioners are set forth in the following extracts from its minutes:

MEETING OF JANUARY 7, 1904.

A. Barton Hepburn—Mr. President, many if not most of the great enterprises that come so closely home to the general welfare and interest of this entire community have had their origin and found the mainspring of their successful accomplishment through the action and activity of this Chamber. Probably no one of the great enterprises to which I have referred comes more closely home to the entire community individually than the Underground Rapid Transit Railway, now nearing its completion. It is fortunate for this community that our merchant princes and successful business men, like the President of this Chamber, Mr. Orr, Mr. Smith and others, can be induced, or gladly come forward, to give to the public the benefit of their services in the accomplishment of these great enterprises solely in the public interest and for the public good. The President of this Chamber, with five other members, together with the Mayor and Comptroller, constitute the Rapid Transit Commission. Their labors have been long and arduous, and it seems to me that we owe it to ourselves, as well as to them, at this particular time to take some fitting notice of the services that they have rendered, which will inure so greatly to the benefit of our community. In that connection I have a preamble and resolution that I desire to offer:

"Whereas, The Chamber of Commerce initiated the plan and prepared the bill passed by the Legislature on the 24th of May, 1894, under the provisions of which the Underground Rapid Transit Railroad is now nearly completed; and

"Whereas, The President of this Chamber and five of its members, with the Mayor and Comptroller of the city, were duly appointed a Board of Rapid Transit Commissioners; therefore, be it

"Resolved, That the Chamber desires to make suitable recognition of the eminent services rendered by the Commissioners, and to this end Messrs. George F. Seward, Jacob H. Schiff and Cornelius N. Bliss be and they are hereby appointed a Special Committee to consider and report at the next meeting what action in their judgment should be taken by the Chamber."

RESOLUTION APPOINTING COMMITTEE

MR. HEPBURN—Mr. President, in deference to your well known modesty, being a member of the Commission as well as President of this Chamber, it seemed well to vary the invariable rule under which we act, and to name the committee in this resolution instead of providing that they be appointed by the Chair. I move the adoption of the resolution.

The resolution was unanimously adopted.

MEETING OF MARCH 3, 1904.

The Special Committee made the following report, which was advised to be printed and a copy sent to each member:

REPORT.

In the City Hall station of the Rapid Transit Subway is to be placed a tablet bearing this inscription: [An engraving of this tablet will be found on page 5.]

TABLET

SUGGESTED BY THE CHAMBER OF COMMERCE,
AUTHORIZED BY THE STATE,
CONSTRUCTED BY THE CITY.

This inscription is right, but it does not adequately set forth the service this Chamber has rendered.

Our city has special need of rapid transit. Its principal business section is at the southern end of Manhattan Island. The island is narrow and the residential section stretches far away to the north. It includes also a great district beyond the East River. The conformation of the city differs in this respect from that of London, or Paris, or Berlin, where there has been unimpeded growths in all directions from common centers of business and population.

PHYSICAL DIFFICULTIES

In each of these great cities the physical difficulties of such enterprises have been less. In each of them the difficulties attending the organization of such work has been less. They are all capitals of great states, so organized within themselves and so associated with the respective national governments that great public works are not halted for lack of intelligent, appreciative and effective support. This city, the second in population on the globe, is not the capital of a State. Vast in the magnitude of its population, yielding place to no other in financial and commercial importance, it is not the mistress of its own affairs. Its local government indeed is often in conflict with the State Government because of constitutional conditions and of the free play of political forces.

While these things are true we yet stand in face of the great facts that harmony has been secured between the State and the city; that the greatest work yet known in the world for the purpose of giving transit facilities to a great population is nearing its completion, and that it is the Chamber of Commerce and a representative body of its members that have so planned and so worked as to bring about the great result.

There is a feature in American affairs that should be recognized by every citizen who appreciates and loves his country. We live under republican institutions. The effective quality of such institutions is seldom so great as that of the older forms of government. Public measures there are generally directed by a compacted body of men who, by reason of ability and experience, have come into supreme control. Under a republican system there is always changeable control, and public measures can never be pushed beyond the point to which public sentiment has progressed. It follows that in any republic public sentiment must be developed and organized by the people themselves. It has come to pass, happily, in our great land, that the development of right sentiment and the organization of measures demanded by the public interest have received the attention of unofficial citizens. The field of work of this Chamber is broader and more important than that of any like body in the older countries. Our people, quick to see the needs of any situation, are constantly organizing unofficial bodies that do good work.

RECOGNITION BY THE CHAMBER

It is said that republics are ungrateful. It may be so. But it cannot be said that the people who live under republican forms of government are ungrateful toward the men who in public or private life serve the public with fidelity. On the wall yonder hangs a great historical picture. It presents the tribute of this body to Mr. Field and his associates in an achievement incomparable at the time and of vast concern to the world. Those who have participated in the transactions of this body have seen it often yield just honors. The man who more than any other created right public sentiment for a sound currency, Mr.

Hanna of Indiana, stood here of late to receive addresses of appreciation and an engraved medal from the Chamber. The man most prominent in the work of devising the basis for the Rapid Transit enterprise received at your hands like honor, and yonder in a corridor of this beautiful hall is to stand his statute done in marble. He was a citizen who served the public officially and who served it unofficially with singular clearness of vision, with devotion and with truth, and the rewards granted to him by this Chamber have been such as will make his memory last until these walls crumble into dust. If it be true that republics as such are ungrateful let us take care that no such charge may be brought against our citizenship at large.

What has been said is general in terms. Facts specific in character should be set forth lest some one may say that the work of the Chamber and of its members has not risen to the height of public achievement indicated in the language thus used. The facts are salient ones and he who runs may read the record.

The State authorized the work. The Act of the Legislature granting this authority and determining the methods to be followed was prepared under the direction of a Committee of this Chamber, approved by this Chamber, and urged upon the Legislature by this Chamber until success was won.

COMPOSITION OF COMMISSION

Under that Act the city was empowered to carry forward the enterprise by a commission of eight persons. The President of this Chamber for the time being and five other persons all members of this Chamber and designated by it were Commissioners. To these were added the Mayor and Comptroller of the city. The Act made the body a continuous one, it being provided that the Commission should itself fill vacancies in its number. It happens in this way that six out of eight Commissioners have always been members of this Chamber. And it happens in this way that the great republican need of unofficial service has been satisfied in a remarkable manner.

WORK PERFORMED

The foundation of the enterprise having been so laid, the duties of the Commissioners began. It was for them to create the thing so planned for. Their work has been of a kind that cannot be told in detail. They determined the route of the subway, having regard to existing means of transportation, to the convenience of the population actually existent and that hereafter to exist, and having regard to the right development of territory shut out from reasonable access to the business center. They determined plans for the structure, fitting them to the streets to be traversed and to the probable exigencies of traffic. They laid the financial scheme, having regard to the prompt construction of the work on economical lines and conserving the permanent interest of the city in the work, by providing that the city, after a term of years, shall come into complete ownership and control of it. They carried through the courts proceedings necessary to legalize the plans so made. They selected and supervised the engineering staff. They reconciled differences with the city as to moneys required and as to the use of streets and interferences with public utility services. They reconciled differences with individual property owners. They determined the construction of the operating plant in order to secure safety for the multitudes who will use the subway.

Is it too much to say that all this duty has called for attention, prudence, and ability of the highest order, and that the harmony secured and the public approval vouchsafed at each stage of the work indicates that attention, prudence and skill have been exhibited in a degree that has left nothing to be desired?

The work nears completion. By July it is likely that our citizens will be in full use of its benefits. What we may do here to set forth the merit of the work and the merit of those who have done it will but faintly express the appreciation of the people who will be served by it. In knowledge of this the Chamber and the members of the Commission will receive their best reward.

Your Committee in submitting this report desires to add that it hopes to submit at the next meeting of the Chamber a further report indicating what means should be organized first, in order that the Chamber may take a right part in celebration of the opening of the Rapid Transit Subway to public use, and second, in order that the service rendered by members of the Chamber may be properly recognized.

Your Committee submits the following resolution:

Resolved, That this preliminary report be received and printed for the use of the Chamber and its members.

All of which is respectfully submitted.

(Signed,) JACOB H. SCHIFF,
GEORGE F. SEWARD,
CORNELIUS N. BLISS, } *Special Committee.*

MEETING OF APRIL 7, 1904.

The report made as stated above was adopted by the Chamber.

APPRECIATION OF THE CHAMBER

MEETING OF NOVEMBER 2, 1904.

The Special Committee, several gentlemen having been added to its membership, offered the following report, which was adopted:

REPORT.

To the Chamber of Commerce:

Your Committee was appointed in January last. On March 2 it made a preliminary report which was printed for the information of members. That report presented briefly the following facts:

That our city is so situated that rapid transit is more necessary here than in any other great city.

That this Chamber, impressed by the importance of the subject, studied it with care, prepared the form of legislation required and pressed it to action by the Legislature of the State.

That these studies involved not only physical problems of a serious nature, but also administrative problems of importance and difficulty.

That the law actually secured provided the means for a right solution of all these problems involved.

That it committed the enterprise to a Commission of eight persons, six of whom were members of this Chamber.

That continuously ever since six members of the Commission have been members of this Chamber, the other two being the Mayor and Comptroller for the time being.

That the Commission deserves high commendation not only because it determined plans for rapid transit broad in scope and fitted to the needs of the city, and has carried these forward under difficult circumstances, but also, and notably, because it has so planned that the city owns the franchise, and will eventually come into possession and control of the entire system with little or no debt outstanding.

It is not the purpose of your Committee to enlarge upon the report so made or to elaborate remarks. It has waited until the subway, so far as it is completed, has come into use, and every citizen may see for himself its magnitude, the fitness and beauty of its details, and its capacity to serve the convenience and comfort of our population at the moment and so long as multitudes of people congregate within our borders.

The subway speaks for itself in these directions. It speaks also upon a further point. In all its parts it bears witness to the forethought of those who were the direct instruments in its construction, and to their skill, capacity, courage and constancy. If it is a great work, it it so as the result of adequate design and effort.

But the subway is as mute as the great pyramid in another direction. It has no voice to name and thank its own builders. That duty rests upon us who have been the human witnesses of their labors.

Your Committee now suggests the ways by which the Chamber may give deserved honors to those of its members who have served the enterprise. We advise:

BOOK

1st. That your Committee be instructed to prepare and print a descriptive and historical memoir of the enterprise to the end that the instrumentality of this Chamber, of its members, and of others in the great work may be properly recorded in permanent form. Your Committee believes that such a record is necessary to a right appreciation of the work that has been done, and, as well, that the record will serve a large public purpose by indicating how similar municipal purposes here and elsewhere may best be promoted.

MEDALS TO COMMISSIONERS

2d. That your Committee be instructed to cause to be struck suitable medals in gold, similar to the one already presented to Mr. Hewitt, and that these medals be presented in this Chamber to Mr. Orr and to those members of the Chamber associated with him in duty.

3d. In order that the matter may proceed in a proper way, your Committee proposes that the Executive Committee be requested to decide to what extent current funds of the Chamber may be utilized for the purposes stated.

GROUP PICTURE

A further proposal has been considered by your Committee. It is this—That a group picture, presenting the portraits of those of our members who have had to do with Rapid Transit work, be procured and given place on the walls of this Hall as a companion piece to the Atlantic Cable picture.

Your Committee is prepared to say that such a picture would adorn our walls, would be of peculiar interest to our members so long as the Chamber exists, and that the services of our members would be fittingly honored in this way. Books go to the shelves of libraries and in the end are lost sight of. Medals remain in the family and are not remembered elsewhere after a brief season. A great painting remains an object of interest, of pride, and of inspiration for an almost indefinite period. Your Committee cannot but hope that such a picture may be placed upon our walls, but it has no thought that it can be provided for out of the current funds of the Chamber nor otherwise than by the generous action of individuals.

Your Committee desires that the way may be kept open to secure such a picture, and to this end asks the Chamber to authorize the Executive Committee to give any needed assurances that a suitable painting, if offered, will be gratefully accepted by the Chamber.

Your Committee respectfully submits the following resolution:

That this Chamber holds in great appreciation the unselfish and highly successful services of Mr. Orr and his colleagues, and with the desire to give this appreciation tangible form requests the Special Committee to give effect, to the best of its ability, to the plans set forth in its report.

(Signed) George F. Seward,
Cornelius N. Bliss,
Jacob H. Schiff,
A. Barton Hepburn,
A. Foster Higgins,
C. Adolphe Low,
Isidor Straus,
Charles S. Fairchild,
J. Edward Simmons,
Isaac N. Seligman,
} *Special Committee.*

MEETING OF DECEMBER 7, 1905.

The Special Committee submitted the following report:

Report.

To the Chamber of Commerce:

At a regular meeting of the Chamber in January, 1904, the following preamble and resolution, offered by Mr. Hepburn, were passed:

Whereas, The Chamber of Commerce initiated the plan and prepared the bill passed by the Legislature on the 24th of May, 1894, under the provisions of which the Underground Rapid Transit Railroad is now nearly completed; and

Whereas, The President of this Chamber and five of its members, with the

Mayor and Comptroller of the city, were duly appointed a Board of Rapid Transit Commissioners; therefore, be it

APPOINTMENT OF COMMITTEE

Resolved, That the Chamber desires to make suitable recognition of the eminent services rendered by the Commissioners, and to this end Messrs. George F. Seward, Jacob H. Schiff and Cornelius N. Bliss, be and they hereby are appointed a Special Committee to consider and report at the next meeting what action in their judgment should be taken by the Chamber.

At the meeting of March following your Committee presented a preliminary report.

At the meeting of November following your Committee made a further report containing, among other matters, the following proposals:

INSTRUCTIONS

1st. That your Committee be instructed to prepare and print a descriptive and historical memoir of the enterprise, to the end that the instrumentality of this Chamber, of its members, and of others in the great work may be properly recorded in permanent form. Your Committee believes that such record is necessary to a right appreciation of the work that has been done, and, as well, that the record will serve a large public purpose by indicating how similar municipal purposes here and elsewhere may best be promoted.

2d. That your Committee be instructed to cause to be struck suitable medals in gold, similar to the one already presented to Mr. Hewitt, and that these medals be presented in this Chamber to Mr. Orr and to those members of the Chamber associated with him in duty.

These proposals were approved by the Chamber.

Your Committee, in pursuance of the authority so given, has caused to be struck seven medals of suitable size and design, and now brings them to the Chamber in order that they may be formally presented to the persons named below:

Alexander E. Orr,
Morris K. Jesup,
John Claflin,
Woodbury Langdon,
Seth Low,
John H. Starin,
Charles Stewart Smith.

APPRECIATION OF THE CHAMBER

Your Committee has to report further that the memoir or book authorized by the Chamber is now in the hands of the printer. It will contain a description of passenger transportation facilities in our city and vicinity from an early day, and a statement of plans now being prosecuted for further developments. It will contain also much matter relating to the underground railway systems of London, Glasgow, Paris, Berlin, Budapest, Boston, Philadeplhia and Chicago. The book, with its pictures, maps and plans will run to more than 300 pages. SCOPE OF BOOK

Your Committee believes that the information presented in this book justifies the following conclusions:

(1.) That the work done by the Rapid Transit Board and the plans determined upon for further work will provide our city in its various sections with a very complete system of rapid transit facilities.

(2.) That this system, to say the least, will compare favorably with that of any other city in the world.

(3.) That the physical difficulties met and overcome have been greater than in any other city.

(4.) That the working out of a right system has been more difficult by reason of peculiarities of governmental control, State and Municipal.

Your Committee has had no duty assigned to it as respects those gentlemen who have served on the Commission in an official capacity beyond presenting to the members a just and appreciative statement of the facts. These gentlemen include Mayors Van Wyck, Low and McClellan, and Comptrollers Coler and Grout. But your Committee has believed that it would be grateful to the Chamber to invite these gentlemen to be present and to witness the honors that we feel free to bestow upon gentlemen of our own membership toward whom we entertain sentiments of gratitude that are enhanced and deepened by the affection generated in years of intercourse on this floor. Some of the gentlemen so invited are present and will know that our gratitude is not bounded by the walls of this room, but extends also to them in full measure. INVITED GUESTS

Your Committee has not failed to remember that one gentleman has served on the Board who was not an official member, and not a member of this Chamber. This gentleman, Mr. George L. Rives, known to us all as a man who has served the city in important ways and always beneficially, has been invited to this meeting in order that he may also be the recipient of our thanks.

Your Committee has invited to be present also Mr. William Barclay Parsons, Mr. August Belmont and Mr. John B. McDonald. These men, in their several departments, have exhibited such broad capacity and such faithfulness that no account of the subway which fails to note their services could be considered at all complete or just.

Your Committee has not been authorized to apportion honor between the members of the Board, official or unofficial. Yet we think that the members of the Board would themselves consider us remiss if we should fail to state that the services of two gentlemen have been especially valuable. Your Committee refers to the late Mr. Hewitt and to Mr. Orr. To the acute mind and wide political and administrative experience of the former is to be largely credited the combination of the theories of municipal ownership and private enterprise adopted and adhered to in the subway undertaking, and which has made the work especially satisfactory to our people. To the trained business intelligence of Mr. Orr, to his fertility of resource, his critical care and sturdy courage, is to be largely credited the solution of the grave problems that were met at every turn in the prosecution of the work.

OBJECT LESSONS

Our great community is to be congratulated in an especial manner upon the fact that the best virtue and the best intelligence of our citizenship have been enlisted in the enterprise. It is not always that this happens under our institutions, and not always that it happens under any institutions. That it has happened here, in a city thought by some to be given over to the lust of wealth and careless as to the course of administration, must give cheer to every man who is proud of his city, and who believes that high integrity as well as high capacity are to be found here in no stinted measure.

Your Committee proposes now to place the seven medals in the hands of the temporary presiding officer, to be by him in your presence, to-day, presented to the several gentlemen for whom they are intended; that five copies of the book shall be given to each of the Rapid Transit Commissioners, official and unofficial, one copy to each member of the Chamber, and that 500 copies be printed for distribution among public libraries.

Your Committee moves the adoption of this report and the approval of the proposals just recited.

Respectfully submitted,

(Signed) George F. Seward,
Cornelius N. Bliss,
Jacob H. Schiff,
A. Barton Hepburn,
A. Foster Higgins,
C. Adolphe Low,
Isidor Straus,
Charles S. Fairchild,
J. Edward Simmons,
Isaac N. Seligman,
} *Special Committee.*

The further proceedings on this occasion were as follows:

The President—Before action is taken on this interesting report you will see the propriety of my calling to the Chair our Vice-President, who is with us, Mr. Charles Lanier. I will ask him to take my place.

Mr. Lanier took the Chair.

Mr. Alfred P. Boller—Mr. Chairman and gentlemen, it is fitting in seconding the adoption of the report just read to make a few remarks in appreciation of the work of this Committee. ALFRED P. BOLLER

In its whole history of public accomplishments the Chamber of Commerce never did a greater thing than become sponsor for the magnificent system of Rapid Transit Subways, with which this city is now blessed, and enabled to march forward toward its destiny of being the First City of the World.

Great as this achievement has been, the Chamber has done even more than create a work of public utility of far reaching consequences. It has shown how a great public work, of incalculable value to the City of New York for all time to come, can be conceived, organized and carried out, freed from those political entanglements, which so often prove a source of waste, extravagance, or scandal.

This is, indeed, an occasion of pardonable self-congratulation for a great deed well accomplished, and the Chamber honors itself in honoring those men on whom has fallen the burden and responsibility of the trust committed to them.

As an engineering work, the New York Subway is, I believe, unmatched in ENGINEERING any city in the world in magnitude and the extent of the difficulties overcome, and is an enduring monument to that youthful brain that the Rapid Transit Commission called in to their aid, to show them how the work they had undertaken could be accomplished. It must have been an inspiration that dictated to that Commission the selection of its technical head, when, instead of following the usual course of seeking an engineer of trained experience, with a record of great deeds accomplished behind him, they committed the responsibility of planning the exceptional work they had undertaken, as well as its supervisory execution, to the hands of a young engineer who had his spurs yet to win, and experience on a large scale to get. It was an unheard of procedure, but the results accomplished have shown that in no respect has the wisdom and judgment of the Commission been vindicated in a higher degree than when they called William Barclay Parsons to be their Chief Engineer.

CONTRACTOR

No reference to the engineering side of this splendid subway system is complete without congratulating the Commission upon the limited tenders they had for the work when advertised for contract, which resulted in the selection of John B. McDonald as contractor, whose genius for organization, coupled with a fertility of resource, was a potent factor in achieving the results obtained. It was a happy combination of circumstances that brought together such well balanced co-ordinating factors as our Rapid Transit Commission, its Chief Engineer, and its Chief Contractor, resulting in a completeness of scheme on bold, broad lines, that has excited not only the admiration of the engineering world, but of all well-wishers of civic righteousness for the high sense of trusteeship which actuated its administration.

May the example set by this Chamber for enlisting "high integrity and high capacity," in the service of the city, shine forth as a standard of endeavor for all future time, as the burnished gold on the medals that to-day are bestowed on those of our members who have so faithfully discharged a great public duty.

Mr. Boller—Mr. President, I would like to add a few remarks upon the report just read by Mr Seward. A limited number of copies of the record was provided for. There was no provision for a stock on hand in the Chamber. They are provided for distribution among the members and for library distribution. We ought to have an edition here in the Chamber, as the material is so valuable that there will always be a demand for it; and, perhaps it is not in order, but I think it would be well for the Executive Committee to take up that question and consider the advisability of printing an additional number of copies for future use.

THE CHAIRMAN—Are there any further remarks? Gentlemen, the question before you now is the adoption of the report of the Special Committee. What is your pleasure?

J. EDWARD SIMMONS—I move its adoption.

The report was then unanimously adopted.

THE CHAIRMAN—I see that the Hon. Edward M. Grout, Comptroller, is with us. We would like to hear from him.

EDWARD M. GROUT

MR. GROUT—Mr. Chairman and gentlemen of the Chamber, I came as a witness, and did not expect to be a participant in your ceremonies. Perhaps the process of elimination, by which I am the only public official here who is not a member of the Chamber, has led you to ask me to speak. I can add nothing whatever, it seems to me, to what is contained in the very full and fair report of your Committee. The noticeable thing in the Rapid Transit law in my mind, as I have seen it in administration, is the recognition of the necessity of the continuous work of a continuing executive body; and that precedent has been adopted, in a measure, in the great and important work which the city is about to undertake of procuring a larger supply of water for the city; and it seems to me that in every public improvement where the plans must of necessity require a long period of time to complete them, the principle which you have caused to be adopted in the Rapid Transit Act, of a continuing body, as against public officials who serve for a short period, is the principle to be chosen.

One personal word I would like to say. It is a matter of great pleasure for one who has sat for four years on the Board with the members of your body who are there, to see them receive at your hands this recognition of the valuable services which they have performed for the city. [Applause.]

THE CHAIRMAN—Mr. William Barclay Parsons is present with us. We would be glad to hear a few remarks from him. [Applause.]

WM. BARCLAY PARSONS

MR. PARSONS—Mr. President, I don't think there is much for me to say, after I have thanked you, sir, and the members of the Chamber, for the invitation to be here to-day and to receive the thanks of the Chamber, and for the very flattering remarks that were made, especially by Mr. Boller, in seconding the report of the Committee. Mr. Boller referred to the work of the "young engineer." But the young engineer could not possibly have succeeded if he had not had during his eleven years of service with the Rapid Transit Commission the full and absolute support of that Commission at all times; and for that support I should like now to make full acknowledgment, and thank the members of the Board for having given it to me so unreservedly and fully as they have done. The Committee state that they have made no attempt to apportion honors. Of course, it is not for me to do so; but I do not think I am stepping beyond the bounds of propriety when I say that in this eleven years of service as the executive officer of the Commission I was necessarily brought into very close contact with the President of the Board, and I know that at many very critical moments, if it had not been for his steadfastness and absolute and unswerving belief in the enterprise of which he was the head, we would not have had rapid transit to-day. And I think, therefore, this city owes the Chairman of the Commission, Mr. Orr, a very great debt, and that this Chamber, of which I am a member, also owes to his efforts the fact that we are celebrating to-day the achievement of his labors. [Great applause.]

The Chairman—Mr. George L. Rives is present. We would be glad to hear from him. [Applause.]

GEORGE L. RIVES

Mr. Rives—Mr. President, for the very great compliment which has been given to me in the report of the Committee I can only express my most sincere and grateful thanks. I was born in this city, have been brought up here; I have lived here all my life. It has always been my desire and my ambition to deserve the good will and confidence of my fellow citizens. I need not say to you, therefore, with what pleasure I feel that such efforts as I have been allowed to make for the service of the people of this city are appreciated and approved by those who represent the commercial and financial interests of the metropolis. Quite apart from any personal question, I want to express my very great gratification that this Chamber has thought it right in this public and striking manner to recognize the value of the services of the members of the Commission. My own membership in the Commission ceased four years ago, so that I can speak in a very impersonal manner of the efficient and admirable work which they have done. It is only those who will take the trouble to inform themselves, as your Committee has done, of the great difficulties that had to be overcome, difficulties of an engineering character, difficulties of what I might call a moral character, difficulties of a legal and financial character—only those who thoroughly understand that can appreciate how complete and striking a victory this Commission has won. Unfortunately a great many people do not understand the subject. One of the candidates for Mayor at the recent election, standing upon the platform of Municipal Ownership, and backed by hundreds of thousands of votes, is now advocating the passage of legislation which will legislate out of office the Rapid Transit Commission, and change radically the law under which they have operated. Such legislation was introduced last year and defeated, but it will be introduced again at the coming session of the Legislature and urged with a great deal of vigor and with a great deal of popular backing. I need not tell this Chamber what I think personally of the merits of the Rapid Transit Act under which these things have been accomplished. We are reminded to-day of the fact, as everybody here knows, that the existing law was initiated and framed under the auspices of this Chamber. If this Chamber desires to see that law continued in force; if this Chamber does not wish to see the conservative safeguards removed which Mr. Hewitt so admirably contended for and so admirably introduced into this bill, I venture to suggest that it is the part of this Chamber to have its voice heard at Albany during the coming session of the Legislature. I need not tell you that the influence of the Chamber in such a matter will be very great and may possibly be decisive. And I do hope that whatever the Chamber may do or leave undone, it will at least carefully examine into this subject with the purpose of retaining the conservative safeguards which have been thrown about this matter. Mr. President, I can only end as I began, by thanking the Chamber very sincerely for the great compliment that has been paid me. [Applause.]

The Chairman—We would be glad to hear from Mr. August Belmont, who is also present here. [Applause.]

AUGUST BELMONT

Mr. Belmont—Mr. Chairman and gentlemen, it was not my purpose to say anything to you, but, of course, I must respond to the request of the Chair. I really do not think that I can add anything, except to ask you to review the work, you who are business men and understand what it means to organize a corporation and manage it in the face of the difficulties which corporations of to-day encounter; and I can only say that I trust that that management has met with your approval and will meet with your continued endorsement. You see the results of it. You know the claim which it has for conservative capitalization and for careful conduct. I speak of that with some pride, and that is as far as I can go. The future will have to speak for itself. [Great applause.]

The Chairman—I am sure, gentlemen, we would like to hear from Mr. John B. McDonald.

JOHN B. McDONALD

Mr. McDonald—Mr. Chairman and gentlemen of the Chamber of Commerce, it affords me great pleasure to be here to-day to do honor to the men of New York who have contributed so much to the great work of constructing the first Municipal Railway of Greater New York.

It would be a twice-told tale were I to recount the story of the many obstacles met and overcome. The facts exist, however, that with the aid and countenance of your body, the patience and forbearance of the public, the unfailing support of the Rapid Transit Commission and its Chief Engineer, supplemented by the co-operation of this and preceding municipal administrations, you have given to the City of New York the greatest Rapid Transit Railroad in the world.

Little more than a year has elapsed since the road was opened for active operation. I think it may be fairly said that but few, if any, anticipated the great benefits to the public which it confers. Even now its capacity is overtaxed.

There remains much to be done to meet the demands for transportation of this Empire City. Build where you will, the ever increasing population of New York will absorb your facilities, and the crying demand of the hour is for more accommodations.

I know that so long as the public interests are entrusted to those who have not failed in the past we may look confidently to the future.

I congratulate you, gentlemen, and the City of New York upon the accomplishment of your gigantic undertaking. That your work has been completed and placed in the public service without a shadow to mar its fair fame will live in history a monument to those who have directed and aided in its construction. [Applause.]

The Chairman then presented the medals to the gentlemen named in the report.

The Chairman—We will now listen to Mr. Alexander E. Orr.

ALEXANDER E. ORR

Mr. Orr—Mr. President and gentlemen, my fellow-members of this Chamber, to whom you have just presented these golden tokens as evidences of your recognition and approbation of their services as Rapid Transit Railroad Commissioners of the City of New York, have commissioned me to express to you in their behalf their sincere and heartfelt thanks for the honors you have conferred.

For myself I cannot help remembering at this moment, with keen feelings of gratitude, the honors which have come to me for many years past from you, my fellow-members of this Chamber. Several times you elected me your Vice-President, then, for five consecutive terms, your President; then you advanced me to the dignified position of honorary membership, and now, as if in confirmation of all that has gone before, you have presented me also with the gold medal of the Chamber as an additional evidence of your appreciation and respect. Truly, the lines have fallen to me in very pleasant places, and for it all I can only tender you, as I now do from the deep places of my heart, my grateful thanks.

It has been both a pride and pleasure to the members of our Commission to know that the very first move toward real and effective rapid transit under municipal ownership was made by this Chamber, and it was for this reason that when designing the tablet to commemorate the building of the first rapid transit road in New York our Commission decreed that the very first line of the inscription should read: "Suggested by the Chamber of Commerce of the State of New York," there to remain as long as the solid bronze should last as the evidence of your contribution to real rapid transit development.

It is true that in the prosecution of this great work confided to our care there were, especially in the earlier stages, some serious set-backs and very many discouragements; but knowing as we did that we possessed the confidence and support of this Chamber, we again and again took courage, till we finally reached the goal that you, after critical investigation of future possibilities, had the wisdom and the foresight to suggest.

We are glad, yes, more than glad, Mr. President, that Mr. Seward's Committee has mentioned names other than our own, of men who have given true and loyal service to the cause of rapid transit, and without whose aid and co-operation the problem now so happily solved would have remained an unsolved problem to-day.

With the Committee's permission we desire to add to the list the names of the late Justice Henry R. Beekman, who, under the supervision of this Chamber, drafted the rapid transit law, and of Edward M. Shepard and Albert B. Boardman, who, with George L. Rives, already named in the report, acted as our counsel and made all rough places in our legal pathway smooth, and then in a few brief words emphasize the names—first, of that great and good and patriotic New York citizen, our dearly loved fellow-member, Abram S. Hewitt, [applause] known to us all as the father of rapid transit. No poor words of mine can add to the luster of his great fame, but I am sure it is a pleasure to us all to remember that during his lifetime we were able to recognize his services in a manner that brought joy and happiness to his heart.

And of William Barclay Parsons, our Chief Engineer, who designed and superintended the building of the subway, and whose professional skill proved equal to every engineering difficulty that was encountered and won for him a well merited national and international reputation. It may interest you to know that Mr. Parsons' direct ancestor of several generations back obtained the original Charter of this Chamber from the British Crown. And of John B. McDonald and August Belmont, who at an opportune moment came to the front, when so many held back, and with faith and courage accepted the contract for construction and operation, which crowned all our previous efforts with success. And of Edward M. Grout [applause] and Bird S. Coler, who as the chief financial officers of the city, were members of all our important Committees, and helped us so much in determining franchise values, which to our minds are the most valuable of all municipal assets. All these names should be held in our grateful remembrance as long as rapid transit is deemed essential to the comfort, happiness, and development of this great City of New York.

In conclusion, it is not for me to forecast the future, but I cannot help believing that passenger transportation through large cities by subway contrivance has come to stay. [Applause.]

CHARLES STEWART SMITH

Charles Stewart Smith—Mr. Chairman, some of my associates on the Rapid Transit Board have made a suggestion to me which I have very great pleasure in communicating to you. Mr. Seward, in his report, and my friend, Mr. Parsons, in his remarks, paid a very merited compliment to the President of the Rapid Transit Board. My friends on my left have suggested that I should say something which would express the convictions of the members of the Rapid Transit Board regarding their President. Mr. Orr has executed his great work and borne his immense responsibilities with absolute fidelity, great industry, and very great ability. [Applause.] There were times when the Board felt very uncertain of public support. A good many of our best citizens in New York talked about a "hole in the ground." But Mr. Orr had unbounded faith that in the end the rapid transit work would receive the approbation of the citizens of New York city. I want simply to say that I wish to confirm the remark in the report made by Mr. Seward in reference to Mr. Orr, on the part of the Rapid Transit Commissioners themselves. [Applause.]

CALVIN TOMPKINS

CALVIN TOMKINS—Mr. President, in 1888 Mayor Hewitt sent a message to the Board of Aldermen of this city on the subject of rapid transit. It was probably the first great rapid transit paper which emanated from a city official. I find extracts from that message have been embodied in a resolution presented to this Chamber, and I think it would be peculiarly appropriate and grateful at this time if by general consent that resolution, which is virtually and practically Mr. Hewitt's message, could be read and receive our consideration. We have heard from the other gentlemen who have been peculiarly instrumental in bringing about this great public work. I think it is fitting that we should hear a few of the words of Mr. Hewitt who was the great leader in that enterprise. I would ask general consent. I believe the Secretary has that.

A. BARTON HEPBURN

A. BARTON HEPBURN—Mr. President, the resolution which the gentleman refers to was introduced and referred to the Committee of which I am Chairman. I embodied the sentiments of Mr. Hewitt as expressed in his message, and with it, I presume, the Chamber would generally agree; but my Committee did not think it right or opportune or proper to report to this Chamber an expression of abstract sentiment. We are practically business men, and when any practical question comes before us for action it is quite right that we should express our sentiments; but for this Chamber to approve formally the sentiments expressed by Mayor Hewitt in a message which he delivered some time ago did not seem to us to be a proper thing to do, even conceding that we approved of the sentiments expressed, and for that reason the resolution is lying in Committee unacted upon.

MR. TOMKINS—I ask general consent to present it.

MR. SIMMONS—Mr. Chairman, inasmuch as the programme laid down by the Special Committee has been completed and the business of the Chamber has been finished I move that we adjourn.

The Chamber then adjourned.

www.ingramcontent.com/pod-product-compliance
Lightning Source LLC
LaVergne TN
LVHW010543110826
845149LV00003B/546

9781418187859